BACK TO BANGKA

BACK TO BANGKA

GEORGINA BANKS

VIKING
an imprint of
PENGUIN BOOKS

VIKING

UK | USA | Canada | Ireland | Australia
India | New Zealand | South Africa | China

Viking is part of the Penguin Random House group of companies whose addresses can be
found at global.penguinrandomhouse.com

Penguin
Random House
Australia

First published by Viking in 2023

Cover images: Fight planes over Tokyo Bay, Corbis Historical collection courtesy of Getty
Images; nurse by Diane Labombarde, courtesy of Getty Images; Shutterstock
Cover design by Alex Ross, Alex Ross Creative © Penguin Random House Australia Pty Ltd
Map by James Mills-Hicks, Ice Cold Publishing
Author photograph © Sally Coggle
Internal design by Midland Typesetters, Australia
Typeset in 12.5/18 pt Adobe Garamond Pro by Midland Typesetters, Australia

Printed and bound in Australia by Griffin Press, an accredited
ISO AS/NZS 14001 Environmental Management Systems printer

A catalogue record for this
book is available from the
NATIONAL LIBRARY OF AUSTRALIA National Library of Australia

ISBN 978 1 76134 113 7

penguin.com.au

MIX
Paper | Supporting
responsible forestry
FSC® C018684

*We at Penguin Random House Australia acknowledge that Aboriginal and Torres Strait
Islander peoples are the Traditional Custodians and the first storytellers of the lands on which we
live and work. We honour Aboriginal and Torres Strait Islander peoples' continuous connection
to Country, waters, skies and communities. We celebrate Aboriginal and Torres Strait Islander
stories, traditions and living cultures; and we pay our respects to Elders past and present.*

For Bud and Jean,
Sally and my father

In memory of those who died on Radji Beach

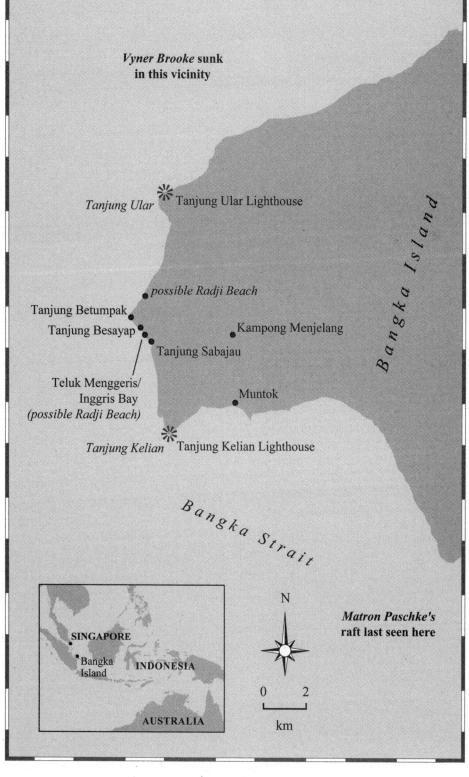

Vyner Brooke sunk
in this vicinity

Bangka Island

Tanjung Ular ✳ Tanjung Ular Lighthouse

● *possible Radji Beach*

Tanjung Betumpak ●

Tanjung Besayap ●

● Tanjung Sabajau

● Kampong Menjelang

Teluk Menggeris/
Inggris Bay
(possible Radji Beach)

● Muntok

✳

Tanjung Kelian Tanjung Kelian Lighthouse

B a n g k a   S t r a i t

SINGAPORE

● Bangka
Island

INDONESIA

AUSTRALIA

N

0   2

km

Matron Paschke's
raft last seen here

Bangka Island

Author's Note

The story of the Australian nurses who were murdered on Bangka Island, the Dutch East Indies, in 1942 has become better known in recent years, but it's still one that many are unaware of. It is a story of atrocious war crimes, the likes of which are still being enacted through the world today in conflict zones, and of incredible bravery amid the brutality of war.

It was a strange feeling to be brought into close proximity with this infamous slice of history through a relative – my great-aunt Dorothy Elmes, or 'Bud', as the family has always known her – and to be drawn into her life in such a visceral way. Because of this I wanted to do Bud (and the other nurses) justice by writing through her eyes, a dramatised account, taking her story out of its historic cage and giving it another life.

Alongside the Bud narrative is my account of being drawn deeper into the history of that time as I attempt to find out what really happened that day in 1942; grapple with the impact of these murders on our family; and see the continuity of history playing out in our present moment.

In researching and writing about injustices inflicted on my great-aunt and many others, the complexities of the historical record became clear to me – what is hidden and what is told. So it is important to acknowledge the context in which I have written this story – in 2023 in Australia, a nation in which much history that needs to be heard is untold and unacknowledged, or dishonoured, by which I mean that of our First Nations peoples.

To construct what happened during Bud's last forty-eight hours, I have used primary and secondary sources from, among others, the National Archives of Australia, the Australian War Memorial, the National Library of Australia; as well as books, journals and newspaper articles, and discussions with relatives of the nurses and others. There are, however, gaps and discrepancies in these accounts, understandable given the traumatic nature of events, the fallibility of memory and the nature of experience, whereby we see only a sliver of what is occurring at any one time. Where there are discrepancies, I have tried to rely on primary accounts, the people most likely to know, or similar accounts from more than one source. Where there are gaps, I have made plausible guesses. I have used my knowledge of Bud's character from family lore and stories, plus her letters, to imagine how she would have responded to what unfolded in her last hours.

A few other things to note. For authenticity's sake I've used the language of the day to talk about the Japanese Imperial forces and referred to 'Japs' occasionally. This language is obviously problematic now and I have kept it to a minimum. Japanese names have been kept in traditional order – surname first followed by given name. Minimal punctuation has been added to Bud's letters. And conversations in the present-day narrative are reconstructed from memory.

Australian Army Nursing Service pledge of service

I pledge myself loyally
to serve my King and Country
and to maintain the honour and efficiency
of the Australian Army Nursing Service.
I will do all in my power
to alleviate the suffering of
the sick and wounded, sparing no
effort to bring them comfort of body
and peace of mind.
I will work in unity and
comradeship with my fellow nurses.
I will be ready to give assistance
to those in need of my help,
and will abstain from any action
which may bring sorrow
and suffering to others.
At all times I will endeavour
to uphold the highest traditions of
Womanhood and of the Profession
of which I am Part.

PART ONE
THE NURSES

Corowa Hospital, New South Wales, undated, 1940

Letter from Bud to her parents

Dear old Tumpy & Dad,

Thank you ever so much for sweet pants & singlet, sponge bag & hanky they are just what I wanted. I got them & your letters yesterday.

Got a wire from Sydney yesterday saying to bring my own uniforms I have been wearing as I start duty on Tuesday so have been living in worn out old things which is a catch so have one of Smithys* & Matron gave me one of hers which is being fixed up for me & two of my own. Went round & said goodbye to the Strongs on Thursday & Mrs Strong sent me a large supply of bath

---

* Smithy – Jean Smithenbecker, a great friend of Bud, with whom she trained and nursed at Corowa Community Hospital, New South Wales.

soap, powder, a sponge bag & soap container which was perfectly sweet of her.

& the kids here have given me all sorts of things, pocket knife, soap, coat hangers & Smithy gave me a most magnificent torch & another towel, so now have to get another suitcase to pack all the surplus in.

Will send home a suitcase containing books & those shoes, which Jean* wants, cardigans & various other oddments I don't want, the only civilian things I am taking are tennis things & a couple of dresses to wear on Monday & Sunday [...]

Will write to let you know my address as soon as I can. Aunt Idie is meeting me & Aunt Evie** rang up the other night & she said she would.

Must hurry hope Boz & Bid*** good & the spuds grow alright,

Love,
Bud

---

* Jean – Beatrice Jean Howard Elmes – was Bud's older sister and only sibling.
** Idie and Evie were Bud's aunts on her mother's side.
*** Bid was Jean's dog, an English setter. Boz may have been a cat though we don't know for sure.

East Sumatra, Dutch East Indies

14 February 1942, before 1 p.m.

The *Vyner Brooke* steams towards the Bangka Strait, a sitting duck in a hostile sea. The afternoon is hot, stifling, like a heavy blanket. Water laps the boat but provides no relief. Earlier, hiding in the lee of the Tudjuh islands, the cramped, grey Sarawak steamer looked for darkness to resume its course down the strait for Batavia. But now Captain Borton takes his chances in the open. Suicidal, he thinks, to remain anchored close to land. Accustomed to carrying twelve passengers in comfort, the *Vyner Brooke*'s steel sheath strains to accommodate the more than two hundred and twenty-five now on board. Squeezed in tight, they grab whatever space they can. The smells of salt, sweat and dread are intensified in the early afternoon sun.

On deck the air is expectant. Sixty-five nurses have made their emergency preparations. Dispersed around the boat are more than a hundred passengers and fifty or so crew. Lulled into an edgy slumber, Bud tries to get some rest, adjusting herself on a canvas stretcher where she has made a makeshift bed, jammed in beside the others, her kit bag close. A lifebelt stands in for a pillow. In the saloon, a group of children play Ludo to pass the time, piercing the monotony with the occasional cry. There shouldn't be so many children on board, Bud thinks. Why didn't their parents leave Singapore earlier? Probably the powers that be wanted them to stay for morale. Deluded to think things would carry on as normal. Bud is fearful for what she suspects may come.

Overhead, at approximately thirteen hundred hours, emerging from the broody sky a Japanese scout plane appears and circles. Already hit by strafing that put holes in some of the starboard lifeboats yesterday, Captain Borton is on high alert. He looks up, spots the scout as it disappears to the north-west, and curses.

'Sound the siren!'

Jarred from her restless sleep, Bud gets up and scrabbles for her tin helmet. This is it, the moment she has anticipated. She stumbles and looks skyward. Nothing, yet. The *Vyner Brooke* groans as the engine strains to go faster. Muffled shouts and footsteps echo as sailors charge to four-inch and Lewis guns. 'Clear the decks!' Matron Paschke commands them. 'Follow your district nurse. I repeat. Follow your district nurse.' Dashing Dot – as they call their much loved Matron, for her brio and enthusiasm – orchestrates their movements.

Bud races towards the top deck, to get all passengers allocated to her station to safety below in the saloon. 'Faster,' she urges those around her. 'We have to find cover before they return.'

'Think we'll make it?' Schuey – Marjorie Schuman, Bud's best friend – throws a backwards glance towards Bud, who bolts up the stairs.

'Hope so.'

Bud grips the rail, heart hammering, and leaves Schuey as she goes up. On the top deck she cranes her neck to check for planes. 'Have these.' Laney hands her a spare helmet and lifejacket.

'Thanks.' Bud doesn't linger on her kindly eyes, or the dread she is feeling. As she moves off, she remembers Matron's instructions to 'grab extra emergency dressings and morphia for the wounded'. She doubles back, takes a fistful to supplement the ones already pinned in her uniform pocket, and shoves them in her coat.

'This way.' Bud beckons the crowd of passengers above the din. A young boy with flaxen hair stands transfixed in the middle of the deck. 'Now!' She gives him a shove.

'Take shelter!' the First Mate yells as the crowd surges towards the stairs, crushing each other as they descend. There is a press of flesh and the smell of inevitability.

'Don't push,' an elderly woman pants.

Bud raises her hand, tries to calm the throng. 'Stop! There's room for all of you.' At least she hopes there is. She squeezes her body – lithe from swimming and tennis – in beside the door and places a hand on the woman's shoulder who, wheezing, is starting to panic.

Within minutes all the decks are cleared and quiet descends. Bud flicks her eyes up, squints in the midday sun. Which direction will they come from? Then she hurries downstairs and checks the passage for stragglers.

Entering the saloon, her eyes skirt around the dark panelled mahogany interior as she takes up her station with the other sisters in her team, strategically dotted around. Nods of understanding pass between them, as if to say, 'We can do this.'

'Everyone got a spot to lie down?' Bud asks, her voice wobbly. 'I know it's tight.'

Passengers reply, with muffled voices, from the floor in her section. Some are lying prostrate, others have crawled under tables, some have gone to take refuge in a bathroom, or under beds in cabins or staterooms. Bud lies down, edges herself in beside a collapsible table and some chairs that are fixed to the floor, and wonders, how long till the planes come back?

'Find something to cover yourself: blankets, clothes – anything to protect you,' Clarice yells across the room. 'There could be flying shrapnel … and glass,' she adds, eyeing the Laycock windows. 'Make sure you have your helmet and life-jacket on.'

People grab coats, blankets, tablecloths – whatever they can find. Bud covers herself with her coat and pins her arms to her side to stop them from shaking. From her vantage point sprawled on the floor she tilts her head up to see Chippendale chairs, cut-crystal lights and polished brass standard lamps with silk shades. By turning her head sideways, she can see cane underneath the padded leather chair next to her. The initials E. B. have been scratched into the wood. Just like the impression she made with a compass under her desk at the little bush school at home in

Cheshunt, Victoria's High Country. B. E. it had read – funny, the reverse.

A hush descends as they settle on the floor. Nothing to do but wait now. Bud sucks in air and holds it, dry in her throat, till her body forces her to breathe out. Mentally, she rehearses her role should they be hit. Her chest pounds and her ribs feel as if they will pop.

A couple of minutes pass. 'Planes at ten o'clock,' a sailor shouts down the passageway. 'I can see the red spots.' Bud closes her eyes, her body tense – every sinew steeled in anticipation. She can hear the scream of the aircraft approaching, feels her adrenaline rising. She lifts her head up to look out the windows but can only see a patch of blue sky and a woman's pale legs in front of her.

'What's happening?' someone asks as they all jolt sideways like skittles. The *Vyner Brooke* turns sharply. Bud reaches to grab hold of the table leg but feels herself slide. A whistle-like sound breaks the silence, accelerating as it gets closer.

'What's that?' another voice calls out.

Deafening cracks as three bombs explode in the water. A deep, sonorous echo reverberates off the seabed and into Bud's body. The boat shudders. Bud's chest thumps.

'Missed!'

'Hold on!' Flo yells across the saloon. The *Vyner Brooke* lurches and zigzags to avoid its attacker but the unmistakeable *ack ack* of machineguns can be heard starboard.

'Us or them?' Bud asks. 'What did that hit?' She sticks her head up, tries to find the others scattered around the saloon. Wishes she could see Schuey, old hound, but her station is beside the staterooms. Bud grabs the hands on either side of her; one is small and soft. The ship turns again, chops up water. Captain Borton dodges planes with a deft hand. The boat rocks and Bud's body swings. She grips the floor; digs feet, arms and limbs in. Was the chance of a lifetime. Now please let it stop!

A tiny sharp fingernail presses into the fleshy part of Bud's palm. She turns her head towards the young girl of about six next to her, with neat brown plaits, who clutches a raggedy teddy. Bud recalls serving her a meagre allocation of bully beef and army biscuits earlier today but doesn't know her name – she wasn't allocated to Bud's care.

The girl reassures her bear. 'Don't worry, Mr Jacks, I'll protect you from the bombs.'

In the panic people have scrambled. Bud strains to hear what's going on outside; the sound of planes circling back, the high-pitched shriek of engines – like mosquitoes – and a whistle falling. 'Four, five, six,' she mouths to herself. Missed again. How many planes up there? Bud tries to work it out. Six? Seven? More? How many bombs each? Her mind is muddy, can't make the calculations. Barely audible, she tries to count them. Each time a fighter plane releases its bombs it strafes the ship and then arcs back up. The *Vyner Brooke* does its best to retaliate, but Bud knows its retro-fit as a battleship is no match for Japanese warplanes.

'Twelve, thirteen, fourteen.' Bud keeps tally. A whiff of gunfire can be smelt as smoke fills the saloon. Her ears have started ringing.

After a while a couple of the bolder nurses, sick of seeing only the floor in front of them and a partial view through the windows, creep over to the door and look out. 'Fifteen, sixteen, seventeen.' From her spot on the floor Bud can see red crosses displayed on the nurses' armbands. Freeing her hand, she touches her own symbol of protection – like a lucky charm.

Clarice breaks the silence. 'Keep this up, Captain, and we just might make it to Batavia.'

A mild cheer goes up. 'Eighteen, nineteen, twenty,' Bud mutters. The ship weaves and Bud's arms throb from trying to hold on.

A crew member sees them through a window. 'Get down!' Knobbly veins bulge in his neck.

The nurses scuttle back to their positions on the floor. 'Twenty-one, twenty-two, twenty-three, twenty-four, twenty-five, twenty-six, twenty-seven.' Bud's chant becomes stronger as her confidence grows.

And then the bombing stops.

'Is it over?' the small voice beside her asks, stroking teddy's head.

'Not sure, sweetie.' The noise of the planes is getting fainter. Are they going back to reload? Bud's neck is tense; she tries to stretch it, pushes knuckles into stiff tendons. 'Just stay as you are.' Extracting the nails from her palm, she squeezes the delicate hand. 'You're doing a fine job there with Mr Jacks.'

A few minutes pass. They don't dare move.

Then Bud hears a faint drone start to get louder. They're back. The ship jerks and the assault resumes.

The bomb hits hard, plummets straight down the funnel of the ship and explodes in the engine room. The force ricochets around the *Vyner Brooke*. Another bomb hits, closer this time, near the rear of the saloon towards the aft. The vessel shakes and the saloon turns a fiery red. In one of the staterooms a woman screams. Shrapnel strikes wood, which splinters and explodes. Crashing sounds – the walls collapsing.

'Stay put!' a sailor yells. Flashes of flames in the engine room and on deck; smoke, sirens and shattering glass. The acrid smells of burning flesh, hair and wood singe Bud's nostrils. A deep, guttural cry forms in her throat but is drowned out by the echo of bombs and otherworldly groans.

'I'm hit! My legs. *Help!*'

'Flo, is that you?' Bud shouts. If there is a response, she can't hear it. The ship seesaws and the onslaught continues. Bud presses her palms hard into the floor but she slips. 'Try to hang on!'

A third bomb hits the front of the ship. The *Vyner Brooke* lifts, almost into the air, and there is the sound of splitting. Is the boat cracking open? Bud covers her head with her arms and is thrown upwards. Something hard, like a piece of wood, whacks her calf. Then her body falls back down and her ribs smack the floor. Her chest compresses and the air is sucked out of her. Over and over planes attack, miss many times with their arsenal, but have hit three times, with a fourth near-miss that feels to Bud as though it has gouged open the starboard side of the ship. She knows that will be the fatal blow.

The *Vyner Brooke* has stopped dead in the water.

Bud freezes. Wonders, is it over? If they now have to take their chances in the water. She starts to call out but stops herself. Doesn't want to scare the children. Yesterday they went over and over the drill with Major Tebbutt, the senior officer in charge of the nurses on the *Vyner Brooke*, and Matron Paschke. Bud has rehearsed it many times in her head.

When the long siren sounds, she scrambles up, knowing what this means. *Evacuation! Evacuation! Prepare for evacuation!* The ship has taken on water and is already starting to list. They can't have much time.

'Are we sinking?' her small companion asks.

'Stay close,' Bud replies, 'I'll get you off.'

But Bud knows they are overloaded without enough lifeboats, the ship full with mainly women and children, plus nurses and crew, a few elderly and the odd serviceman. Matron Paschke's instructions ring in her ears. *All civilians are to be evacuated before you nurses can leave the vessel. Your first responsibility is to the physical wellbeing of those in your care.*

Bud is determined this will not be a repeat of Singapore. Ordered to leave their patients by Lieutenant-General Percival and Major-General Bennett, when they wanted to stay – whatever the cost. They had taken an oath, had a job to do. She still feels upset. The male orderlies were allowed to stay. A patient of hers, a soldier from the 8th Division, gave her a feeble smile and insisted she go. 'For your own safety, you must,' he told her, but his strung-out eyes etched guilt into her starchy collar. Bud had stared at the cracks in the hospital wall, engorged with tropical rain. She left a glass of water by his side, with a straw so he could sip – if he could lift his broken arm – and against her will she fled with the other nurses, in an ambulance, through the burning streets of Singapore to Keppel Harbour, stopping at go-downs for shelter from air raids on the way. Tears on their cheeks. Guts in their boots.

Bud looks around now at mutilated bodies: ruptures, flesh wounds, hernias and heavy losses of blood. Though there was shelling and a few fatalities in Singapore at Oldham Hall, where her hospital unit, the 2/10th, were most recently located and often needed to don tin hats in order to keep working, she has previously been spared the sheer scale of this level of trauma. She suppresses her horror and exhales slowly.

Betty and Caroline have started getting one of the civilians, Mrs Bull, and her three children out. They envelop a child each in their arms and head to the lifeboats.

'Sister, help me,' a feeble voice calls out.

'Who's that?' Bud can't see through smoke, bodies and debris. 'Where are you?' She stands and can feel her ribs ache. With her fingertips she traces the bones. Hopes they are intact – fingers crossed no hairline fractures.

'At the rear ... starboard side.'

'I'm coming,' she replies and pulls the emergency dressings from her coat pocket. 'Smoke's in my eye.' Bud wipes it with her sleeve.

'Hurry ... please.'

'I'm trying to get there.' She moves towards his voice. 'Think I can see you up the back.'

'I'm shaking.' His voice is faint.

'Hang on.' Bud picks up her pace. 'Nearly there.' She clambers over a sandy-haired teenage boy and his mother, who's dressed in a peacock blue suit, lying entwined. Bud can see the man now, emerging through the haze, right beside Clarice and Rosetta who, also injured, are being fixed up by other sisters. The bomb must have landed right behind them near the passageway to the cabins. Shrapnel wounds to soft tissue, gluteal area, Bud thinks after a cursory glance their way. Bit of blood loss, but nothing fatal.

'Hello.' She squats down beside the man. From his deeply impressed crow's feet, she thinks he is about sixty. One of his legs is blown out the back. What is left of his hamstring hangs semi-detached from the ischial tuberosity. Bud braces. 'Let's get you fixed up, then.'

'Can't move my leg.'

'Lie still – you have shrapnel wounds.' She starts to wind the field dressing firmly around his leg so he stops haemorrhaging, then inserts gauze to stop the flow of blood and applies pressure to steady his twitches. At any moment it's likely that Captain Borton will make them abandon ship and take what casualties they can. Already, as she glances around, she can see other nurses moving people out, following the directions of a ship's officer in the whitest of whites. Veronica, from the 2/13th, moves among the chaos with hypodermic needles and morphia, giving extra shots to those who won't make it.

'All done,' Bud says to the man as she fixes the bandage with a safety pin.

'This blood on the floor, is it mine?' His head jerks to the side and she can feel his heart-rate quicken – is he having a cardiac arrest?

Bud places her hands on his sunken cheeks. 'Just focus on

me,' she says, and she turns his head to centre and locks her eyes on his.

'I don't think I can make it.'

Her hazel eyes forbid his dissent. 'Yes, you can. I'll give you a shot of morphia to take the edge off.' She works fast – the ship lists to starboard and the smell of burning has intensified. The man raises his hand just off the floor. She clasps it. Liver spots and knotted veins speak of a life lived outdoors. Plantation manager probably. Bud tries to control her rising alarm as she stands.

'Stay …' He grips on tight.

'I'm sorry, I have to help others.' Bud gently uncurls his stiff, arthritic fingers. Still so many to get off, she thinks, how will we make it in time? Mona Wilton and Wilma support an injured Kath right past her. Bud wants to cry out, *Neuss, are you okay?* But she tells herself to stay calm and focus on her patient.

'I don't want to die alone.' His spongy hand quivers.

'You won't. I promise.'

Rutherglen, Victoria,
13 December 1940

Letter from Aunt Evie to Bud's mother,
Dorothy Jean Elmes

[...] We are very sad Benda* is leaving the district she is going to be missed by many [...] She is full of beans and very delighted to be going – the Showground camp will be nice and central – she will be able to get away to friends – one of the country camp hospitals would have been much lonelier.

Idie was very pleased Benda is to go to them, and I'm sure she will be good to her, it will be nice for her to meet the girls – Benda is to wear a grey hat, Idie will have a navy hat with white bow & they must find each other.

The 2nd class is all booked up but one seat. B is going 1st and can get a seat in a lady's carriage – I shall try and make her take a

---

*   Benda was another family nickname for Bud.

cushion – and a few sandwiches. It will be interesting to hear how she gets on [...]

I warned her not to carry much money with her – but have it transferred to Sydney Savings Bank which she is going to do – I don't think she will get such good pay in future – but I am not sure. It is very doubtful that she will get overseas for many months – As things are going the war might end sooner than we thought – Let us at least hope for Peace in the New Year.

In case I cannot write again a happy Christmas to you both. So sorry you will not have the child with you – but she is doing her bit nobly [...]

Much love,

Evie

Mouth of Bangka Strait, East Sumatra

14 February 1942, 1.30 p.m.

'Time to go.' Bud reaches down and helps up her young companion. Still talking to Mr Jacks, the girl stands and tugs at her mother, who swaddles a baby. Bud diverts the girl's attention away from the woman they pass, whose abdomen has been perforated, who is haemorrhaging. Her intestines are spilling into clumps on the ground through the bloodied hand with which she's trying to keep them inside. Next to her lies a man disembowelled by shrapnel. Bud could swear he sings 'Rule Britannia' as he takes his last breaths. She yanks at the girl's sleeve, places her hands like blinkers on both sides of the girl's face and drags her, and her mother and baby, along the smoky passageway littered with shards of glass. Through the heaving mass of passengers trying to stay calm, Bud can smell burning oil and desperation. Her eyes still sting. Down the passageway and up the stairs they go.

Out on the top deck the sky is an inky grey unfurling with smoke and the sun has turned black. Bud sees a ship's officer and thrusts her three charges at him. 'Get them to safety!'

Passengers with ill-fitting lifejackets hurtle headlong into the water, hit the sea's surface with such force that Bud fears for their lives. Another bomb explodes and a spout of water shoots up in the distance. A child screams. Bud throws herself down to dodge machinegun bullets that are pelting the ship, hugs up into a ball and cradles herself for a moment. As quickly as they came, the planes retreat. She gets up, trips, the deck is smeared with blood. Her stomach lurches. The ship tilts to a steeper angle. She grips the metal railing and her shoes start to slide.

But the *ack acks* and shrapnel have put holes in the port side lifeboats – who knows how many are still seaworthy – and some of the ropes that secure them have split. The crew are trying to lower these lifeboats first. Suspended by a thread, one filled with women and children hangs, creaking, then drops into the sea, spilling out some of its passengers. Another one drops – on board are a couple of unsuspecting sailors whose shouts decrescendo as they fall.

'Hurry,' Matron Paschke yells, gesticulating forcefully. 'We haven't got long. Get everyone off this ship!'

Eric Germann, a thirty-one-year-old brewer from New York, is frantically untying and throwing rafts into the water with his brawny arms before the *Vyner Brooke* sinks. He wears thigh-high leather boots. 'Anyone allocated a lifeboat, climb down the ladders and get in!' Eric pushes forward a reluctant boy and then descends the ladder himself to free a lifeboat that has got lodged under a water condenser outlet and is now filling with water. From above, Bud sees him hook his leg over the bottom rung and lean back, submerging his head. Once the lifeboat is freed, he pops back up again. At the same time, a couple of society women are climbing down in high heels. Bud could swear she sees them use his head as a stepping stone. Eric yells at them, irate, then starts to climb back up against what is now a downhill tide of passengers. Back on deck, water drips through his scraggly beard. Bud notices he now has bare feet. 'Accused me of looking up their skirts.' She moulds her face into a scowl. Has a mind to grab a pair of those heels and dole out a few whacks.

A little boy, Isadore, is thrust into Eric's arms by passengers. Bud thinks he must be only about three years old. His mother has collapsed, inconsolable, at their feet. Bud feels useless standing as an onlooker to the poor woman's grief.

'Her husband has gone,' one of the passengers explains. 'She saw him jump off the ship in shock when the first bombs hit. He can't swim.'

'Don't be afraid,' Eric says to Izzy, the man's gentleness softening the impact of his bulk and deep-set, livid eyes. 'We're just going to jump into the water for a nice cold swim.' He places his hand over Izzy's mouth and nose, then envelops the boy with his body and leaps them in.

'Move quickly!' Matron Paschke keeps shouting, her arms thrusting forward like signposts. 'We only have a few minutes.'

Bud remembers her promise to the man in the saloon who, she is sure, hasn't yet been loaded into a lifeboat. She doubles back inside, wonders if she'll be able to get him off, or if he is too far gone. She navigates the swarm heading in the other direction, and spots Rosetta, Flo, Florence, Clarice and Kath, all injured and being helped to evacuate. One of the crew sticks an arm out to slow her. 'We need to get off this boat!' But Bud weaves past. 'I have to check for someone.'

The boat groans, as if aware of its plight. Bud can't see much and has to feel her way to the saloon, sliding her hand along the polished wooden panelling of the passageway. The boat tips further to starboard and Bud's right arm braces against the side to counterbalance her weight so she doesn't fall. She traces the grain till she feels the edge of what must be the door into the saloon, using both hands to steady herself on the lintel. Smoke and the smell of gunpowder have filled the room. Water sloshes around on the floor. Bud moves with haste towards the corner where she left the man. Now lying on an angle, his smudgy figure has slid further towards the side. Closer in, she can see blood seeping through the field bandage, forming an outline of soupy red. She squats beside him to check his vital signs. Minuscule movements around his jaw and twitches on his lip line can be detected. They must've thought he was too far gone. Bud touches him, hopeful. 'Told you I'd come back.' No response bar the slight compression of his jugular notch and a barely audible moan. He has slipped into Cheyne-Stokes breathing and for a long fifteen seconds there is no breath at all. Spongy, cold skin meets hers as she clasps his hand and places her finger on his weakened pulse. His pupils dilate. Bud hears that wet crackle sound. 'I'm giving you another shot of morphia.' She talks fast, reaches for her syringe and sticks a needle in his upper arm. She hopes he can hear her beyond his aqueous eyes that gaze into mid-distance, strokes his hand, knows her touch is the last he will feel.

Bud looks around. Soon all these bodies will vanish. Up and up the water will climb, past her calves, over her knees. She blinks and can picture everything floating. She has to get off! Her legs are like bricks but she forces them to move. She reaches down and closes the man's papery eyelids, drops his hand, and pitches herself up the debris-strewn passageway and stairs, out into the open. Past Beth, who is responsible for the being last to check, and Jessie, in charge of the saloon. Bud wonders where Schuey is, it would be good to see her face. Last time she saw her was when they took up their stations just before the bombs hit. The ship is at a steep angle now – must be about forty-five degrees. Bud runs as best she can at this tilt, stumbling along, and doesn't look back.

Up on deck Matron Paschke gives the final order: 'All nurses are to evacuate. Now!'

Earlier in the day, Bud, being one of the better swimmers, had volunteered to jump into the water instead of taking up space in a lifeboat. Half the lifeboats are ruined now anyway, hopefully these last few are left intact. Thank god for the lifejackets, lifebelts and rafts. Matron Paschke has calmly briefed them – though she can't swim herself and has asked for their help – to jump in and find a raft, or, if that's impossible, to cling to anything that floats. Bud fastens her lifejacket between her legs, hopes it's tight enough – she knows it could break her neck if it isn't. She double-checks, tugs again. Should she go down the ropes instead? 'Hand over hand' is how they were briefed, but shrieks from the nurses she's spotted doing this stop her. They must've slid straight down instead, the ropes shredding the skin off their hands.

Bud takes off her helmet and goodbyes the shoes that Smithy – still at the hospital in Corowa though she has signed up – has only just sent. 'Sorry, Smithy, can't swim with them dragging.'

Crimson-faced Major Tebbutt yells at them above the noise. 'Evacuate. *Now!*'

The boat tips even further to starboard. Bud wraps her fingers around the rail so tightly that her hands cramp. Behind her on the listing ship are the remaining nurses and crew; below her at least a hundred passengers are strewn in the sea. She can see children bobbing in the water, their mothers clutching at them, determined to hold on. A girl slips from her mother's hand. Bud tenses. She holds her lifejacket down, away from her neck, and prepares to jump. Now or never. The water is a fair way, her legs tremble.

'Now!'

Bud jumps.

'Watch *oouuuuut!*' For a few moments she is suspended, weightless in air, then she freefalls into the sea. Her body hits and the surface bites. Cool water erupts and she descends down, down, down, gurgling as she plummets. It is quiet in the depths, far from the cries and groans. Muffled, distorted sounds filter through from above. Her descent slows and the sea wraps around her like a shawl. Pausing in the stillness, she drinks in silence and consolation. Then pressure in her ears and lungs starts to build. With a kick she propels herself up and scrabbles back to the surface. She coughs, tries to ignore her aching ribs, and expels the seawater she inhaled on the way down. Treading water, she looks around to figure out what next. A life raft whistles past her. 'Watch it!' she yells and ducks. But there is no way to be heard above the death throes of the ship. The *Vyner Brooke* tips further sideways so that everything on deck becomes a hazard for those in the water. A rail flies past, just misses the back of Bud's head. She spins around. Her lifejacket of unbendable cork squares sewn into canvas is gouging her neck. This is not like the lazy off-duty afternoons at the club doing lap after lap.

Bud looks around her, swears she can see Mona Wilton and Wilma jumping out of a leaking and crowded lifeboat, dog-paddling away from the ship, which creaks like it's about to break up. Not long till it goes under. If Mona and Wilma don't get further away, they'll get caught underneath. Mona can't swim at all and Wilma is only slightly better.

'Mona, Wilma!' Bud shouts to get their attention. 'Hurry!' Bud could swear it's them – they usually travel together. The ship lists again, violently, more life rafts fly over the side. Rip and slice up the water. Now Bud can't see them – doesn't know if they've been hit or just obscured by rafts and debris. The current pushes her back as she tries to swim over. Two bodies appear several yards from where she last saw them. She can see outlines and uniforms of grey. Are they alive or floating in their lifejackets? Bud cries out again, but the water is silent. Her wail intensifies. It looks like the bodies are moving – she can see if she squints – but are they drifting or swimming? Bud tears at the water in frustration, smacks it with her hands. Keep moving, no time to …

what's that? Something touches her shoulder and as she turns, the corpse of a boy, no older than four, brushes her arm. His mouth is open, she can see his milky teeth. She whirls around, tries to pre-empt the touch of sodden, waxy bodies. Looks back at the inclining ship just in time to see the outline of Matron Paschke – she must be one of the very last to leave – climb onto the railing of the partially submerged vessel and hurl herself towards a group of nurses, who catch and pull her onto a raft. Something inside Bud settles knowing Matron is safe.

The sun beats down and the smell of bombs and gunfire lingers. Bud starts to shake; she can't control her convulsing body as the currents pull her this way and that.

Creaking sounds snap her back to attention. The *Vyner Brooke* is in its death throes. From her watery perspective, Bud takes in a scene made colourless by the smoke that tinges everything. In ghastly slow motion, the ship turtle-rolls, teeters on one side and groans. It hovers aloft for what feels like a couple of minutes. Finally, it succumbs, inch by painstaking inch, until it glides, bow first, with a whoosh into the sea near the entrance to the Bangka Strait. A wrinkle on the water is the only sign of its existence.

'There she goes,' says Captain Borton, who clings to a piece of wood nearby. The words hang where the ship was.

Bud checks the watch her parents gave her for her birthday. It has stopped.

And then comes silence, intense and eerie.

A few metres in front of her a teddy floats by. Mr Jacks? Surely not? Bud's stares at it blankly. It's the same mustardy colour, with dark brown, leather paws. Bud wonders if the girl and her mother are safe. Her heart bleeds. She feels the water's welcoming embrace, the soporific effect of the sun and how easily she could lie back and succumb.

2/10th Australian General Hospital, Malaya, 22 February 1941

Letter from Bud to her parents

Dear old Tumpy & Dad,

There is not much news since I wrote last time. Haven't heard from Jean or Smithy yet [...] some of the shops [here] are very cheap have just had a frock made for 4/6 and the material only cost about 9[pence] a yard but whether it will wash without shrinking remains to be seen.

Had a game of tennis the other afternoon, don't know whether it was the climate or my fault but was much worse than usual; as the courts are slow in a way but beautiful to play on, more like grass [...]

Hope Jean & Rowley* are with you now; the change will do them good.

---

* Rowley was Bud's two-year-old nephew, her sister Jean's son.

I will be disgustingly lazy when I get home, as we have women or they are called Amahs – they do all our own personal washing make our beds clean up in general, very nice in a way but occasionally like to do a spot of work.

They seem to grow a good bit of rice about here, it looks very much like rye or millet in the distance and they apparently cut all year round, but mightn't be right in saying that.

Glad Boz is alright and the fowls are condescending to lay again.

Sorry this isn't frightfully interesting but can't think of much to tell you at the moment [...]

Love,

Bud

2/10th Australian General Hospital, Malaya, undated

Letter from Bud to her friend Jean Smithenbecker

Dear Old Smithy,

Not very much news this week, although was rather social last week. On Friday night several of us went to a Malayan girls training college for about an hour to a concert given by them, it was very clever although some of the sketches were a bit hard to follow as it was all spoken in Malayan (we aren't so hot at the language yet). On Saturday morning we enticed an ambulance (our means of conveyance) to take us to the swimming club with several pounds of steak which we had cooked there which was delicious; and that night six of us were invited to a Rotary club dinner consisting of eight courses; but altogether it was most interesting, some of the speakers were very good and clever, the majority of the members were well educated Chinese and Singalese. The Chinese particularly are frightfully proud of never having intermarried with the other races, although most of them have lived here for dozens of generations. Suppose you think we don't do any work; except as a little recreation but we do really, although it doesn't sound like it [...]

By the way we discovered the most delightful drink, a mixture of sweetened condensed milk & Bournvita messed up together with water and a little dash of ice, most soothing to the nerves [...]

Sorry this is so boring but the intelligence is high; they say that in this country after a while the appetite goes, then the mind, followed shortly by the morals so it looks as though have started in the middle, don't know what will come next.

Cheers old hound to all the other tripe hounds,

Love,

Bud

Mouth of Bangka Strait, East Sumatra

14 February 1942, mid-afternoon

Bud looks back to where the *Vyner Brooke* once was, and where a vortex swirled after it sank. A trail of debris is strewn across the water: suitcases and trunks, helmets, galley utensils and planks of wood. Scared of being hit, she circles around to see what's behind her, hands poised to react. People grasp rafts, lifebelts, spars, anything that will float. They yell to each other over flotsam in a mass meeting attempt. 'Take off your tin hat, Tweddell' bounces over the water, and, 'Does anyone need a hand?'

Soon currents are snatching and dragging everyone in different directions. The contents of a suitcase rolls by on the swell. A leather-bound bible and letters on translucent pages, now soggy in the sea. A blade of sunlight pierces the smoke, illuminates a collection of floating underwear – girdles, bras and undies. Matron would tut-tut to see it so exposed. Aquamarine, green and orange fish, now lifeless and shot up from the seabed, float into Bud's peripheral vision. Urgh, they brush her cheek. She grabs the skirt of her uniform, which has bunched up, and pushes them away. Despite the blackened sky the heat belts down.

Oil covers the water, smears and smothers her skin. Bud squints and blinks – it has seeped into her eyes. She wipes off what she can with her sleeve but it is oil-soaked too. She'll have to keep her head out of the water till it clears, look ahead through blurry eyes. Down and around she pushes her legs – like a bicycle – treading water.

Another corpse floats by. A boy of about two, with a cherubic head of blond curls, now streaked – like a tabby cat – with oily stripes. Keep going. Can't help him now. Bud prays she won't see any of her friends like this. Where's Schuey? She remembers the photo they took on leave in Singapore, after the Eton crop. We both looked foul, Bud thinks. With her hair cut shorter, Schuey looked as though her neck was stretched, and I just looked smug.

A clearing in the wreckage around her opens up. Bud takes her chance to get an unobstructed view of the island. Swims as fast as she can, arms like eggbeaters, and her head jutting out to get to clear water. Panting, she takes a moment for her heart-rate to lower and work out what next. It is eerie over here, adrift in the sea. People being propelled in different directions. Bud can hear a rendition of 'We're Off to See the Wizard', which echoes with distortion. Who's singing that? She can see now the large island about ten miles in front of her. Between the two lighthouses, she reminds herself – that's the beach we are aiming for, with the mountain behind. Where Matron Paschke instructed us to meet up. Must keep it firmly in sight.

What would she do if the planes returned? She's a target out here, so exposed. Dive under, she thinks, but for how long could she hold her breath? Her ribs hurt. She looks up to scan the darkened, smoky sky. Blotches, like ink blots, appear in her vision. She blinks her fuzzy eyes and is relieved to see nothing up there.

Then Bud spots an empty raft – at last! – swims over and heaves herself onto it. Her arms wobble with her weight as she lets the hard wood buttress her. Made of canvas-covered slats, the raft is just big enough for one, or two if you sat back to back. She lies on it, extends her arms wide, like a T, and floats as if she is cushioned on a cloud. A minute or two passes while she musters her strength. Then she sits up and inspects the raft. There is a canvas water bottle with fresh water, two paddles, and looped ropes fixed to the sides for swimmers to hold on to, or tie up with.

Matron Drummond, on a lifeboat not too far away, spots her and calls out, 'Sister Elmes, paddle over – we'll attach your raft to the lifeboat.'

Bud isn't as familiar with Matron Drummond – in charge of the 2/13th – so she feigns a brave face. 'I'm okay, Matron Drummond … don't want to weigh you down.'

'Nonsense,' Matron shouts across the water, 'we must stay together.'

So Bud grabs a paddle and plunges it below the surface. 'Yes, Matron,' she calls, grateful – not really keen on the idea of facing this solo. She pushes the paddle down, her entire weight thrown behind it, grunts, and forces it back against the current.

Her arms burn with the strain but despite the dense water she manages to manoeuvre the raft towards the lifeboat. She unfixes the rope from the side of her raft and ties it onto the trailing rope of the lifeboat, as Sedgeman, first officer of the *Vyner Brooke* and a merchant officer in the Royal Naval Reserve, instructs her to. Sub Lieutenant Bill 'Ginger' Sedgeman is in his early thirties, Welsh, with a comfortable command. Bud can see about twenty people on or around the boat: Bessie Wilmott and other nurses; Mr Watson, an elderly magistrate; some injured passengers; and a couple of sailors bailing water out. They don't take much notice of her, immersed as they are in their own ordeals.

'Buddy Elmes, you okay?' She looks up and sees Laney hanging on to a trailing rope. A grin transforms Bud's frown.

'Laney, so good to see your face.' She and Laney had clicked instantly when Bud was attached briefly to the 2/4th Casualty Clearing Station. 'Have you seen Schuey – you remember her? 2/10th, same as me?'

'Not sure.' Laney tugs at her lifejacket and adjusts the strap, but something about her response unnerves Bud. 'So many trying to get off …'

They settle into an uneasy silence. Vacant-faced men, women and children sit on the lifeboat and stare blankly. Some contort in pain. It would be a clear, bright day but the haze of bombs still cloaks the sky like a shroud. After a while, the lifeboat starts to creak with the weight of its human cargo. Despite the furious bailing it sits lower and lower in the water. Bud's raft is now right up against the boat, although, as Sedgeman has told her to, she has tied the ropes slack enough to keep it at a distance. But the current has changed and the raft bangs back and forth, creating a drag.

'Some of you will have to swim.' Matron Drummond looks around and assesses the group. 'Can the strong swimmers get in the water. You'll need to alternate between paddling and swimming so we have a chance of making it ashore.'

Bud volunteers. Perched on the raft, she unties her lifejacket, yanks it off and awkwardly takes off her uniform, which is a relief since it created friction in the water, bunching up around her legs. 'Lucky I've got my voile on.' She lays her uniform out on the raft so it doesn't slide off, and ties the hem of it to one of the ropes to make sure. Though her lifejacket chafes under her chin – a blister is forming – she knows she must put it back on. She secures it tighter between her legs so that it sits away from her chin. She slides back into the water, which laps around her, viscous on top and unknown below. Damn, the lifejacket is already working its way back up. It feels a little cooler now – she'll have to swim faster. Then she remembers sharks. Surely they've been scared off? But there's a tremor in her legs as they stretch out behind her and she thinks of the trails of blood in the water.

She falls into a rhythm of strokes and breath. It's hard to swim with the lifejacket on, she has to keep her arms stuck out wide at an angle, but she doesn't dare take her chances without it. She opts for one-armed freestyle and alternates with sidestroke. One stroke at a time, her attention on the sensation of breath as it comes in and goes out. The rhythm of her belly as it rises and falls is soothing and familiar, despite her sore ribs. The lapping sound and swoosh of the water as her hand glides in, up and out reminds her of happy days spent at Malayan and Singaporean clubs.

Good fortune is on their side and Bud feels a current catch and lift them. It's pulling their small flotilla towards the island, the one that Matron Paschke urged them to head towards.

Meet you there, she said, and then we will get ourselves teed up.

As they head for shore, the rafts are siphoned this way and that. Bud watches as some are drawn further and further away. She thinks she can just see the outline of Matron Paschke in the distance on a raft with other nurses. One of them seems to be holding a couple of children, and some are alongside, gripping trailing ropes. They paddle with urgency as they are dragged out to sea.

'Let the current take you out and then try to make your way diagonally to shore,' Sedgeman yells out, though Bud thinks it's unlikely they can hear him.

Laney starts to sing. 'Row, row, row, your boat …' Known for captivating audiences with her favourite, 'A Nightingale Sang in Berkeley Square', on the trip over on the *Queen Mary*, the effect is poignant but comical. A lone voice, her song lilts on the tide.

Soon some of the others chime in: 'Row, row, row, your boat gently down the stream …'

Bud is tone deaf but wants to join in too, doesn't think there'll be any objectors, though it is a bit of a struggle to sing and swim.

'Merrily, merrily, merrily, merrily, life is but a dream …'

Bud swims sidestroke as she sings, grips the rope on the side of the boat and keeps her head above water. For a while they warble with enthusiasm but they peter out, exhausted from their efforts to steer the lifeboat towards shore. How long till we make it, Bud wonders, trying to gauge the distance to land. She can see two lighthouses winking to mark the coastline. That's where we're headed, she repeats chorus-like, the beach in the middle.

They've been in the water for a couple of hours now, she thinks, though she has no working watch to verify the time. She can feel her hands going numb, it's starting to get cold, and a blister is forming where the rope rubs. She looks up, thinking how exposed they are out here.

An elderly man floats by on his back, wrapped in a lifejacket, and still as a corpse. An unlit pipe is clenched between his teeth. Is he alive, or at rest in his watery grave – his last experience a pleasurable peccadillo? His body floats off into the distance, like a wax figurine.

The smell of death pervades the air. Beside Bud on the lifeboat, a Malay sailor with his hair and clothes burnt off struggles to breathe. A sister she doesn't know tends his wounds and talks in a low, mellow voice, using a borrowed shirt rinsed in seawater as a cool compress to treat and keep sun off his wounds. Fluid loss will become a real issue, Bud thinks, but how do we prevent it?

Under their breath some recite the Lord's Prayer. 'Our Father who art in heaven …' Some call out their loved ones' names. All are at the mercy of the currents near the Bangka Strait. An indiscriminate lottery in a giant sea.

And Schuey? Bud stops swimming, thinks she sees her drift by about forty yards away. 'Schuey, over here! It's Buddy.'

No response. *Is* that her? Or is Bud seeing things? 'Schuey!' She pitches her voice as far as she can. No one turns or calls back. Is that her crop of bobbed brown hair? 'SCHUEY!' Bud waves wildly. Still nothing. Bud's chest contracts, like it's about to crumple. Their bond feels stretched to the point of snapping.

Images of the wounded on board flood her mind. How shattered she feels at leaving the old man, and, in Singapore, the soldier with desolate eyes. Did that last shot of morphia ease his transition from this world? And the young girl with Mr Jacks? She can't think about that.

Bud sobs, just a little, as she continues her strokes that help drive them forward, shoreward.

Melbourne

November 2016

I fell into Bud's story, I think, if I'm honest. There was no hero's journey, no desperate discontent. Maybe my gradual uncoverings began with a murmur from the other side of the grave. Or a crack in the family silence when Dad lent me a book about the massacre on Radji Beach, Bangka Island, and awoke my curiosity. Perhaps the events were always in my bones. And it was time, seventy-five years later, to open the door to our family history. Close enough that Dad, and his sister, Sally, were still alive. Not so close that the grief would envelop you. Though at times I felt it did.

When amateur historian Michael Pether wrote to me at the end of 2016, Bud was barely on my radar. Michael told me that a seventy-fifth memorial service of the massacre on Radji Beach was to be held there the following February. He explained he was trying to write the memorial entry on my great-aunt, 'Buddy' Elmes. He'd found her in a blog I'd written, in which I had mentioned her name once in passing. The blog was about resilience and my grandmother, Jean. In a few short years Jean had lost her sister Bud (Dorothy Gwendoline Howard Elmes) and her husband, Arthur Rowland Banks, who was known to us all as Dolly. Both in traumatic circumstances: not long after the family found out that Bud was likely dead, Dad's father, Dolly, went missing for a week and turned up dead in the Yarra River. It was said to have been a heart attack, but Aunt Sally thought it wasn't. 'Cause of death: Drowning (open)', the death certificate read.

When Michael's invitation to the memorial arrived, I was interested – how could I not be? – but I prevaricated. I was busy, working, co-director of a learning and development consultancy. Two teenage girls to look after. Couldn't possibly go to Indonesia in February; I would've just had four weeks' holiday over the summer break. Then again, this was an invitation to wrest myself from my usual routine. To retrace my relative's steps, to find out more about a story of national significance, of women in war, that seemed not well enough known for my liking.

The email from Michael contained a Facebook link: 'Muntok Nurses and Internees'. I clicked it. Up came photo after photo of nurses, in black and white, or sepia tones. The images took my breath away. The page was like a shrine, a public eulogy. I scrolled and scrolled, searching for Bud. There she was. My fingers tingled, my heart did a little leap. The shot registered as familiar. Had I seen it before at my grandmother Jean's home? I circled through her Wangaratta fibro in the bank of my memories, crunched along the gravel drive with the whiff of peppercorn trees, around the living and dining rooms, down the hall, adorned with Jean's art, which led to the apricot tree she had planted out the back.

But I couldn't place its whereabouts. Later, my Aunt Sally told me it had hung on Jean's bedroom wall, so I would have seen it. A boring old war photo in my childhood mind, no doubt, Jean's false teeth far more impressive. Jean had kept the portrait close and private. It shocked me, though, brought me to a halt when I realised that I had never heard my grandmother mention her sister Bud's name. Not once.

I leant in to the image on the screen and took a closer look. Must be her army shot, the one you got when you signed up. 'Look this way,' *click*. Bud was handsome, chestnut hair pulled back in a bun, hat set at a jaunty angle. She looked a little rakish, androgynous even, in her uniform. Her eyebrows and fulsome gash of a mouth arched up, as if to challenge, *are you up for it?* I wanted to reach back in time through the computer, like a portal, say, 'Hello, Bud.'

When I told my husband, Kingsley, he looked like tearing up. He was listening to Human League in the kitchen. 'Pretty sobering,' was what he said and blew out some air.

'Yep,' I replied. 'It was a war crime.'

I broadcast the news to the family: 'There's a seventy-fifth memorial service for Bud and the nurses – on the actual beach. Who wants to come?'

I didn't want to go alone – bit of a wuss, plus this was an experience to be shared, preferably with Aunt Sally or Dad. Would they want to go, though? I wasn't sure.

I made a cup of tea and waited. I could hear echoes of girl world upstairs: grunts when a bathroom was used too long, late-night laughs, dance-routine thuds, whispers and Netflix shows.

Our dog, Lola, positioned herself on my lap. Lola was barely there, three kilos of black curls. She was supposed to be a small dog but must have been the runt. Feisty though, like a ferret, when needed. She had been known to round up sheep.

Ping. Aunt Sally was *desperate* to come, but couldn't. She'd had a car accident in her youth and struggled to walk nowadays, in her early seventies. She'd need a wheelchair on the beach and the heat was not kind to her. I could hear her regret through the screen: 'February in Indonesia? Too hot. You go, George, in my place.'

'Clive?' I asked my uncle hopefully.

'We've just moved to Warragul.' Of course he couldn't go without Sally. He would consider this hers to remember. Clive was protective of his wife in all the right ways.

Ping. Imogen, my sister, responded. 'Love to come. Have to get out of my leadership thingy though. Leave it with me.'

It would be great to have her with me. Imogen always knows what to do, or has an opinion on how to deal with difficult things.

Ping, ping, ping. Responses were coming in fast. Tim, my cousin, a group captain in the air force and responsible for the F/A-18A Hornet Force (official title Officer Commanding No. 81 Wing). Surely he could fly in – like when he did the flyover for the Australian Grand Prix. But no. 'Apologies,' he said, but he was commanding a trilateral activity with the US and Japan. The irony. Tim's brother next, Alex. He and his wife had just had their third baby.

I refreshed my emails. Nothing from Oliver, my brother. Living in Dubai, with a busy job and a young family, I knew he was unlikely to say yes. My mother replied next: she hadn't renewed her passport. Not the best excuse, but she would have to be loyal to Dad, who said, 'No. Don't want to open old wounds.'

It was a statement of finality, his shield of protection firmly in place. The memorial could have been a chance to understand a little more; something of him, something of his past. I didn't push it, though, I never did.

I wasn't getting far, so I decided to dip a toe into the memorial club, post on the Facebook page – say who we were, that we were hoping to come. An hour or so later, another Michael, Michael Noyce, posted back. The administrator of the Facebook page, he explained that he was the nephew of Kath Neuss. His side of the family had changed their name after the war.

I jumped online. Sister Kathleen Margaret Neuss had dark-brown hair rolled back off her face and a motherly air. She and Bud were both posted with the 2/10th Australian General Hospital to Malaya, and later Singapore just before it fell. Kath was thirty when she died and Bud twenty-seven. Perhaps they'd reached for each other at the end, on the beach, under the glare of the sun.

Twenty-seven. At twenty-seven, I was engaged and living in a flat facing the Sydney Opera House, possibility and the Harbour stretching out before me. I tried to run my hands through Lola's coat. Matted curls met my fingers. Clutching her so she couldn't get away, I grabbed the brush with metal teeth and started to work it through her coat. Lola growled and bared her teeth.

About eighty people are coming, Michael Noyce explained – relatives, the Australian and British defence attachés, plus the Australian ambassador to Indonesia.

What about you? he finished.

*

Lola needed a walk and I needed air, so I put her on her lead and headed for the Melbourne Botanic Gardens. Ears back like a rabbit, she bolted up the hill, stopping to sniff the granite wall of the Shrine of Remembrance. Panting, I caught up and paused to admire the building, monolithic in the afternoon sun. Though I passed it at least once a week, I read for the first time the words on the side of the memorial: 'Let all men know that this is holy ground.'

I looked down the manicured hill and along St Kilda Road, all the way to the city. Traffic was bad. Cars were creeping along. A tunnel was being excavated for the train line underneath. The contents of the earth were spewed up; gravel, dirt, detritus. Grey barricades fenced off parts of the pavement, which was now unsafe to walk on. A horn beeped its impatience, not that the traffic could move any faster.

Maybe I should leave things as they are, no need to churn them up. Our family has always been minimally interventionist, maintained an Anglo-Saxon sense of restraint. Not too 'full-on' as Dad would say. You had to read the vibe with us; undercurrents instead of conversations. I had become well attuned, had sensitive nerve endings.

I turned away. Across the road was Victoria Barracks, sombre, bluestone and covered in ivy. My inner-city sanctuary was surrounded by monuments of war. A cannon sat centre stage on the lawn. I imagined Bud, a knock away from enlisting (though later I found out she had enlisted in Sydney). All those nurses who wanted to do their bit, signed up for King and country. Dead in the water. Brutal, senseless violence – it was hard to take in.

Back I looked towards the shrine, where we mourned them yearly at the dawn service, stumbling up from our house nearby, kids in tow – if we could convince them. It was easy to eulogise heroes here, beside the walls of Tynong granite, the eternal flame and marble stone of remembrance. But if I went to Radji, my feet would be walking where they were slain, my toes imprinting the same sand.

The eucalypts glinted in the afternoon sun. Lion-like statues guarded the entrance. The word 'sacrifice' jumped out at me like an optical illusion. Unnerved, I headed home.

A couple of days later Imogen called. 'Can't come, sorry … I *really* have to go to the conference.'

'Oh no. I *really* wanted you to come.' Imogen was the adventurer in the family and I was the domestic one, or so Jean had once said – I resented the comment at the time. Visions of us sisters unearthing our history together had been playing in my mind. Together sifting through our past.

'Me too.' Imogen said. 'Have you read her letters?'

'No.'

'I read them at Clive and Sally's house … stayed up late one night.'

Did I know there were letters? Sort of. Maybe I'd dismissed them as old war stuff that wasn't relevant to my life, or had I not been paying attention? I was known to be vague. Now I couldn't stop thinking about Bud, the nurses, the memorial, and Michael Pether finding me by chance like that.

A while later, Kingsley's sister, Amanda, called. 'I'll come, if you want me to.'

'Will you?'

Focused as I was on my side of the family, I hadn't thought of Amanda. She had been a nurse herself, in palliative care, and was now studying grief counselling. Ebullient, a lover of people and life, and good with her hands – she made quilts; would wrap you up if you needed, soothe you with her words. Amanda had five grown-up kids, and now, recently divorced, she was on the move, finding her place, sorting through her things and life.

'I'd love you to come.'

'It would be special for me ... as a nurse.'

'Yes, of course,' I replied, though I hadn't considered that angle.

I hung up and emailed Michael. 'Yes. I'm in.'

Not long before my trip, Sally came over and gave me Bud's letters and related documents. Previously housed in a rattan box, they were now filed in a repurposed cardboard folder with white stickers lining its spine to cover up the details of its previous contents. The folder was kept in a black shoulder bag. Not quite the rattan box of romance, but practical and designed for protection.

Sally appeared reticent but there was a sense of unburdening as she handed me this most precious of gifts.

'I'll look after them,' I promised.

The folder was heavy; I clutched it awkwardly, felt its weightiness in my arms and wondered what I was accepting. Was this a passing of the baton?

'She was a character, you'll see,' Sally said. 'Used all these funny names. "Old Tumpy" for her mum, "Nifty" for Jean and "Old Tripe Hounds" for her friends. Real jolly hockey sticks type stuff. Old fashioned … colonial. You can't believe they used to talk like that.' Sally paused. 'They should go to the War Memorial eventually.'

'Kooky,' I chuckled. 'She sounds like a real eccentric.' Or maybe nicknames like that were normal at the time. I clutched the nylon bag tight, already forming an attachment to these papery things of the past and the enigmatic woman who had written them.

'I'm *so* pleased you are going,' Sally stressed, gave me a big hug, sighed as though a weight was lifted, and said goodbye.

Closing my front door, I stood in the hallway gripping the letters. I was the next link in this history chain. Herstory, in this case. Now that they were my responsibility, I needed somewhere to keep them. A dry place, a watertight spot. Away from kids, moths, pets, damp and accidents. Sally had guarded these letters since Jean had died. They were her connection to her mother's only sister, who she never met. Down the hallway and through the kitchen I raced. Banged cupboards and drawers open and shut till I settled on a spot in my study, where I placed them on a clean, dry shelf, satisfied they would be safe in there. Relieved, I closed the door.

*

Later that night, when the house was quiet, I retrieved the bag, its Velcro making a ripping noise as I dipped inside. One by one I laid the yellowing letters on the dining table. The dim light revealed about forty, all filed in date order in plastic sleeves marked with little white stickers. Thank you, Sally, for doing this tedious work – she had even filed the envelopes. Alert with anticipation, I rubbed the tips of my fingers to make sure they were dry, blotted them on a tissue for extra precaution, and inserted them between a plastic sleeve. The paper felt brittle and chalky to touch and as I pulled a sheet of rice paper out, I was thankful it didn't crumble with age. Peering at the writing, I adjusted my glasses in the night light – they weren't quite strong enough. It was all a bit hazy. I blinked a couple of times to refocus my eyes.

'Dear Old Nifty', the first one started. I smiled. The next one I read through its plastic protection: 'Dear Old Tumpy'. Bud didn't disappoint. Quickly I flicked through all the plastic sleeves. The first few were addressed to Willow Cottage in Cheshunt, where Bud's parents had lived after their first house, The Willows (also in Cheshunt), burnt down in the 1939 bushfires. How charming the cottage sounded, like a childhood tale. At the top right-hand corner of the letters was the address of Corowa Hospital, where Bud had trained and nursed before she signed up. Scrawly handwriting, almost indecipherable in parts. It tended to deteriorate as the letter went on, as if she was in a rush – we have that in common. Bud was left-handed, so that too. Fanning my left hand, I twinkled my fingers.

Keen to read a missive about the war, I leafed through pages. Found one. No date on it except Saturday. 'Got a wire from Sydney yesterday saying to bring my own uniforms I have been wearing as I start duty on Tuesday.' And just like that she announced her starting date to her parents. How would they have received the news? A chasm of pride and unease opening up inside? Dread crept over me as I read, knowing the fate of the author of these fragile pages. It settled right up under my ribs, where it spread out and made itself at home. Shopping lists and mundanities filled the rest of the page: uniforms, sponge bags and hankies, plus social chit-chat about people the three of them knew. I pictured Bud as she packed for war; ticked off her list, folded uniforms – or maybe scrunched them in her case – and made decisions about what she would need in an unknown destination: tennis clothes – Dad had said she was an excellent sportswoman – and a couple of dresses. Also, what she would send home from Corowa – books and cardigans.

Sifting through the rest of the bag, I found telegrams, photos and clippings. One newspaper article caught my eye – the page was not as aged as others in the collection. I unfolded it and to my surprise a large photo of Sally in *The Age* appeared. It was dated 1996 – she would have been about my age. She was seated at a desk, pen in hand, her curls bouncy, cropped. 'Old letters unearth a wartime nursing hero' the title said underneath.[1]

The article reported that Sally 'cherishes a treasure trove of letters written by her aunt that she now hopes will be collated and published as a book'. What? I squinted to make sure I had read this correctly and dropped my head a little. Sally hadn't said anything to me about this. Would Dad have known about it, or seen this article? Smoothing out the paper, I reread it slowly to make sure. Stunned, I reached for the phone, but the screen said it was almost midnight – I'd have to wait till morning. There was no way I could sleep now; my thoughts were zooming. I read the next letter, and the next, my fingers at the ready to turn the gossamer pages.

By the time I read the telegram sent to Bud's parents by the Red Cross, it was one in the morning. On 23 June 1944 Vera Deakin White (the director of the Red Cross Bureau for Wounded, Missing and Prisoners of War) wrote, 'It is with deepest regret that we heard that your daughter – NXF70526 S/ Nurse G. Elmes, is now officially believed to have been killed on or after the 11th of February 1942.'

I clutched the edges of the oak table. My great-grandparents, Mummum and Dadee, as Dad and Sally called them, may have done the same, seated at their dining table as I was now, reaching for the silver letter opener. Perhaps Dadee moaned and Mummum let out a cry. It was enough to stop your heart from beating.

I shut the folder and walked silently to bed.

Next morning, I rang Sally. 'I didn't know you were writing a book about Bud.' I was breathless. 'What happened? Why didn't you finish it?'

Sally was quiet on the other end. 'I'm not really sure,' she replied eventually, apologetic, searching for an answer. 'Umm …'

We paused. I couldn't think what to say next, what to ask, my mouth went dry. Didn't want to push or pry.

We both drifted into silence. It was familiar, what we did.

Radji Beach, Bangka Island

14 February 1942, late afternoon

Bud crawls out of the water and collapses on the sand, her body shaking as it surrenders to the ground. Squinty-eyed, she scans the scene. Beach, jungle and more beach. Threat-ready, she tucks her legs underneath her, like a beetle, so she can jump up and flee in an instant. Her shallow breath pumps in and out. How far away are the Japanese, she wonders. All around these islands. There seems nothing untoward, but they could be hiding beyond the tree line. She scans to double-check, and the thump of her chest starts to slow. Her ribs still ache from being slammed into the floor after she was thrown upwards when the bombs hit. Seems like days ago. She can barely open her salt-stung lips. Bites her tongue to try to extract moisture. She has half a bottle of water left but it's attached to the raft. She grabs a fistful of sticky sand and watches it clump in her puffy, waterlogged fingers. Though she has never felt entirely at ease with sand, it is *terra firma* at last. Bud sinks into it and exhales.

Images scored in her mind form deep grooves of ghastliness: corpses mutilated by bombs, bodies floating in the water. Willing her thoughts to heel, she flicks them away; *think on good things, think on good things.* But her senses assault her – the stench of burning flesh and guttural, otherworldly sounds. She shudders to think of all those last moments. Were the passengers still on the ship unconscious as the *Vyner Brooke* descended? Or did they make their transition wide-eyed, gasping? She dry-retches and it pulls her back to her own fleshy body.

When she sits up she spots her lifeboat companions slightly further down the beach. In the last couple of hundred yards she lost hold of the rope attached to the side and had to swim for shore. Turned her head towards the others to keep them in her periphery. From her vantage point now she takes in an agreeable half-moon-shaped beach fringed by jungle, palms and vines. Boulders poke out of the sea and a rocky headland at one end punctuates the horizon. Though nothing looks amiss, Bud is wary. She knows she should get up, reunite with the others and put her uniform on, but she cannot seem to move. Just needs a moment. It is late afternoon but still, out of the sea the heat bites; it bounces off the sand and stings her face, which has that tight, stretched-out feeling, baked from drifting in the water.

Flicking sand from her arm, Bud tries to block out the smell of putrid seaweed. She conjures the rivers of her life; the King River she knew growing up in Cheshunt, and the mighty Murray at Corowa from her days training at the hospital, majestic and constant, snaking its way across arid land. In winter a kind of whoosh and in summer a lazy ebb and flow. The haze of heat and the river red gum, *Eucalyptus camaldulensis*, which fringed its banks – timber of deep red and interlocking grain – the smell and crackle of the bush. Bud recalls crawling into a tree hollow to hide and have a cigarette. At dusk, sulphur-crested cockatoos would leer and squawk in search of a spot to nest. Bud blew smoke rings right back at them. Her desire to nestle once more into that hollow in Corowa intensifies; the place she whiled away hours playing gin rummy with Smithy, belly-laughing so hard she had to run for the loo. After tennis at the hospital courts, they would rip off starchy whites and pull on comfy clothes instead. Bud would saunter through the corridor in her gawky way, open the catch and burst out the door. Pop a cigarette in one corner of her mouth, wedge a book under her arm, and head towards the river.

Prostrate on Bangka Island now, she wonders, how long were we in the water? Maybe only a few hours. Three? Three and a half? It felt like forever. Could do with a cigarette. Her palm throbs and she glances down to see a red, irritated wound, a burn from holding onto the rope on the side of the lifeboat. She hadn't really noticed it when she was in the water because her hands were numb. Needs a dressing, but that's pinned inside her uniform pocket, and antiseptic – not sure if any of that made it onto a lifeboat.

She summons strength to extract herself from the cumbersome lifejacket, which by now has chafed the skin raw under her neck and irritated her armpits – all that bobbing up and down in the water.

'Ahh.' She pulls it off and slumps down onto the sand. Her body is stiffening. Weariness threatens to engulf her; she hasn't had decent sleep for days. Her limbs are listless but the sand supports her. She flexes her puffy fingers and tries to get some feeling again.

'There you are!' Her reverie is broken by voices.

Bud looks up and sees some of her lifeboat companions walking along the beach towards her – Matron Drummond, Laney and Sedgeman.

Matron summons her: 'Sister Elmes, up and away from the edge unless you wish to resume swimming.' Bud laughs, a matron's reprimand has never been more comforting – and she's had plenty. 'And put your uniform on while you are at it.' Matron hands it to her. Sedgeman looks down and turns red. Bud whips it back on, shakily doing her best to make herself decent. Matron continues, 'We have made it here, but now we must prepare ourselves for the night and whatever faces us tomorrow.'

Bud glances behind her over her shoulder out towards the Bangka Strait. Thinks of the countless other survivors, adrift, still at the mercy of the currents. Pulled back and forth in the fading light, would Schuey and Matron Paschke be clinging to whatever they could, trying to reach shore?

Bud gets up. Lightheaded, she doubles over to catch her balance and steadies her hands on her knees.

2/10th Australian General Hospital, Malaya, 11 May 1941

Letter from Bud to her friend Jean Smithenbecker

Dear old Smithy,

[...] Many thanks for getting Ambie* to send my shoes. They should arrive next month some time, these beastly things seem to develop corns. Tomorrow Schuey & I hope to go to Singapore for a few days as we have all been granted two days leave, so it should be rather pleasant.

It seems hard to think we have been here three months, in a way it seems years, but hope it's not as long as that.

Have only just crawled out of the old flea bag so at the moment the grey matter isn't working well but seeing it's Sunday & no one wants their appendix or anything else removed will refrain from going on duty till after breakfast; as a matter of fact, rather

---

*   It's not known who Ambie was.

wish someone would get an acute appendix because am the only member of the theatre staff at home today, still suppose I mustn't be blood thirsty [...]

We left here on Monday morning at seven & arrived at Singapore just in nice time for lunch; had a nice trip down, the country varies very little only some parts are wetter than others; and slightly more hilly, but it's the never ending greenness of the place you get SO sick of. However patches of it were beautiful; passed the usual native villages all very much the same only the smell varies slightly (stronger), one sign in front of one of the shops amused us, 'Talmid Molomel' 'Oculist' Eyes. piles. woman decease'. So he must have had rather a wide range to cure; don't know what Oculist means in this country. Anyway after having a very nice lunch at Raffles where we were staying a Major of some description had a car lent to him took us round to see the sights, which included the civil airport, but of course we weren't allowed to see much, after that to the swimming pool which was very nice & most select and really beautiful ... After feeding the face we drove through the botanical gardens where there are dozens of monkeys, quite tame scampering about all over the place ... then to a Chinese garden which was absolutely beautiful ... along one side was rock with tunnels carved through it with the most exquisite china figures of Chinese & tiny temples done in vivid colours, don't know what they indicated; some Chinese fairy story; or pilgrimage ...

After that we got back to Raffles for a bath and some dinner, Schuey knew a couple of air force lads so we changed into our evening frocks (don't noise it about that we wore evening clothes because we aren't supposed to, but you have no idea how people stare at you when in uniform, anyone would think we were something the cat dragged in), and went round to various cabarets, stayed at the quietest one most of the evening, & thoroughly enjoyed it. After that went for a drive round again admired the moon etc, had supper and retired to bed.

Love,
Bud

2/10th Australian General Hospital, Malaya, 18 May 1941

Letter from Bud to her parents

Dear Old Dad and Tumpy,

[...] Alas the only change in colour in the country are the rubber trees which lose their leaves & go slightly red. Otherwise everything is green undergrowth, trees & palms so it is terribly monotonous. There are a few hills about as high as the Black Ranges but nothing else to write home about [....]

This afternoon the band from one of the units entertained us so it was quite enjoyable.

Talking of cigarettes, the shortage isn't so acute now evidently they have another shipment in, so it doesn't matter about trying to send any, as can always get tobacco and roll my own.

Also tell mum not to bother about an evening dress as may never wear one for some months, also taffeta isn't much good because they have to be washed nearly every time, so some time may get myself a pale blue linen one as things are much cheaper here, or rather that class of stuff is.

[...] That isn't me in the *Womens Weekly** – was out swimming when that was taken; by the way if that woman writes to you (that reporter for the *Womens Weekly*) asking for any of my letters, kick her in the pants as she wrote the most awful tripe and half of it was a gross exaggeration; saying we were treated like film stars [...]

Have horrible idea that I am going on night duty next month; as am being moved from the theatre worst luck but suppose I shouldn't growl as have been there ever since we landed and the others have had much more experience so it's only fair [...]

Love,
Bud

---

*   There was a series of articles published in the *Women's Weekly* by Adele Shelton Smith that caused a furore among the troops and back in Australia: Shelton Smith's articles glamorised both the nurses and the 8th Division's lifestyle. This article, entitled 'They treat us like film stars, says A.I.F. matron in Malaya', was from vol. 8, no. 48, 3 May 1941, p. 7.

Radji Beach, Bangka Island

14 February 1942, dusk

The sea threatens to draw Bud back into its azure embrace. 'Move!' she orders her leaden legs, then steadies one foot in front of the other and trudges up the beach behind Matron Drummond and Sedgeman. From the sun's position she knows it won't be long until it sets.

Though pleased to be on firm ground at last, Bud is still distressed about the nurses being forced to abandon their patients. *Pro humanitate*, she mumbles to herself, *not* abandoning humankind. We took an oath. So why did we have to leave Singapore when the men were allowed to stay? Bud knows how to take orders but her sense of independence is irked.

She and Laney head for the shade at the edge of the jungle and turn to survey the sea. Waves curl back and forth in formation but belie strong currents beneath. Currents that had worked in their favour. Behind them the vegetation is well watered and lush, as it was in Singapore and Malaya. How Bud longs for geraniums, red-hot pokers and love in the mist from their garden in Cheshunt. Pretty cottage garden flowers – a mixed posy in a jam jar perched on the windowsill. Even a field of dry summer grass would do. Here, there are no seasons to speak of – apart from rainy. What she would do for autumn, winter and spring. The crisp air of a winter's day to lick her face. Place her hands on icy cheeks till her fingers tingle, then warm them by the fire and try not to get chilblains. Still, we signed up to do a job, she reminds herself, and we're certainly doing that. Bet that journalist from the *Women's Weekly* would eat her words now. Would pay to see her face.

Looking around her, Bud notices signs of local activity. She points out remnants of dried fish scattered among seaweed, which she and Laney inspect. Perhaps they string the fish up between the trees to dry. They bend down, sniff and both pull away.

'Pongy,' says Bud.

'Must be a recent catch,' replies Laney, who moves back towards the others.

But no villagers have come to welcome them. The beach is abandoned, except for them, the interlopers. The locals must live up there in the jungle. Bud's eyes try to penetrate dense foliage. Her tummy flutters. Are we being watched? Maybe the Japs have taken the beach and the terrified locals have scattered, far enough to monitor them at a distance. She stands as still as she can, trains her eyes on the jungle beyond the sand and its grassy apron. Peers into impenetrable green past the curtain-like vines. She narrows her eyes. Nothing. Tilts her ear to hear the tiniest of sounds. The crackle of a leaf, an imperceptible whisper, the click of a gun. After a while she tires and turns away.

Matron Drummond and Sedgeman summon them to where they have positioned themselves, with a good vantage point, at the centre of the beach. A crimson hue bleeds the sky. Bud shields her face with her hand and turns her back to the glare of the fading sun. Soon it will fall completely into the sea.

'We must organise ourselves so we are safe and comfortable for the night,' Matron Drummond reiterates, her voice upbeat but its urgency betraying her. Still, she galvanises the crowd who have made it ashore so far: nurses, sailors, civilians and a few hurt from the bombing. Bud does a quick head count, about twenty all up, including women and children. We can't be the only survivors. Where *is* Matron Paschke? Perhaps she and Schuey have been swept by currents to another part of this island. Bud wraps her arms around herself and clutches her shoulders.

Sedgeman motions them to come closer. 'We'll make our way along the beach and do a quick recce of the area,' he says. 'Two squads will be formed. The wounded are the first priority. Blankets and coats will be arranged in sleeping positions around the bonfire for them. We'll build that here, where we're standing. It'll be a beacon for those still in the water.

'The other squad will check the beach. Our second priority is to find fuel for the bonfire and clear the area of potential hazards. Look out for snakes and other nasties. Not to mention the Japs.' No one laughs. Sedgeman, having misfired, nudges a bit of sand with his toes. He ploughs on. 'Keep alert for aircraft. Scour the immediate area for anything that could be useful – wood for the fire, materials to construct stretchers. Don't go far. We'll do that tomorrow – it'll be dark soon ... Questions?'

'No, sir.'

Matron Drummond briefs her squad of nurses, instructs them to administer whatever first aid they can. Basic medical supplies, including morphia, bandages and field dressings, were thrown into the lifeboat as they abandoned ship. Hopefully they've survived in better condition than I have, thinks Bud, inspecting her gashed hand, which is starting to bother her more now. She tries to straighten her palm but it throbs. Matron Drummond prays aloud for protection for those still at sea. Collectively they pause and bow their heads. Bud searches for signs of life in the water. None of them speak but they all choke on the same question: how long could you survive out there?

Bud is told to go with Sedgeman's squad – she will be on the second nursing shift. She grabs a bandage and a hankie to stuff inside as a gauze substitute. There is a small amount of sulfa powder among the limited first aid supplies but she leaves it for others.

'Can you fix me up?' she asks Laney. 'Don't think there are any rope fragments in there.'

'Course. That's a nasty burn.'

Bud curls her toes as Laney places the folded hankie on the wound and winds the bandage around her palm. 'Did tweezers or any surgical gear make it into the boat?' Bud asks.

'Not sure.'

'Least it was in saltwater. Should be clean enough.'

Combing the tideline, they search for bonfire fuel. 'Watch out for snakes, Laney.'

'I know my browns and my red bellies, but these tropical types tend to blend in.'

'Chameleons.'

Mona Tait has joined them and retorts, 'Don't want to end my days in a python embrace. I'd prefer it to be a soldier.'

'Tommy Arthur for you, Tait,' says Bud. 'The most wonderful man in the world.' She impersonates Mona with a mock swoon. They laugh. When Mona smiles she has crinkly-up eyes, visible behind her dark-rimmed glasses, which somehow have emerged from the water with Mona.

Bud continues. 'Long as it's not a Japanese soldier ...' The trio falls quiet. Bud wants to open her mouth and stuff back in what she has blurted. News of a massacre at St Stephens Hospital in Hong Kong was whispered to her by others. She tries to ban thoughts of the Chinese and British nurses molested and killed by Japanese soldiers, some women used as human shields as they tended to patients. It happened on Christmas Day. Bud shuts her mouth, unsure what Laney and Mona know, stares at the ground in front of her and feels her eyes sting and pool. She picks up a piece of timber. 'This should burn well enough.'

Mona replies, 'That looks like driftwood. Probably washed up on the currents – like us.' She's attempting to be bright.

Bud looks towards the jungle. Her stomach feels queasy, it's starting to churn, as if a ferment has been added. She gulps in air, determined to stop the swirl. 'Careful when you lift things up. Remember our bush training,' she says, but their banter now has a nervous edge. 'Still can't believe you met Billy Jones in Sydney. Heard anything of her?' Her words tumble out. They avoid each other's eyes. 'She pass the medical?'

They have drifted close to Matron Drummond's group. 'This isn't summer camp,' Matron calls out. 'Keep it down.'

They work in silence as they continue to scour the beach. But Bud cannot erase the images of the fate of the Hong Kong sisters from her mind.

The twilight hour has almost passed and the sky is a purplish pink. In the last of the light, they redouble their efforts collecting wood for the fire.

'Hurry.' Bud adjusts the bandage on her hand and picks out a short splinter of wood before it pierces the bandage and sticks in her wound.

Back and forth they travel between the bonfire they are building at the centre of the beach and the tideline, which has proven to be the best place to collect driftwood. Plenty of debris has washed up on the shore.

'Think this is all from ships that have sunk in the last twenty-four hours?' Mona asks.

'Guess so.' Laney scans the horizon. 'Lots of them out there.' She turns to Bud with anxious eyes. 'It'll be getting cold out there now.' Bud takes an involuntary step towards the sea and shivers. The idea of Matron Paschke and Schuey facing a night in the water. Will they roll on waves and plead to stay awake? Hope that a current will catch and carry them this way to shore? Pinch themselves so they don't slip under, no more than a bubble to say they are gone?

Bud and Laney meet each other's eyes. Bud wants to ask Laney about Schuey but can't bring herself to. Instead, she asks,

'Think any of the boats leaving Singapore made it through?' Laney gives a forlorn shrug. Then she turns back to Mona and they resume their search for wood, either dry or oil-drenched from sunken ships. Bonfires at Cheshunt come to mind. Her father's lessons to her as a young girl, teaching her to sort young wood from seasoned, to find the grey, dried-out bits that would burn. Difficult in the tropics but they do find plenty of driftwood that should give the fire a good start. They call out to Sedgeman to let him know they have enough.

'Hurry and stack it,' he replies. They pile spare wood up high beside the bonfire. Calculate how much they need for it to burn all night. Sedgeman pulls out his lighter and they huddle round. With a flick, the flint sparks and a flame leaps up. Sedgeman lights the fire in a few spots and they fan each, using hands, breath and anything useful. Accustomed to bonfires in Cheshunt, the gravity of this one is not lost on Bud. Flames start to lick, kindling first, then, as the fire gathers strength, driftwood as well. Orange light jumps up high. Alert to sparks thrown out – it must be the oil that coats some of the wood – they step back. Bud and the nurses bunch together, arms locked around each other's waists. Soon they are tranquillised by the dance of the fire. They rest their heads on each other's shoulders. The heat mollifies their wounds and their thoughts drift inwards.

An urge to surrender to sleep comes over Bud. She lies down on her back. From her vantage point she gazes at the sky, dark now but still foggy from smoke. Stars attempt to glow through the veil. How different the sky is here, she marvels – closer, heavier. The Southern Cross has shifted position from where she usually spots it at home. There are the pointers – she can just make them out. Would Mum and Dad be looking up now at these same stars, sitting on the verandah at Willow Cottage? The night sky sharp and the crisp, country air warmed by summer. Would Jean and Rowley be admiring them too, now that they were back from the heat of Whyalla? What about Dolly, her brother-in-law – where was he, having been called up? Had they heard the impossible – that Singapore has fallen? That must have made it home and into the papers by now. Mum would be scouring them for news.

'Don't you worry about me,' Bud whispers, relieved that her parents and sister cannot see her predicament, the bombs that struck the *Vyner Brooke*, the deaths in the water. 'I'm okay.' She sends her thoughts to the sky and watches them turn southward.

Around eight-thirty, Eric Germann and his raft and boat train land. Bud sticks her head up, wipes her weary eyes. Is she dreaming? Little Izzy Warman – where's his mother? – and another teenage boy, who turns out to be English, emerge from the shallows. Others trail behind them: a maimed soldier, a civil engineer, around half a dozen in total.

Eric lowers himself down next to the bonfire and drops his head between his hunched-up knees. Bud notices he is without his shirt and thigh-high boots. Sculpted muscles on his shoulder blades twitch with cold. Matron bustles over to help him. The bonfire roars and pulses.

Bud falls asleep and dreams of life rafts close to shore. The bonfire, the only light in a dark and merciless sea, beckons them like moths. She sees her friends raise their white hands, illuminated, ghostly. So near, Bud feels she could reach out and touch their uniforms from where she lies by the fire. *Sshh. Listen. Someone's out there.* 'Schuey?' Bud cries out to parched figures, desperate for a flicker of recognition. But those in the water don't respond to her voice over the roar of the ocean, the quiver of the flames. All Bud can hear is the bluster of the sea and the pounding of her heart.

2/10th Australian General Hospital, Malaya, 24 May 1941

Letter from Bud to her parents

Dear Old Tumpy and Dad,

[...] Today am working among the officers not a bit exciting, the same as any private block, but still nothing like vanity, don't know where I will be next month as the staff is changed every month so far have been lucky to be in the theatre for the last three but am being moved this time worst luck [...]

By the way have been thinking it might be a good idea if I made an allotment to you and dad as don't use much money over here and if anything ever prevented us getting back it might be more use to you and it would save dad the necessity of getting a pension in later years.

Anyway, let me know what you think [...]

Love,
Bud

2/10th Australian General Hospital, Malaya, 26 November 1941

Letter from Bud to her friend Jean Smithenbecker

Dear Old Smithy,

Gosh I am glad that you have been accepted, hope you will feel contented about it but Matron is right if you want to pull out now it's not too late, my only fear is that you will be sent somewhere miles from me & we will be parked here for the duration.

Smithy if you are going away, I would get plenty of voile underwear even bloomers if you have to wear them as they don't wear out nearly as much as the cotton and milanese ones do. Also smuggle in a few pairs of silk stockings because usually you can get away wearing them on leave, if you ever do get attached to us wouldn't bring any woollen clothes at all except a lightweight pullover.

Have just had five days leave in Singapore which was very pleasant. & thoroughly enjoyed it. Got through a terrific bit of money but it was worth it. Must go and have breakfast.

27.11.41

Well old hound have been in a pretty fierce temper all day. At the moment have the settlement job in the place doing occupational therapy which consists of going around all the wards, and teaching the convalescent patients raffia work, needle work, leather work, luckily there are two of us as I don't know one thing about it & don't want to. Also organising amusement such as concerts in one of the wards every week and taking the convalescent patients for drives and generally messing in if it was hard work wouldn't mind, work from nine to five approximately, the amount of work should only take about two hours. However it has amused the staff very much the thought of me teaching anyone needlework, specially left-handed. However luckily only have a week of it.

Thank goodness you have that certificate from Dr Collins, it was worth it. Also, glad it doesn't matter about the age. Matron Kearey [?] is usually fairly decent to you except when you fail to report when she tells you: warning from me who knows.

Sorry Morris doesn't approve.* I can understand his point of view but still don't see why you can't go away as it is the chance of a lifetime, anyway you may do a spot of home service for also most of the girls seems to do several months camp life now. Be funny if you go to the showground. By the way do you ever hear from Billy Jones, has she joined up yet? Tait writes to her & Skeet quite regularly so must get their address some time. Now you

---

* Morris is most likely Smithy's boyfriend. In another letter from 19 October 1941, Bud says to 'give him [Morris] my kind regards and love and kisses provided you deliver them'.

have been called up my Christmas present to you won't be much use. Anyway, give it to your mother she might find it quite useful [...]

Got down to Singapore last Wednesday evening had quite a nice trip down even if our driver did do eighty some of the way on a narrow windy road in the rain, don't mind a bit of speed but there is a limit to everything. However, got to Raffles and found no room had been booked, eventually they admitted having one for four being five of us it didn't make any difference so we went and inspected it, it was like a flat an enormous sitting room two bedrooms and a bathroom. So we were quite satisfied with it, the first night retired to bed early. Second day shopped and went to the pictures saw Charles Boyer and Olivia de Havilland in 'Hold back the Dawn' very well done: Came back and went to bed, at least two of us did the others went out. Next day spent at the pool which is really beautiful, stayed there until fairly late, I went out again for dinner came back to Raffles and danced but the chap I was with had to be on duty so left early. Crawled to the old fleabag. Saturday wandered around the shops, tried to get into European shops again and not have to bargain [...]

[...] Now some words of advice, firstly don't work too hard, no one else does & the more you do the more you will have to do. Also pretend you know what they are talking about if any strange new name is mentioned & ask someone afterwards who is not looking superior. Eat well and frequently even if you don't like the food because it is good for you and keeps your temper more or less even.

Don't drink to excess???

Bath once a day because the smell irritates your roommates.

Don't talk to strange men in the railway carriages. Also look after yourself because no one else will. More I see of life the more it is self first [...]

Enough of this tripe give my love to all the kids and Matron [...]

Love,

Bud

Radji Beach, Bangka Island

14 February 1942, around 10.30 p.m.

Just as the survivors have settled into a stupor, four ashen figures emerge from the darkness and walk towards them. Bud squints, wonders if she's looking at an apparition.

'Vivian!' Matron jumps up. Vivian Bullwinkel – who Bud does not know well as they served in different units – steps towards them. Tall with a striking, unguarded face, now weary and crumpled, her pupils are dilated. A grin replaces her strained look. Bud also recognises Jimmy Miller, second officer of the *Vyner Brooke*. Blond, Kiwi, with sticky-out ears, he is about her age. Two other nurses, who Bud does not know by name, stand slouched on either side. The group shuffles round to make room for the newcomers. Vivian leans limp into Matron's arms. 'Sit down, you must rest.'

'No, there are others, wounded,' Vivian hauls herself up straight, 'as well as about twelve sisters – unwounded, relatively – and three civilians.' She sways on her feet, though she

75

looks determined to stay upright. Bud grabs her arm, streaked in oil, and anchors her. Dares to hope though, when she hears that number, twelve – surely one is Schuey? 'We only just managed to pull them up onto the beach,' Vivian continues. 'Had to leave them there … lying on the sand, so we could come and get help.'

'How far away are they?' Matron looks up the beach and searches the darkness.

'A mile or so – some distance.' Miller steps forward and Bud notices his cheek is crisscrossed with oil and red gashes. 'We need to get back to them.' Beads of sweat dribble from his temples and mingle with dried blood. He wipes the sweat with the back of his sleeve.

Matron insists Vivian sits down. Those on either side move in to prop her up, weaving their arms around her waist. 'How'd you get here?' Matron asks.

'On a partially submerged lifeboat … some of us got in and some held on to the side for dear life.' Vivian's parched skin speaks volumes.

Alice Rossie – also a nurse but with the British QAs* – offers Vivian water, which she sips between dried-out lips. 'Thank god you are strong,' Alice says. Vivian coughs and the water splutters back up.

'There wasn't much space, so the wounded had priority,' Vivian continues.

---

* Queen Alexandra's Imperial Military Nursing Service (QAIMNS), known for short as the QAs.

'We'd've sunk if we'd all got in,' Miller adds. Vivian presses her hands to the flames and stares straight ahead. 'Those who were capable had to hang on and kick.' Sounds familiar, thinks Bud. He goes on. 'We managed to push against the strong currents … saw the bonfire from the water and headed towards it. We came ashore about a mile or so along the beach.' His speech speeds up and Bud notices he's puffing as he tries to get his story out. 'Those who could, staggered ashore … took a moment to recover … then pulled the others out. Dragged them up the beach and away from the tide.'

Mona places a hand on his shoulder – he looks unsteady. Miller continues, 'We decided to make our way towards the bonfire and pray those gathered around were friends.'

Vivian takes over. 'Some of the nurses were badly hit by shrapnel. Florence Salmon had her breast almost ripped off.' Bud stiffens – her breast, poor Florence – and recoils just imagining it. Florence is one of her own – 2/10th Australian General Hospital – and around Bud's age, a couple of years younger. She's upset by her friend's too-awful injury – such a sensitive area. 'She can't move and will need to be carried back. Flo Casson has damage to her legs, one of which is possibly fractured, and Rosetta Wight has wounds in her buttocks and upper thighs. They can't walk by themselves and will need support – they may have nerve damage. Kath Neuss has a shrapnel wound in her hip. She's not too bad but still needs a hand.'

Thank goodness they did make it off the ship and are here, Bud thinks, recalling them lying prone and being fixed up in the saloon after the bombs struck.

'So we need help,' Miller says. 'Do we have anything resembling a stretcher for Florence? Plus, the elderly look stunned … probably in shock.'

'Are there any doctors here?' Vivian asks.

Dr Tay Soo Woon steps forward. As the only doctor on the beach his expertise is vital and he was quick to board the lifeboat with Matron and offer assistance. But where is his wife, Bud wonders, remembering them sharing the meagre rations she doled out to them on the *Vyner Brooke*. Since she hasn't turned up, he must be perturbed. 'I'm sorry, but I can't leave my patients here in the state they are in.'

Jimmy and Vivian beg him. 'Please help us.'

'No.' He is definite. 'I'm needed here.'

Matron's arms gesticulate in protest. She presses again but he won't budge. Her fury can be felt in her energetic gait and the downward movement of her lip.

Eric Germann and the English teenager who'd arrived with Eric on his raft volunteer. Bud doesn't know the teenager's name and is too tired to ask. Everyone else, impassive by the fire, avoids eye contact.

'You'll need to construct a makeshift stretcher,' Matron tells them. Worst-case scenario, thinks Bud, they'll have to half-carry, half-drag them back. Eric grabs a couple of oars and ties shirts, which people pull off and lend, to improvise one. Matron indicates to Bud that she wants her on duty to prepare for the new arrivals. She pulls herself vertical.

The sea is flecked with bright dots, as if glow worms dance their mating ritual luminous on the swell. Bud's eyes linger, mesmerised, on the pinpricked water. A sudden blip of light flares above the horizon. Her jaw tightens. What was that? A plane? She looks up. Could've sworn something flashed in front of her. Now gone. Bud doesn't blink, she wants to catch it if it returns. Hard to believe it was nothing – but maybe her tired eyes are playing funny buggers. Or it could've been a shooting star.

She can't help but let her mind wander back to Cheshunt. When will she see home again? Her new home, Willow Cottage. Lying beneath the willows sprawled out on a blanket. Reading, lolling and spending an afternoon doing fat nothing. Mum nagging her not to get too much sun. Watching Jean's pet magpie anting while echidnas and platypus play on the banks of the King River.

On the other side of the bonfire Bud can see Alice trying to entertain Izzy, who has woken with the arrivals. They recite nursery rhymes and she can hear the odd muffled giggle – a welcome change from the blank look of shock that was imprinted on his young features. She hopes his mother is still alive. Izzy holds Alice's hand tight as she tries to resettle him.

Bud starts to sort supplies for those about to arrive. She lines up on a blanket – it is the most sterile environment she can create – bandages, field dressings, morphia and syringes, gauze, and a small amount of antiseptic, plus a pair of surgical scissors. Already some of the bandages are soiled and need to be washed and dried to re-dress patients. Plus they need enough for those being fetched. Bud grabs the soiled pile and walks towards the water's edge to rinse them in the sea. Careful not to get pulled back in, she bends down and swishes them in the shallows.

Rubs them together to give a good scrub. Till, as far as she can see in the moonlight, blood rinses out, dilutes and disperses in the water.

A couple of hours after they left, Bud, dozing, hears Jimmy's voice. 'We're back!' She sits up to see the faint outline of a train of walking wounded. Runs to meet them.

'Neuss!' Bud calls to her friend, relieved to see Kath, who's limping along propped up by two other sisters. Every second step, she falters. In the dim light Bud scans the dozen nurses for Schuey, but can't find her familiar face, crop of tightly wound curls, or Roman nose. No fruity remarks or Schuey guffaw. She sucks the inside of her bottom lip and sinks her teeth into it. Disappointed, she pushes away defeatist thoughts. 'You okay?' she asks Kath.

'Except for my hip,' Kath pulls her uniform up to show Bud her wound, hurriedly dressed on the *Vyner Brooke*. No doubt caused by shell splinters.

'Ouch. We should re-dress that.'

Eric Germann and the English boy carry Florence on their improvised oar-and-shirt stretcher. From the way they stagger, the last fifty yards are a struggle. They place Florence down and have a breather. Eric braces his back with his hands and arches to release the tension.

Bud touches Florence's hand. 'How are you?' She's disconcerted by Florence's chalky stillness and lack of response. Her breast wound site has been bandaged using what Bud figures is a ripped-up petticoat – perhaps done on the lifeboat to stem the bleeding.

Rosetta and Flo appear next at the rear of the train, half-dragged, half-carried by sisters doing their best to support their weight. 'Hang in there, that's it.' Bud can hear words of encouragement and sobs on the midnight air. Step, by step, by step. Each step won with a wince for the sisters carrying, and presumably stabs of pain for Flo and Rosetta.

Bud and Laney take over for the last push. 'I'll take Rosetta, you take Flo,' Bud says to Laney. 'Put her weight on me.' Bud bends forward and the relieved sisters who were half-carrying Rosetta help to lay her over Bud's back. Bud figures this piggyback style is the least likely to stress her hand. Rosetta is heavier than she is, but she only has to shuffle a small distance and then ease her down onto a coat. Laney is performing a similar operation with Flo.

'Okay, both of you?' Laney asks.

'Okay,' Flo replies, 'but please move slowly.'

'Please,' echoes Rosetta.

A crack of thunder and flash of light cleave the sky.

'What's that?' Bud instinctively swings seaward to peer out. Rosetta groans. Bud can't believe what an idiot she is – having gone to such lengths to minimise the impact on Rosetta's thigh. 'I'm so sorry, Rosetta. You all right?'

'Just.' She replies.

'Storm?' Laney suggests.

'Sounds like gunfire.' Bud searches the inky black.

'Could be a battle.'

'They're everywhere,' Bud replies. They stand transfixed, Rosetta and Flo still half on their backs, staring into the void, which is pierced with occasional flashes. 'Surely some of the boats that left Singapore will make it through these waters – even back to Australia,' Bud says, though the hope now seems foolish.

The whole sorry group waits for what comes next but it is quiet out there now. No storm follows, no thunder either. Uncertain as to what they have seen, they stare into the jet-black expanse.

'Not much further,' Bud tries to reassure Rosetta and Flo. Rosetta nods, in too much pain to talk as Bud inches forward as smoothly as she can. 'Soon be there and we'll place you by the fire on a blanket.' Bud is perturbed by the fact that every move she makes only inflicts more pain – and she's only carried Rosetta a short way. Her spine grinds against Rosetta's ribs, her back spasms, and heat builds within her.

'I need a moment,' Laney pleads beside her. Flo is making a mewling sound.

What was it we saw, Bud wonders? How close by are the Japanese? This bonfire is signalling our position. No doubt they can see it too and might come to investigate. Bud wishes she had telescopes for eyes, could see into the distance to where planes might be massing. Armies might already have landed in boats that glide with stealth under the cover of night. She tries to shrug off her agitation.

A couple of hours after the rescue party departed, they have all finally made it back. Almost continually, Bud hears the low sound of moaning. She looks at the wounded train, all visibly upset by the pain their colleagues have endured, and sees Eric stumble away from the crowd, heading to the back of the beach like an injured animal. It looks as though he has found the wreck of what might've once been an old fishing hut. He's picking up a few planks and fronds from the ground and pushing them into the sand to create a sort of shelter.

'How was it?' Matron asks as she helps gently lie Rosetta and Flo down on blankets.

Bud gestures towards Eric in reply, who is behind the few remnant planks of wood he has managed to erect into a patchy screen.

'Harrowing,' Miller, who has dropped to the ground nearby, replies. 'But we've got them all back.'

Radji Beach, Bangka Island

15 February 1942, after 1 a.m.

Quiet has now descended on the group settled around the bonfire. Matron has instructed Bud to get some rest. Bud is in that place twixt sleep and wake, riding high above Cheshunt through the gums, when she startles. 'What's that?'

'Don't know,' Laney sits up and peers towards the sea – she's heard something too. Voices down on the shore. Female voices? Blurry silhouettes emerge and walk towards them.

'Survivors!'

Bud feels a surge of hope and pulls herself to her aching feet. Sisters Peggy Farmaner, Lorna Fairweather and, from her own unit, Clarice Halligan, Esther Stewart and Ellen Keats, plus some civilian women, materialise and walk in dribs and drabs into the light of the fire. No Schuey. Bud tries not to let her panic show.

'Have you seen Schuey?' she asks Clarice, Esther and Ellen, who are shivering from so long in the water, looking haunted by the day's ordeal. At least they are now in the balmy night air.

They shake their heads. 'Haven't seen her since the siren went before the bombs hit,' Ellen replies. 'Caught a glimpse of her then, heading to her station.'

Bud crumples like a paper bag to the ground. She is, of course, pleased to see more of the sisters, but feels the dull ache of her missing friend. Too spent to ask about how they made it here, she promises herself she'll find out in the morning.

The rest of the group stares ahead, like hollow men and women, barely registering the newcomers and overwhelmed by the maimed, the elderly and exhaustion.

'Welcome,' some of them whisper, trance-like, and they edge a little further out from the bonfire to draw the newcomers to the comfort of the flames. 'Come, come sit down.' They grip listless hands and place arms around slumped shoulders. Clarice is hurt, Bud notices, being propped up by others and limping. She's older than Bud by almost ten years, mature and surgically experienced. She was stationed as a missionary nurse in Wedau in Milne Bay Province, Papua New Guinea. Christian stoicism with panache. Bud recalls hearing about Clarice's convertible Ford with a canvas roof. She wouldn't mind getting one herself. That'd be something to drive down to the Whitfield pub. Or pick up the old hounds from Corowa in it and race along the Murray River. Matron lays Clarice down on one of the coats and starts to examine her wound. Bud remembers she was near Rosetta at the back of the saloon when the bomb struck and shrapnel flew out. Matron reassures Clarice that all she needs are a few stitches to the back of her thigh, which has been lacerated by a bomb splinter.

'So many hurt ... got to get some sleep,' Bud mutters. 'Be back on duty in the morning.' She lies back down. Dreams come like waves and pummel her frame. In and out of consciousness she drifts for a few hours.

A voice sobs in Bud's ear, starts to babble.

'Who's that?' Mrs Warman, Izzy's mum, lies next to her. She must've arrived while Bud slept. She's scratching at the earth, sand under her fingernails, and talking in what Bud assumes is Russian. Night terrors. Bud grabs her hands, curls back her fingers to empty them of sand and rolls her onto her side, restraining her arms so she calms. No doubt reliving the moment she lost her husband, when he plummeted to his death off the side of the ship. Bud breathes loudly and evenly. Hopes Mrs Warman will fall into synch, that the lung crackling Bud can now hear will clear and Mrs Warman won't wake Izzy – with whom she has only just been reunited, and who now sleeps beside his mother tranquilly, curved up tight into her frame. '*Shhh*. It's okay, it's okay,' Bud soothes. Mrs Warman opens her eyes for a second, convulses and closes them again. Bud holds her till she quietens.

Now that sleep has departed, Bud decides to join those who have congregated in small clusters and are discussing their fate on the periphery of the bonfire. She needs to go to the loo first, so she drags herself up and trudges far enough away from the group to be discreet, but not too far. Bad things happen under the cover of night, she reminds herself. Sand squeaks underfoot and she feels an ever-so-slight breeze in the air. She sniffs it in and relishes the cool stream of air against the inside of her nostrils as she walks up the beach, keeping a cautious distance from the jungle. As a distraction she focuses her eyes on the night-sky twinkle and counts stars.

About a hundred yards away from the camp, where the light of the fire dwindles, she hears a snap.

What's that? She stops rigid on the sand. Ears alert, body coiled, she pivots. She feels her thighs tighten and her feet push downwards. Moves her weight forward ready to run. She can't see what's in front of her.

Snap again, this time to her left. Bud lifts her hands, ready to defend herself, her fingers like talons. Saliva fills her mouth – fear. Her hands twitch as she trains her ears to hear the tiniest of sounds. What was that noise? She sniffs the air. When will they make themselves known? Rustling starts a few feet from her. It's barely audible but she hears it edging closer. Her chest drops and caves, heart-rate quickens. Ever so slightly, Bud dips her head and rotates her eyes left and right. She can only see a soupy darkness. Her muscles flex and clench. If they are going to take her they'll do it now. The rustling continues. What are they playing at? A minute passes. Finally, she breathes out and waits to ensure she can't hear anything else. Must have been an animal or the wind. Or *is* it soldiers, unable to see her but observing the others round the fire from a distance? Bud tells herself it's not, and on the count of three moves quickly to find a spot to wee, keen to get on with it. She rubs her arms and looks back towards the bonfire, caught in an otherworldly hue, as if in limbo between this place and the next. Even from far away she can hear low chatter around the fire and a battle out on the horizon.

What's in store for us, she wonders, as she squats down to pee.

Something definitely moves behind her. She twists on her haunches and it brushes her neck. Bud shrieks, her arms go out in front of her and she falls forward onto the sand, jarring her wrists. But there are no voices, no Japanese commands. What is it – a possum? No, they don't have them here. What, then? Bud stands, pulls her underwear up and runs. Sprints as fast as she can, determined not to look back.

Close enough to be safe in the night light, but where they can't see her alarm, she stops and waits for her heart-rate to calm. Once her panting has subsided and she can pretend all is fine, she rejoins the others. Next time she'll hold on till morning.

There is not much sleep to be had that night. Bud listens to the lap, lap, lap of the sea as it pulls in and out. Like a film on a loop she sees Singapore fall, over and over. Oilfields burn and sirens scream as they push their way to the dock. Crowds shove, cars blaze and the desperate plead, 'Sister, please … take us with you!'

2/10th Australian General Hospital, Malaya, 19 January 1942

Letter from Bud to Jean

Dear Old Nifty,

Sorry I didn't write last week, but we did do a spot of work at a Casualty Clearing Station for a couple of days & have now moved again & starting another hospital, so have been pretty busy: only arrived yesterday at dinner time we went straight on duty got off about dark and have been working until just a few minutes ago [...]

We live about fifty yards from the hospital itself so we don't get much exercise walking there and back. By the way if Dolly ever calls here and gets shore leave he might come and see me. Although I can't give him my address so there is a bit of a catch as this place is fairly large (any Australian Army lad would have a fair idea where we were). You should guess by this time where we are. Don't know if mum will worry or not if she knows where we are.

Anyhow the place we were in has been taken and bombed etc. So we got away in good time.

A lot of our unit has been detached to another unit so there aren't the usual crew we had; but that happened some weeks ago. Anyway it is just as well as we are rather crowded. Four in a room, small at that, just room for our stretchers and kit bags hold alls etc [...]

Think you are rather wise keeping Rowley in the country wouldn't think it would be so good having him in a city.

Don't take any notice of the postmark as got the envelopes some days ago. If we move again we will end up in the sea any how we are seeing Malaya by ambulance: might write a book about it some day most likely it wouldn't be allowed past the censor

Sorry there isn't any more news. Couldn't tell it to you if there was! [...]

Love,
Bud

2/10th Australian General Hospital, Malaya, 20 January 1942

Letter from Bud to her friend Jean Smithenbecker

Dear Old Smithy,

Haven't heard from you this week but the mail isn't quite so regular as it was. Or perhaps it is because we have been moving: Anyway, we have at last settled hope this time for the duration: Had a very nice holiday in the [?]; did two days work at the C.C.S. [*Casualty Clearing Station*] which was very interesting, wish we could have stayed there but we are now in quite a nice place. Old and very dirty but we have had a good bit of cleaning scrubbing and scouring etc. Externally it is most picturesque, built early in the eighteenth century (or looks like it), situated in beautiful grounds nice trees and lawns etc; also some nice air raid shelters (we hope) as am getting quite partial to getting there first to avoid the rush. As often get bits of shrapnel lying about from ack acks and have no desire to stop a bit unnecessarily:

Our quarters are in a way most comfortable although a bit crowded as it is only a flat but have a wireless and a Frigidaire, amahs to do our washing and cleaning etc which makes a lot of difference to our personal comfort.

Sorry there isn't a great deal to tell you Smithy: We were just saying what an interesting letter we could write if there wasn't a censor who might open it but will try and remember the tit bits to tell you when we get back.

Suppose you have more or less guess where we are now by this time as don't think you will need to stretch your imagination much.

Cheers,
Love,
Buddy

Radji Beach, Bangka Island

15 February 1942, dawn

Throughout the early hours of Sunday morning Bud keeps waking in fright. Screams in her ears, the creak of the *Vyner Brooke* and bodies floating in the water.

Now it's daylight she jerks awake once more. Sand has got into her ears and her mouth. She scoops it with her tongue and spits it out. Spits again. Then she rubs her heavy, blood-shot eyes. Thank god it's morning.

As a kid, when the family lived in Melbourne, in the summer Bud loved to go to the beach. One summer day the family took a tram from Armadale to St Kilda with buckets and spades. Bud and Jean constructed a giant sandcastle surrounded by elaborate moats, then took turns burying each other in the sand. For hours they played; pat, pat, pat, their hands smoothed the surface under which one of them lay.

'Don't move,' Bud said to Jean, 'or you'll crack it.'

Lazy days of an Australian summer, the chalky blue of the

bay and the open sky of youth. When they moved to Cheshunt, on those airless thirty-degree days they swam in the King River and swung from ropes above the water, keeping an eye out for snakes and bull ants hidden in parched grass.

'Don't like this coarse sand sticking to me,' Bud croaks now, as she brushes it off.

Schuey visited her in her dreams, admiring the moon – like they did in Singapore. Though they were meant to be in uniform there at all times, except when on leave, some evenings they would sneak out in dresses and silk stockings, dance with air force lads, and laugh in the warm, fragrant air till their bellies ached.

'Schuey, old hound, where are you?' Bud's slits of eyes scour the horizon. Her throat is dry – no moisture to swallow. Out on the bay, the smoke from bombs dropped overnight lingers, contributing to the general fog. Onshore, remnants from the bonfire smoulder. Ash, salt and sweat – a battle aroma. Where was Schuey when the *Vyner Brooke* was hit? When the room turned red from the glare of the bomb and the ship was thrown upwards? Bud rakes through her memories. Out beside the state-rooms, presumably. All she can hear is Flo's voice, 'I'm hit. I'm hit,' over and over.

'Schuey, are you out there?' Bud pleads to an impervious sea. It's about seventeen hours since they were bombed – that's a long time to be in the water. Bud still hasn't been able to bring herself to ask Laney what she knows.

Better get out of the old fleabag, grey matter isn't working so well. She stretches, rolls over and pushes herself up from the sand, wishing she *was* getting out of a comfy bed, careful not to bump others – they are all packed in like sardines. Mrs Warman sleeps soundly, still cuddling Izzy. Bud's right palm throbs – she tries not to put any weight on it. More debris has washed ashore overnight. Then it dawns on her, the numbers have swollen. Another lifeboat sits at the water's edge.

'You awake, Neuss?' she pokes Kath.

'I am now, what's up?'

'Another lifeboat came in the night.'

Kath looks at Bud. 'You're kidding me? You helped settle them.'

'Did I? Thought I was dreaming.'

'That battle we saw at sea last night … they came from that. Plus, ones and twos who made it ashore.'

Bud taps her forehead. Is she delirious or just exhausted? How can she not have remembered? She's grateful, though, to have had a few hours' sleep, since she's on duty soon with the stretcher cases and Matron is bound to put her on nightshift tonight.

'I'm sore … how 'bout you?' Bud says to Kath.

'Same.' Kath stretches her arms above her head. 'But we're alive and mostly intact.' She glances down at her left hip. 'Not like those poor things over there.' Kath nods to some of those suffering with burns and shrapnel wounds. Won't complain about my gashed palm or aching ribs, thinks Bud. Kath's soft tissue wound is deep and no doubt painful.

'Let me take a look at that.' Bud moves towards her.

'Better get moving.' Kath brushes her aside and sits up. 'Matron's bound to put us in charge of breakfast.' Bud watches to see just how much of a brave face Kath is maintaining. Should she insist on having a look? She decides to leave it till after breakfast.

'What'll it be, madam? Porridge and eggs?' Bud asks sardonically, 'Or toast and Vegemite?'

'How 'bout biscuits and water?' Kath staggers to her feet, her face tight with pain. 'Just a sip, though – we'll have to share it evenly.'

'Surely Sedgeman will send out a search party soon?' Bud's lips are cracked and her mouth is so dry she almost has to prise it open. 'There must be fresh water somewhere.'

Matron Drummond marches over as expected and asks Bud to help divide up the small amount of food they have left. All they have are hard biscuits and some cans of condensed milk. They walk the shoreline – though Kath is supposed to be resting – hoping to find rations that have washed up overnight, but there is only driftwood, helmets, seaweed and detritus. Kath hobbles around the wooden lifeboat that came ashore in the night.

'Think you should be walking?' Bud asks.

'Success!' Kath replies, her arms behind her back, ignoring her question.

'What?'

'A can of condensed milk and a packet of hard sweets.' She holds them up, jubilant.

'Good haul, Neuss,' says Bud. 'Sweets might be a bit soggy ... but good for energy. We can divvy them up among the patients.' Bud offers Kath her arm and they start to head back to the others.

'If only we could make that drink with Bournvita, that'd pep us up.' Bud pretends to swish it around in her mouth. 'To calm and soothe the nerves – plenty of those.'

In the end, breakfast is a couple of bites of biscuit dipped in condensed milk and a small ration of water. They heat the milk on the remains of the fire and give most of it to the children. Bud notices that the majority of the canvas water bottles are at least half-empty. 'Our supply won't last long – especially when the sun's up,' she murmurs to Kath, who gives her a sideways look, as if to say, *I know but don't tell them that.* 'We need to find water soon, or we'll be in trouble,' Bud continues quietly.

Breakfast is over in about twenty minutes but they're still hungry. Bud's stomach growls – she and the other nurses haven't eaten, forgoing their share for the others.

Matron rosters Bud on duty with a couple of other nurses, under Dr Tay. Kath is ordered to rest.

'Move the patients to the grassy area at the back of the beach out of the sun. There is a strong risk of dehydration.' Matron's face is red and, judging by the irritated lump on her right arm, Bud thinks she must have been bitten by something. Hopefully not a mosquito carrying malaria. 'Assess the severity of their injuries and provide what treatment you can. At least wash and change dressings, if nothing else. Maintain as sterile an environment as you can. Plus water at regular intervals. Try to keep the patients cool. Use fronds and leaves as fans.'

'Yes, Matron,' they reply.

'Going to be a tough day for them … not a lot we can do,' Bud whispers to Kath, now lying down at Matron's bidding.

'Rinse their dressings, keep them hydrated,' Kath suggests. 'Hold their hands, wipe their brows, and,' she drops her voice, 'save the morphia for those in most pain.'

Kath looks at Bud, who knows what she's thinking; they will lose some today.

Bud glances around the beach – there must be about sixty of them here now – and heads off to help move patients. Stuff that has washed ashore from ships – spars, bits of metal and oil-soaked wood – litter the sand. There's the odd trunk or two – the contents spewed up all over the place, shoes, diaries, trinkets, now intertwined with seaweed. Bud remembers last night's ordeal: Florence on the makeshift stretcher, in the salty midnight air. Rosetta and Flo half-dragged, half-carried back down the beach. Clarice turning up with shrapnel wounds.

Bud assists the able-bodied men to move the patients to the shady, grassy area till her hand won't take it anymore. Then she starts her rounds. Mr Betteridge, an elderly man, sixty-ish, who arrived last night in the lifeboat with Kath and Vivian, is up first. Dr Tay has assessed him and concluded that he has an abdominal solid organ injury due to an embedded fragment – presumably from a bomb – in his kidney. Need to watch for haemorrhagic shock and infection, Bud thinks – peritonitis will be a real risk. She cleans his deep wound and prays it won't get infected. As she works, Mrs Betteridge sits by her husband's side and clasps his hand.

'Have you two been married long?' Bud distracts him to take his mind from the pain: from the way he tenses his torso whenever she comes close, she can tell he is suffering. She places her middle and index finger on the inside of his wrist to check his pulse, presses gently and notices irregularity. She counts to sixty, his heart-rate is about one-fifty. High, but no sign of fever, she thinks, relieved, as she feels his forehead with the back of her palm and looks for flushing. Mr Betteridge regards his wife with sallow eyes. He doesn't speak.

Mrs Betteridge nods – they have the kind of shorthand that takes a lifetime of marriage to perfect. 'Decades ... longer than you've been alive,' she says. 'We've never been separated in all that time.' Bud detects South African accents, though Mrs Betteridge tells her they have mainly lived in Kuala Lumpur, and lived there well, Bud thinks, judging by the fine cloth and cut of their clothes – though both are now grubby and torn.

She grabs a fresh field dressing and wraps it around Mr Betteridge's wound, which seeps a bit of serous. Flies try to land on his exposed skin and she shoos them away; he can't afford to get an infection. Surgery is needed soon to remove the bomb fragment she assumes is still in there, and any dead or contaminated tissue. If only she had surgical equipment – scalpels, forceps – she could remove the fragments herself, though they are possibly too deeply embedded and would need a surgeon. Plus, it's risky in a non-sterile environment. But what's the risk of doing nothing? They do have a pair of surgical scissors – she'll talk to Matron, see what she thinks. Maybe she should continue her surgical training when she gets home. She's always wanted to, and being here intensifies that desire. Would she ever become a matron? Possibly – you never know. She tries not to think about whether she'll ever make it off this beach.

'Not even a night apart,' Mr Betteridge manages to say as Mrs Betteridge strokes his knotted hand. Bud thinks of her own parents and their habits woven together over time, how Dad doesn't say much and her mother does most of the talking. Both of them grumbling about chicory as a coffee substitute due to the war.

Matron, Sedgeman and Miller assemble under the vines. The temperature is already fierce and Bud feels her flesh start to sear. The chafing under her neck stings. Matron asks Dr Tay to report on the general condition of the patients.

'Many of them have severe wounds,' he stresses, his voice agitated. 'Some need surgery to remove shrapnel and others treatment for burns. Infection, sepsis, ulcers, dehydration – these are all real risks. They're not going to last longer than a week without proper treatment.'

A week? That's optimistic, thinks Bud. Perhaps they'd have been better off going quickly with the *Vyner Brooke*. She'd rather drown – at least die trying to leave – than have this beach become a graveyard.

'Thank you, Doctor Tay,' Sedgeman says, stepping forward to address the group. Dr Tay heads back to his rounds.

'Today we must make a thorough assessment of our position,' continues Sedgeman. 'Water and food are the priority. We'll send three search parties to survey the area. Two will visit the lighthouses nearby and the third party will go inland on the bush track, to try to find a village.' Bud looks around at dazed and worn faces. 'We'll ask the villagers to give us food and water and help us make contact with the Dutch Resident.'

We can't have much time, she thinks. Japanese are everywhere in these waters. If only we could disappear into the jungle, hide out till things settle down.

Bud wants to join the village party, she hates waiting, being reactive, but she's on duty. Sedgeman calls for volunteers. 'We'll send women and men, it's less threatening – the women of the village may only talk to other women.'

We can only hope they'll talk to any of us, thinks Bud, trying to imagine how she would react in their position.

Clarice, Ada, Janet, Mona, Nancy and Vivian all volunteer for the village party, as well as Alice, the British nurse, and a couple of the civilian women, Mrs Hutchings and Mrs Langdon-Williams. Sedgeman also selects a few sailors. Bud thinks, hopes, the village isn't too far up the bush track – they are all exhausted and bare-footed. And Clarice is injured – she shouldn't be going.

Other men volunteer for the two lighthouse expeditions, one of which Miller leads, the other led by Leading Seaman Victor Spencer. Those heading inland to the village set off behind Sedgeman. Bud watches the grey of the nurses' uniforms snake up the jungle path till they are swallowed by green foliage.

The remaining group have been instructed to scour the beach for anything useful: food, driftwood, clothes to make bandages or stretchers. After that they should rest and conserve energy. The nurses have patients to tend.

Bud checks on Florence, who still lies on the improvised stretcher at the back of the beach. Bud approaches and finds her, brown hair scraped back at the nape of her neck, immobilised and staring at the sky.

'How are you, Florence?' The nurse half-closes her eyes.

'Need to go to the loo?' asks Bud. Florence still can't walk and needs help with basic functions. Bud can see that some of the men are creating toileting areas. One for the women and another for the men. They grab oars to dig a couple of pits.

Florence shakes her head. 'Mona just helped me.' Her voice is throaty.

'Have a drink.' Bud puts her hand behind Florence's head and tilts it to give her a few sips of water. 'I'm going to change your dressing.' She unwinds the white muslin petticoat dressing from last night and notices blood loss from the wound – have to watch that. She cleans the wound site as best she can, dabbing with seawater – their saline substitute. Unsterilised. Hopefully nasty micro-organisms won't cause inflammation or infection. She grabs a fresh field dressing – thankfully a few are left – and gauze, and wraps Florence's breast and torso, positioning herself behind her patient's head to lift Florence's upper body into her lap so she can thread the bandage underneath. Florence's skin feels clammy. Bud ties the bandage securely.

'Any news of Leonard?' Florence's older brother is with the 2/12th field ambulance.

'Nope,' Florence replies. She is sweating and Bud gently strokes the beads from her forehead. 'Struggled to hear anything since they did their training in Darwin.' As she talks Bud assesses her lung capacity – she can hear a slight blockage. Does she need chest drainage? It's probably tolerable for now but they'll need to monitor her. Blast lung, ruptured alveoli, oedema and cardiorespiratory collapse might develop in the next few days. Florence's feeble volume and listlessness indicate how weak she is from blood loss, but she continues, 'Some of them went to Timor and Ambon. I think he's in Darwin, still at the camp at Winnellie.' The muscles at the corner of her mouth fight to turn upwards.

All these nurses with older brothers. Bud thinks she should do a tour when they get back, pop in and visit them, hope for introductions. She is turning twenty-eight soon – in April. Will she marry, have children? Bud feels young, unencumbered. She isn't sure which path she'll take. Might she decide by choice? Fate? Or lack of options? At least if she had no children of her own, she has her nephew Rowley to tell of her time in the Far East. And Jean will surely have another. She'll be Aunt Bud – regale them with tales. Teach them to swim, shoot straight and play tennis. She can make them cakes for birthday parties – elaborate ones, fashioned into shapes, like ships, and decorated in whatever coloured icing they choose. Bright green would be her pick. As long as there's no grey to remind her of the *Vyner Brooke*. Not that she's such a great cook. Her sponges are not known for their rising. Bedtime stories, she can do that. *Swallows and Amazons*, the 'Billabong' books – Norah was a good role model for a girl. Not too sissy or prim. Bud'll teach them to be adventurers, whatever their gender.

In the midst of her daydreams she notices that Florence has fallen asleep. Bud carefully removes the nurse's head from her lap, stands and drifts towards the others.

They work in silence to conserve their energy and because it's bloody hot. Bud's face is so tight it pings. Her skin is itchy from the heat, or has she been bitten? She is so tempted to give it a scratch, but knows she mustn't so chews her nails off instead.

Eventually, bone-tired, she drops and spreads her limbs out. Nestles her head on a pillow of vines, where sleep finds her willing.

2/10th Australian General Hospital, Malaya, 20 January 1942

Letter from Bud to her parents

Dear Old Dad and Tumpy,

[...] now settled in a new home, really a flat so at the moment a bit crowded but quite comfortable as now have a wireless, frigidaire and amahs which is much easier as haven't to worry about washing clothes etc.

The grounds are really beautiful, lovely trees and nice lawns. The last few days have been quite busy settling in and cleaning the hospital up as it was pretty dirty from the look of it, built in about 1700; and old fashioned sort of architecture turrets and columns etc. [...]

There is a tennis court but don't know whether we will be able to play on it yet but it would be rather nice while we aren't hectically busy. Pay day tomorrow but at the moment am rather well up in the money line. Its very economical not going out much.

[...] Let me know if you would like more onto that allotment as can increase it anyway, use it all as I have £70 in my pay book at the moment ...

Think I told you we had an interesting trip down. Passed all the convoys going up to the front line. Gosh they look a good cheery crowd.

Love,
Bud

Radji Beach, Bangka Island

15 February 1942, early afternoon

Footsteps wake Bud. She rolls over from where she has been dozing in the shade under palms, her head nestled on a pillow of vines. The group that headed off to the lighthouse with Jimmy Miller has returned. Bud wipes sleep from eyelashes and sits up, hopeful.

'We've found a spring with clean water,' Jimmy calls out, 'and a fishing hut – not far away, just behind the headland.'

Good news at last! Bud looks over at Kath, who was also asleep nearby and now gets up, her hip wound still sore, judging from her ginger stance.

'Get the most severely hurt into the hut,' Matron Drummond directs. 'Make stretchers from some of this wood and use belts, rope, shirts – whatever you can find – to hold them together.' Bud stands, keen to get moving. 'The rest of you, take water canteens to the spring and fill them. You can have a proper drink now.' Matron looks relieved.

Bud has had only the bare minimum to drink since they were bombed and has tried to ignore her sandpaper throat. Her parched tongue sticks to the roof of her mouth – like when she used to eat peanut butter. The nurses have prioritised their patients – many of whom are also on the verge of severe dehydration – and hoped not to get heatstroke themselves, though Bud did feel woozy last night.

'You should stay and rest, Kath.'

'I'm okay,' Kath insists.

'Doesn't look like it.' Bud can tell by the tentative way she places her foot on the ground and then quickly transfers her weight to the other side that she most certainly is not okay.

'Can't sit here doing nothing. I want to help.'

Bud grabs a couple of once-starchy shirts that have washed up in a trunk. Hands them to Kath. 'Rip these into bandages, then.'

'Yes, ma'am.' Kath gives her a mini salute.

Bud and those who can mobilise their bone-tired limbs grab empty canteens and dash towards the relief of fresh water. They follow Miller behind the headland to where a spring bubbles from rocks and flows inland in a small stream. Others transport patients into the hut.

As she waits her turn, Bud curves her body back, soothed by the burbling sound, and opens her chest to the sky. For a moment serene, she sighs. Mona is at the front of the line ahead of Bud and when she has finished Bud moves quickly forward, brings her face down close to the spring. Cool, delicious water – she sniffs it. How sweet it is. A kingfisher calls its staccato squeak in the distance. Bud's mouth wants to salivate but it has no moisture left. With the reverence of drinking Eucharist wine, she cups shaking hands and watches them fill till they brim over. When she puts them to her mouth she gulps in the water and swirls it all around.

Her body resists with a spasmy cough. 'Don't be greedy' – she hears her mother's words, she always was a bit of a guzzler. She splashes water over her face. Down her neck and chest it trickles, with a pleasant, tingly sensation, creating rivulets in the dirt. Once she has quenched her thirst, she fills the canteens she has brought to give to others.

Sometime later Sedgeman's party, which headed inland for the village, returns. What about the other group, wonders Bud, the one that went to the second lighthouse with Victor Spencer? It is mid-afternoon now; the sun is still high. The village group looks hot, worried. Once they arrive back on the beach they sit, frazzled, back to back or sprawled out on the grass. Before he beckons the rest of them over, Sedgeman goes across to Miller and Matron to debrief. Bud can see nods and looks of consternation.

Sedgeman comes back to address the group. 'It's not good, I'm afraid,' he says.

'Great start,' whispers Bud to Kath and Laney.

'The Japanese have taken the island.' He pauses. Bud puts her hand to her mouth. Looks to Clarice nearby – who looks pallid – for confirmation.

'Where?' Mrs Betteridge asks. The group holds a collective breath.

'Stationed at a nearby town called Muntok. We think it's an hour or so's walk along the jungle paths from the village,' Sedgeman replies.

'How do you know?' one of the British sailors asks.

'Villagers told us. They live up there ... a couple of miles along the track. I know a few words of Malay and between that and sign language we managed to work it out.' Sedgeman's face is drawn. 'The Japs may have captured some of the *Vyner Brooke* survivors.' Bud immediately thinks of Schuey, Matron Paschke and the others. At least then they wouldn't be out at sea. Almost as a reflex she scans the horizon, which is laced with streaks of white.

'Will they take us too?' Rosetta asks.

'We don't think they are this far afield, yet,' Sedgeman replies. 'The villagers told us to walk into Muntok, hand ourselves in and the soldiers will give us food and water.'

'Not likely,' Bud mutters to those on either side. 'Yesterday they shot at us and bombed our ship.'

'We've found water, already. A spring,' says Stoker Lloyd, a naval rating who was on the *Vyner Brooke*, having also, Bud was told, survived the sinking of the Royal Navy's *Prince of Wales*.

'How do we know they'll treat us well?' Kath speaks up.

'We don't, but look at us – we're hardly a military unit,' Sedgeman replies. We were hardly a military unit on the *Vyner Brooke* either, Bud thinks. A rush of heat floods her body. 'We have an important decision to make,' Sedgeman continues. 'The villagers were scared, wouldn't give us any food, said they'd be punished for helping.'

Bud wipes sweat from under her arms where it pools in her armpits. She fans herself with a palm frond – the cool relief of the spring has evaporated with this news.

Vivian steps in. 'While Sedgeman was speaking to an old man from the village, a group of women beckoned us over. They gave us a drink of water and were about to give us clothes and food but the men pushed them aside and forbade them to help.'

'We have three choices as I see it,' Sedgeman continues. 'One: hand ourselves in under the Geneva Convention. Two: repair the lifeboats and try to find an island nearby that the Japanese haven't taken.' Sedgeman squints, the strain of his position as the most senior officer on the beach showing. 'Three: hide in the jungle and convince the villagers to help us find food till we can make contact with the Allies.'

We could eat coconuts and pineapples if we could get them out of these trees, Bud thinks, looking up. Wonder if anyone could get up there in their current condition? Otherwise we'll have to wait for the ripe ones to fall.

Matron Drummond interrupts, emphatic in her defence of those in her care. 'Whatever decision we make, we have to consider the number of seriously wounded. Plus, the elderly.' Matron takes off her thick glasses – now grimy – and gives them a wipe with the hem of her uniform. She can't see without them.

'I don't think we have any choice but to hand ourselves in,' Sedgeman stresses. Though he could give the order he doesn't. 'We'll make the final decision in the morning.'

He moves towards foamy water littered with debris, squats and scrubs his hands using sand as a loofah. Bud watches him pick up a chunk of oil-streaked wood and hurl it at the horizon.

Mumbling can be heard as people talk their options over. Matron stresses the point. 'There's not enough food and too many injured for us to realistically attempt any option but the first. But as Sedgeman says, we'll decide in the morning. We can't do anything now anyway – by the time we'd walked into Muntok and got the Japs to come back with stretchers, it'd be dark.' Matron moves back to her patients, her broad shoulders drooping.

'Doubt those soldiers will be helping us with stretchers,' Laney whispers under her breath.

Matron looks at her sharply. 'Prepare yourselves for whatever lies ahead tomorrow. Get some rest.' She moves off to one side and sits on the sand staring out to sea, her legs stuck out in front of her. After a minute she gets up, rubs her lower back and resumes her work. Her face, though sunburnt, is peaky.

Clouds have gathered and are poised, threatening to dump. Airless and humid – this at least is familiar after Malaya and Singapore. Bud turns to Kath, Laney and Clarice. 'Thoughts?'

'Looks like rain,' Kath replies.

'We should take our chances in the jungle,' says Laney, 'try again to get help from the locals ... Surely we could live on coconuts and pineapples for a few days? There must be some herbs and plants we could use to make poultices. We can help you walk, Kath, and find a spot for you to rest.'

'The wounded won't last long – they need surgery,' Kath counters. 'They'll get infected and go septic, plus there's risk of malaria from mozzies.'

Clarice speaks up. 'If the Japanese have taken the island, they've taken the Resident too. Say we survived a few days, what then? How do we get off this place? We'd have to go by sea and with those currents.' She clearly does not want to continue, and she is not easily deterred, thinks Bud, given her time on a mission in Papua New Guinea.

Must be another way. Bud feels an urge to move and flail around. What else could we do? Think. Think! She walks backwards, forwards, in circles, pounds the sand and watches it fly up until Laney touches her on the shoulder.

'What?' Bud startles and turns around.

'I have something to tell you.'

Bud turns to face her. Laney looks at her with alarming empathy, like nurses do when they have bad news.

'Schuey …' Laney starts.

'Yes?' Bud is holding her breath. Laney touches her hand on Bud's cheek.

'Tell me.'

'We think she went down with the *Vyner Brooke*.'

Bud feels a pain in her chest.

'I've asked everyone, no one has seen her,' Laney continues.

'Did you actually see her dead?'

'No, but if she were alive surely someone would've spotted her – either in the water or on a raft.'

Bud turns and hurtles herself towards the shoreline. At the

edge of the sea she stops and collapses. Folds herself into a ball, plants her head in the sand and sobs.

After a while Laney comes over, kneels down beside her and strokes her brown hair like her mother used to do.

'It's okay, Buddy, it's okay.' Laney cradles her friend's head tenderly.

And then it starts to pour.

Muntok, Bangka Island

15 February 2017

Taxi, two planes, overnight in Palembang, plane, and finally minivan. Amanda and I arrived in Muntok twenty-seven hours after we'd left Melbourne. I gulped some water from the snack box we had been handed on arrival and stretched as much as the cramped seat would allow. My fingertips pulsed, alert to Muntok memory, ready to trace history.

Out the window, tropical vegetation framed Dutch colonial buildings. Shops were shuttered in metal and concrete construction streaked with damp. A muddy river ran through the centre of the town. Through the tipping rain the Hotel Yasmin appeared, blurry in a wall of water. It looked like it had been built in the last few years. Muntok was known for tin, not tourists, and we were the largest group of Europeans to visit since the war, Deanne from the Muntok History Volunteers Group – who'd kindly met us at the airport – told us, though we were mainly Australians. Running a hand over my clothes

I decrumpled myself for the introductions and climbed out of the minivan.

'*Selamat siang*. Welcome to the Hotel Yasmin.' The manager ushered us onto the recently mopped white-tiled floor and handed us a lemongrass drink.

Julie Willes, assistant defence attaché, shook our hands. Julie had blonde, practical hair and looked like she knew how to take command. 'Plans are fluid due to the rain,' she said. 'We've had to cancel formalities for today because the nurses' memorial is flooded. Plus, other military personnel aren't flying in till later. Flight delays ... the election.' I frowned at Amanda, impatient to get to Radji – so close now I could feel it.

'You'll get there,' Julie reassured us.

Judy Balcombe, a GP from Clifton Hill, smiled at me in sympathy. Judy had dulcet tones and a forensic eye for detail. My sister Imogen and I had visited her cottage in Clifton Hill and eaten homemade fruitcake with her. She'd helped to build the Muntok Memorial Peace Museum (with David Man, who ran the associated website, and whose grandfather, Gordon Reis, was on the *Giang Bee* and died in the men's camp in Muntok). A plantation manager in Malaya before it fell, Colin Campbell, Judy's grandfather, made it ashore to Bangka Island near Jebus, about 60 kilometres from Muntok. He'd come from the bombed *Giang Bee*, which had left Singapore in convoy on 12 February 1942 with the *Vyner Brooke* and *Mata Hari*. Colin was captured and interned. He didn't survive the men's camp and now his remains languished under a petrol station nearby, which was built on top of the graveyards in the 1980s.

Michael Noyce came over to introduce himself. Retired as a lawyer, he was now a vigneron and memorial organiser. He had an enthusiasm that fuelled both him and our plans. 'Good to meet you,' he beamed.

I beamed back, pleased to meet another relative of the nurses.

'We've already been to Radji.'

'Have you?' I asked with a bit too much eagerness.

'We got bogged.'

I looked out the window, pelted by sheets of rain.

'We tried to push the minivan uphill, but the wheels were spinning. We got completely covered in mud!' Michael's stylish-looking wife, Val, raised her eyebrows.

'Look at these.' He waved his iPad at me, a screen of photos.

'What are they of?'

'Fish. We met some fishermen from the nearby kampong on the beach.* They invited us to share a meal.'

I peered at the picture. It was hard to make out the fish.

'Small,' Michael conceded, 'but they tasted good.'

'That was kind,' I said. I couldn't believe I was seeing photos of *the* beach. I felt a bit cheated; had wanted my first experience to be in person, not via a screen. I wanted to cover my eyes and ears, press rewind. My desire to put my feet on the sand intensified.

'We've found a spot to lay the plaque,' Michael continued. 'We thought we'd bolt it onto one of the rocks on the headland the men were led around. What do you think?'

---

* Kampong is the Indonesian word for a village.

Since I'd never seen the beach or the headland, it was hard to say, but Michael had carried the twenty-kilogram plaque all the way from Sydney in his Qantas hand luggage. It read: 'This beach is hallowed ground.'

I told him it sounded good.

Laney Balfour-Ogilvy's nieces, Eve and Kate, arrived. Laney was a singer, they told me. She was born in Renmark, South Australia, and apparently the family was descended from aristocracy. Kate and I – looking for connections – discovered we were both married to Tasmanians.

'You're kidding!' we said, our emotions, magnified, echoed on the tiled floor.

'My mother-in-law was evacuated during the war,' I told her. 'Hard to imagine Japanese forces would have made it to the depths of Tasmania.' We laughed. No one thought they would make it to the 'impenetrable fortress' of Singapore either. That was a costly miscalculation of colonial and racial arrogance.

The room was getting warm – I tugged at my damp clothes, reverberating with transgenerational introductions.

'I'm Clarice Halligan's niece, Lorraine.' I whirled around and a woman with a sleek bob of white hair greeted me. She placed a crocheted poppy into my hands, red with silky, black stamens and a safety pin stuck in the back. 'I'd like you to have this.'

'Thank you. Did you make it?' I replied, stroking the woollen gift.

Lorraine nodded and clutched my hands. 'Clarice was thirty-seven when she died. One of the eldest. Ballarat-born, she nursed at the Royal Melbourne and in Papua New Guinea as a missionary nurse.' Lorraine was well-versed.

I had never worn a poppy before, and now I had my own, crocheted by a woman whose aunt was killed alongside my great-aunt, seventy-five years ago, not far away from where we now were, smiling and drinking our welcome drinks. I took another gulp. My head whirred.

Exhausted, Amanda and I retired early.

'Tomorrow will be a big day,' we said, stepping over bath mats with our names spelled out in red petals, to enter our room. Rooms were in short supply so we'd gone in together. Tiled, without windows, we named ours 'the bunker'. The shower hung over the toilet to save space and there was a pungent camphor mothball in the corner, which we binned.

Amanda opened her bag, brimming with kaftans in bright colours. Some even had sparkles and runs of rhinestones. This was a once-in-a-lifetime nursing pilgrimage for her, I was starting to realise. I looked down at the contents of my suitcase, tightly coiled and spartan. I had come to remember old wounds.

'How'd you end up being a nurse?' I'd never asked her before.

'I wanted to since I was five,' she replied. 'I used to write to the director of nursing at the Alfred Hospital every year from the age of ten till I sat my entrance exam at eighteen.'

I imagined the director with a pile of letters tied up in a ribbon, 'Amanda Slipper – wants to be a nurse' written in thick texta on top. At eighteen, my career aspirations were less

Florence Nightingale, more Meryl Streep – creativity, self-expression, being on stage.

Amanda continued, 'I'm not afraid of dying, and I think that is a gift I can give to my patients.'

I pictured Bud with the stretcher cases on the beach, the injured on the *Vyner Brooke*. Had she felt the same?

'Sleep well.' Amanda moved the sculpted swan towel onto the floor. I climbed into my single bed with napkin-like corners. Hemmed in and hot, I pushed my feet to the edges, scissored them back and forth – like a snow angel – to free the tucked-in sheets. Eventually I fell into a sleep of anticipation. Tomorrow, Radji.

Muntok, Bangka Island

16 February 2017

The day dawned and I was expectant. Seventy-five years to this day. Seventy-five years, I said to myself again, as though repetition would somehow make it real. What would Jean have made of my trip? She'd be so proud, Sally had said – not something often uttered in our family. Given my grandmother's silence, I suspected her response would have been more complex.

My mouth was dry. The heat and the aircon in our hotel room sucked the moisture out of you. I took a sip of water from a flimsy, plastic bottle which crumpled as you drank. Touching the little bronze Buddha Bud had sent Jean from Singapore, I traced its solid, metallic curve. So small you could hold it in your palm. It came with a detachable frond which required precision and twenty-twenty vision to insert into the pinprick hole on which the frond balanced. Coming from a half-Christian family – my mother a believer, my father an atheist – I found its presence an uncomfortable friend. It had sat on Jean's sideboard along with the silver cannister which, if we were well mannered, she would open for sweets.

Seven a.m. and Bud's last three hours were about to begin. I grabbed my green dress from the wardrobe and ran a wand of waterproof mascara over my eyes.

Descending the stairs to the lobby, we glimpsed an aerial view of our party. The women in our group were draped in grey and red poppy scarves, the colours of the nurses' uniforms, like a military art installation. Arlene Bennett, the vice-president of the Australian Nurses Memorial Centre (which memorialises those nurses who died or were imprisoned in Japanese prisoner-of-war camps), handed us a scarf each. Transparent, ethereal and gauzy to touch, mine floated around my shoulders and I skewered it with my crocheted poppy.

The *Vyner Brooke* nurses who survived the camps walked out in their tattered uniforms at the end of the war, their emaciated frames engulfed by them. They had vowed to wear them only on important days and to keep them safe in the meantime. Vivian Bullwinkel's uniform is on display at the War Memorial in Canberra. (She died in July 2000, aged eighty-four.)

Numbers swelled, as members of the embassy and defence forces joined us. I prickled with anticipation. *Pleased to meet you. You too.* Medals were pinned, admired and inspected. Some had so many they almost stuck out past their shoulders. Though they were probably safer at Sally's place, in Warragul, framed and behind glass, I wished I had Bud's to wear. Dressed in civvies, I felt a little plain, unadorned. There was a blatant display of uniforms in this foyer. My crocheted poppy was pride of place, just above my heart.

Julie gave another briefing and I felt as though I was floating, swept up in the seamlessness of events, choreographed by these people in uniforms. Julie instructed us to step outside and onto the minibus. In front of me was a day of memorial events and visits to significant locations. First stop was the Timah Tinwinning Museum which told the history of tin mining on Bangka Island and was home to the Vivian Bullwinkel Gallery, dedicated to the war.

I grabbed my umbrella, avoided the puddles, and stepped onto the bus.

Lauren, an Australian journalist living in Jakarta, approached me from across the room at the museum where she had been sizing me up.

'Can I interview you about your great-aunt?' she asked.

I agreed, but wondered what I'd say. Since the family had been so silent on Bud's death, I didn't really know a lot. I had started to do some research but I was third generation, after all. I had been wondering how loss is passed down through families. How it could deaden your responses, blunt you to life. For a while I had been feeling flat, like the joy had been siphoned out of me. Was it an existential moment, menopause, or both? I wouldn't tell Lauren that. Perhaps it was why Dadee hadn't talked much. He'd lost his daughter here, his brother in the Somme, and had fought in the Boer War himself. Taciturn by nature, he'd probably also had PTSD. And my father, who of course had lost both his father and his aunt: he didn't talk a lot either. I'd recently heard an interview about epigenetics and trauma; how it may be passed down at a cellular level. If I could extract my own cells, place my epigenome under the microscope, what would show up? Would there be epigenetic markers from off the coast of Zeebrugge, Belgium, where Dad thought my grandfather Dolly had served in the First World War (and received a distinguished service cross). From Vietnam too, where my father was the day I was born, on HMAS *Hobart*. And what about from Radji?

The interview took place on a white terraced area overlooking plantation fields at the back of the museum. Lauren and I sipped coffee without condensed milk and ate delicate layered treats. These evoked for me Raffles in Singapore, where Kingsley and I had once drunk Singapore Slings and thrown down peanut shells on the Long Bar floor. On leave, Bud had written that she and the nurses had frequented Raffles. 'And had a *very* good time,' Eve, Laney Balfour-Ogilvy's niece, had told me earlier. Moon-gazing and dancing late into the night with air force lads, Bud's letters said. Air force *lads*, so generic. Tell me more, Bud, I had pleaded at her scrawl. Names, details, crushes, love interests, plans? But Bud's letters refused to divulge the hungers of her heart.

Lauren directed her first question at me. 'What sort of person was Bud?' Lauren had the kind of girl-next-door look, with swinging hair, that made you want to confide.

'She was a country girl ... quite a character,' I replied. 'Had all these nicknames for her family; Nifty for her sister, Jean, my grandma; Old Tumpy for her mum.'

Lauren laughed; she seemed to appreciate Bud's quirkiness.

'I have her letters,' I continued, 'written home from Singapore and Malaya.' That grabbed her interest. 'My Aunt Sally said they used to sit silently in the corner of my grandmother's dining room, housed in a rattan box.'

Lauren angled forward, her gaze upon me. 'Why do you think this is an important war event for Australians to commemorate?' She stopped, waited. I leant in too.

'I think this event, because of its shocking brutality, is a potent symbol of women's sacrifice in war.'

Lauren didn't flinch, I watched her, assumed she knew the story. That I needn't spell it out. I waited to ensure that what I was about to say would land. 'Like a female Gallipoli.' We locked eyes, one woman with another. Knowing Lauren would ask me something like it, I had prepared my answer. Was I over-pitching, though, with Gallipoli? There were more than 8000 Australian deaths there. But Lauren didn't protest, her face didn't betray thoughts unvoiced, and I didn't need to explain further or justify my claim. That women weren't much on the front line, more on the home front; in shops, factories, fields and families. So this was *significant*.

'What was the family story about Bud?' She started to dig, like an intimate archaeologist.

Bit of a blank here, and I shifted in my seat. Family story … family story? Dredging through my past for something to say, I glanced around. I hadn't realised we were lacking a family story until now. Dead silent was how it was. I flicked back into the filing cabinet of my mind, but I couldn't pull a helpful file.

Only an image of Dad sitting at the table, shaking his head with rueful eyes. If he didn't want to get into a subject he would just clam up, shut the conversation down. Simply, we didn't go there with difficult things; it felt uneasy, unstable ground. I felt a dull, hollow feeling and, unsure of what to say, I reached for some banana cake, took a bite and started to chew. It was stodgy and stuck to the roof of my mouth.

Some members of the Muntok History Volunteers Group lounged in my peripheral vision dressed in camouflage gear, smoking. A wall of graffiti framed this tableau of Bangka cool. Intrigued by Lauren, perhaps, they were looking over. These volunteers had rebuilt the road to Radji and even cleaned the beach for this anniversary occasion. I wondered what their families had suffered at the hands of the Japanese Imperial forces – who had supposedly come to liberate Asia from colonisers – though they were colonisers too.

Lauren awaited my response. Turning back to her I mumbled something about not having a family story about Bud. That it wasn't spoken about in our family – too traumatic – plus the stiff upper lip stoicism of my forbears. Lauren nodded, and I added how resilient the nurses were, but I could tell by her absent eyes that I'd lost her. The interview came to an end. She tapped the red button on her iPhone and said she would like to get some photos on the beach.

We headed in minivan convoy to the site of Muntok's former women's and children's prison camp, Kampong Menjelang.

It was a relief to climb into air-conditioned comfort and rest my head against the glass. I thought of those who had washed ashore on Bangka Island, fleeing Singapore, and were interned here between October 1944 and April 1945 in the women's camp.[2] Ongoing research by Michael Pether indicates that around 100 vessels, including boats, launches, tugs, praus, sampans and junks, left Singapore between 11 and 14 February as it fell to Japanese forces. Only around twenty of these made it to safety.

Sixty-five Australian Army nurses left Singapore on the *Vyner Brooke* hoping to make it home. Twelve died when the ship was bombed and sunk – either at the time, or later lost at sea. Twenty-one were killed in the Radji Beach massacre (twenty-two were shot but Vivian Bullwinkel survived). Thirty-two women were interned in the camps on Bangka Island and Sumatra. Thirty-one of them had landed in different locations on the island, thus avoiding the massacre, and the thirty-second woman interned was Vivian. Eight died over the next three-and-a-half years. Only twenty-four made it back home to Australia at the end of the war.[3]

Vivian Bullwinkel was the only nurse to survive both Radji Beach and the camps. Fearful the Japanese would finish her off if they realised she had survived the massacre, she hid her wound with a water canteen when she and Private Cecil Kinsley – one of the male survivors – handed themselves in twelve days later. The nurses in the camps made a pact never to mention the massacre till they got out. Instead, they whispered about 'the girls on the beach'.[4]

*

Traipsing across an empty field towards the former prison camp site, we soon passed a primary school, where rows of children hunched over notebooks. A little further on, past the Muntok Memorial Peace Museum, Judy Balcombe motioned us to stop. 'This is the only remnant of the Muntok camp left standing.' Judy pointed to an old stone well. She had become an expert in all things camp-related. Hoping for revelation, I peered down, but the well was pitch-black and silent. Amanda looked at me as I pulled my head out, her face said underwhelmed. We walked on. The village of Kampong Keranggan Atas had sprung up on the prison camp site. Where once there were barracks, bamboo with palm-frond rooves under which the women slept on sacks filled with dry grass, now, smack-bang in the middle, was a plaque. We congregated around it for the service. The plaque spoke of a darker past, carved it into the ground. Part of it read:

> In loving memory of the women and children interned in
> Muntok …
> Civilians and army nurses were held captive here, experiencing
> hardship, ill-health and often death. They cared for one another
> and shared the very little they had.
> Despite the squalor, they sought beauty in song.

A mango tree framed this stone nod to history and I watched as a woman picked mangoes from high above us with a long, hooked rod. You would never guess what had gone on here – the landscape was transformed. The evidence buried beneath us; soil shifted out to make way for the new. And if you dug even deeper you would hit Dutch colonialism and a brief period of British rule. I wanted to excavate, to see what I found deep down in the ground. Perhaps, if I did, a pit would open and swallow us all.

Judy stood on a platform to give the address. Only partially shaded by the mango tree, we stood in the midday sun, the air thick and sweaty. My body felt limp. The women interned here had been placed in the sun and forced to kneel for hours for a misdemeanour, some slapped, or hit with rifle butts. Tenko – the Japanese name for roll call – took place twice a day. Each time, the women were made to line up, bow deeply to the guards, the Emperor and Nippon, and be counted.

Judy was softly spoken, villagers were in and out on motorbikes and there was chit-chat in the background. Conducting a service in English in the midst of village life felt odd. How much did the people whose land this was know, I wondered, of the history of this site, the suffering on which the foundations of their homes were built? As the visitors here, interrupting their daily routine, I found the normality somehow reassuring, puncturing my eerie pictures of the past.

Relatives of those who'd survived these camps travelled here from Australia and England year after year. Why? Remembrance, grief, obsession? Or a yearning to make sense of how their families had been affected through the generations?

My legs were getting sore, I shifted my weight, tried to do it subtly – those in uniform stood so still. Maybe it was as simple as a devotion to history. There's always one in every family who wants to know, Amanda had said – and in this story that one was me. Why? Unfinished business. Not that I knew exactly what that was. But I felt that somehow the responsibility had been passed to me. Perhaps because I am the eldest, or because I was available and curious to take it up. Or was it something that I did not understand? I looked up. The sky was humid, overcast, like blots of charcoal dense with matter. Wiping the sweat from the back of my neck, under my mass of hair, I took my hat off for a second to release the heat.

I would go to the beach, lay a wreath, and finish this memorialising.

We had been given a service sheet, and at the bottom I spied in tiny font the words Sister Pat Gunther, a camp survivor, had written about her time here:

> We had reached the stage where we envied those who had been
> lost at sea, and even the nurses who had been massacred. They
> had not known the misery and wretchedness of life in a Japanese
> internment camp. It was all over so quickly for them.[5]

I wanted to protest. Look into their gaunt eyes, argue, 'You got to go home.' But the captors of these prisoners starved them nearly to death and denied their existence – and the men's – at the end of the war. They were hidden away at Belalau, an abandoned rubber plantation near Loeboek Linggau, Lahat, in Sumatra. Major William Alston Tebbutt, in charge of the nurses on the *Vyner Brooke* and also an intelligence officer, was interned in Muntok before later being sent to Changi, and knew there were survivors somewhere.[6] He, along with Major Gideon Jacobs, who was sent to liberate Sumatra, agitated successfully for them to be found.

In August 1945, Captain Seki Kazuo announced to the prisoners that the war was over by telling them:

> Now there is peace, and we will all soon be leaving Sumatra.
> If we have made any mistakes in the past we hope you will
> forgive us, and now we will be friends.[7]

Seki is said to have thrown open the ration store and revealed enough food supplies for all the prisoners – as if the cruelties of the guards were so trifling that they could be brushed aside with this gesture. The Red Cross had sent these supplies so no one would die in the camps. There were boxes of canned vegetables and medical supplies – quinine, vitamins, bandages, serums – and powdered milk. Things the women had begged for. The nurses had buried their friends from beriberi, dysentery, malaria, tropical ulcers and starvation. Dug their graves. Burnt names and dates into wooden crosses with a hot wire, so none of them went uncounted.

My fingers stiffened and clenched. On release, the women were chronically underweight. One, Betty Jeffrey, weighed only 31 kilos, while another, Jenny Greer, was an alarming 20. The Australian public, it was decided, would not cope with seeing them, bones protruding from their skin. They were sent to Singapore first, for medical treatment – where doctors at St Patrick's hospital said five of them would have probably died within a week had they not been rescued.[8]

We dispersed, lost in the past, but it didn't take long for village life to resume. Four young girls were balancing nearby on a motorbike, their hair veiling their faces. 'Can I take a photo?' I asked. I could tell they weren't expecting to be approached, hugging the periphery as they were. They eyed each other, nodded. Tentative at first, they started to experiment, attempted some risky poses, leaning far out off the side of the motorbike, their arms jutting out.

'Careful!'

They smiled, pleased with their boldness.

Other more confident girls thrust cameras in my direction. Hugging me around the waist, they started to pose. A universal-selfie-dance ensued – if only my daughters were with me – culminating in a crescendo of lollies, trinkets and souvenirs. A gesture of thanks for our village intrusion.

Radji Beach, Bangka Island

15 February 1942, dusk

'If only we could get to those coconuts,' Bud says, as she gazes up at laden palms and shakes off large droplets from the deluge that has just passed. For a moment everything feels fresh until it starts to steam again. 'Hurry! Ripen!' she instructs the coconuts. A couple have fallen and been hacked into bits with pocket knives. They each ate one small piece of flesh, which Bud sucked till the sweet, creamy fibre disintegrated in her mouth. She wonders if a few of them could try to shake the trunk? But she's weak from lack of food and her gashed palm would make it impossible.

'I'd like a big chunk of juicy pineapple right about now,' says Kath, who is soaked but doesn't seem to mind.

Once more for dinner all they have are ship's biscuits and a sip or two of condensed milk. Again, the nurses forgo almost all their rations to share among the others. They are desperately hungry and so worn-out. Though they move slower now, they do what they can for their patients, which continues to be a struggle without proper medicine and surgical equipment; as well, the supplies they do have are running down.

'The other lighthouse party hasn't returned, you realise,' Bud mutters to Kath. 'The one that went with Victor.'

Throughout the afternoon Bud has been filing memories to share with Schuey's family if she ever makes it home. Schuey's parents are George and Eleanor; she has a sister called Dorothy (like Bud), and a brother, George, after his father. She will tell them what a fine friend Schuey was. What larks they got up to. Bud feels the loss of her friend like a phantom limb. But it might not be true. They don't know for sure. She could still be alive out there. And what about Matron Paschke – might she have made it ashore?

Clothes have washed in on the waves: some are spread out to dry and some torn up to make bandages. This, plus the fresh water supply, makes it easier to wash and redo dressings. Mind you, there could be nasty bugs in the spring, thinks Bud. Perhaps they should stick to cleaning with seawater, at least it is saline. The nurses wipe brows, toilet and adjust their patients to get comfortable – which for many is not possible. Most underrated comfort of all, they sit alongside them.

A Malay sailor badly burnt in the bombing of the *Vyner Brooke* finally passes away.

'Thank God it's over for him,' Bud says, recalling the rasp of his breath and rawness of his skin.

'I gave him as much morphia as we could spare,' says Mona.

Nearby, two men dig a hole in the sand using an oar and their hands as shovels. They place his body into it with some difficulty – rigor mortis has set in. Though they pat down the sand to bury him as best they can, the mound protrudes above the ground. Ill-equipped and too weak, they cannot dig deeper. Bud wonders how long the sailor will stay covered. Hopefully till his muscles slacken. They congregate and pay their respects. Laney sings a funereal tune as twilight falls, her voice hovering on the diffuse rays of the setting sun.

Bud fantasises about all sorts of escape plans, each one crazier than the next. Where there's a will there's a way, she says, over and over.

In the last vestiges of light, a couple of fishermen appear on the beach and gesticulate the bad news the survivors already know. Sinewy arms point down the beach. 'Muntok. Japon. Japon,' the fishermen say. They point out a path through the jungle that will take them on a shortcut.

The sky is spectacular tonight – hues of red, pink and purple. Subtle shades stain the sky, and gradients of colour weep. This will be the last sunset we see free, thinks Bud, etching the sky in her mind's eye, archiving images to contemplate in captivity. To lift her when she is flat. At twilight in Cheshunt during summer, the family would sit on the verandah, swat mozzies and listen to cockatoos screech as they battled for night-time perches in the trees. Bud has never imagined herself behind bars. Would the Japanese prisons even have bars? More likely barbed wire and jungle huts. And a bed? Probably just a platform. Thoughts of home come thick and fast. King parrots in multicolour flocks; Dad's tobacco crop – hope it's a good harvest this year – Smithy and her old hounds at Corowa. Jean's life as a young mum.

How long till she will see them again, Bud wonders. Saunter on in as a surprise. At least if we're taken prisoner we'll be fed, she thinks. Rice, probably. Bread is what she'd like, and butter spread thickly, topped with homemade plum jam. Her stomach grumbles at the thought. The Red Cross will make sure we have supplies, at least, she figures, and since we are non-combatants we might even get sent home. Wouldn't that be the best surprise to give her parents? Turn up one day at Willow Cottage. Knock on the front door. 'Hellooo, I'm home!' Walk up behind Jean and wrap her arms around her waist.

The sunset fades. Grey starts to overshadow the skerrick of pink in the sky. In the last of the twilight, she looks over to the mound where the sailor is buried and swears there is a limb sticking out, like some ghoulish island horror show. How would George and Eleanor bury Schuey? Bud wonders if her friend's body is still out at sea. She feels the urge to sprint away and never look back. Into the jungle, to the other side of the island, out to sea to find Schuey and swim with her for home.

The glow of meteoric dust hovers after the sun drops. Fairy-dust-like, Bud wants to bathe in this tropical phenomenon. Maybe it could inoculate her against what is coming. When the moon is up, Bud lies down to rest. She'll be on night duty soon, needs her sleep, but she can't settle. Finally, she rolls over, and as she drifts off darkness descends.

Singapore, 8 February 1942

Last letter from Bud to her parents

Dear Old Dad and Tumpy,

Sorry I am a few mails behind but we have been fairly busy, not so much busy but am on duty over 12 hours a day and don't get much time when I get back to write. However am on night duty for a fortnight, go on from seven until seven, but at the moment business is slack; all we have by way of light is a lantern with blue paper wrapped around.

Haven't had any letters from you for nearly a month now but have hopes of getting some every mail day. Got quite a lot of papers from Dad, it was quite good reading about Malaya which seems perfectly true the way the *Bulletin* described Kota Baru, although some of the *Melbourne Sun* seem to be making a bit of a howl but more worried about themselves.*

How is Dolly, met a naval lad the other day and told him to tell Dolly to call on me if he ever landed here which I don't think will be likely now. Is Jean still with you, think it would be very advisable to keep young Rowley up with you.

[...] Will write to Jean in a couple of days' time.

Hope you are both alright and Dad isn't working too hard.

Love,

Bud

---

* The battle of Kota Bharu on the north-eastern coast of Malaya (Malaysia) began on 8 December 1941. It was the first major battle of the Pacific War and occurred about an hour before the attacks on Pearl Harbor (7 December due to time-zone differences). The ensuing hostilities eventually prompted the relocation of all Australian nurses, 2/10th and 2/13th Australian General Hospital and 2/4th Casualty Clearing Station, to either Singapore or elsewhere in Malaya first.

Singapore, 8 February 1942

Last letter from Bud to her friend
Jean Smithenbecker

Dear Old Smithy,

No news and no letters, haven't had any from home for a month
& from you for a fortnight. Sorry if these are so uninteresting but
there is a lot of news but can't tell you at the moment; anyway
the papers seem to put most of it in print. At the moment am on
night duty four nights on. We do a fortnight on day duty & fortnight on night, only catch, don't get any days off. Worked till 2 pm
& went on again at 7; but managed to get about an hour and a
half's sleep this afternoon, anyway hope for a snooze later as two
of us do theatre & we aren't admitting tonight so things should
be pretty peaceful as far as that is concerned. At the moment
we are sitting round theatre both writing with two hurricane
lanterns wrapped around with blue paper as it's supposed to be
a black out.

The orderlies have scrounged us a pretty good supper from the QM store so it looks as though we are going to have pretty good food on night duty. Hope you can read this on this dark paper but it shows too much on the other side.

Have you heard anything of Skeet or is she still in New Guinea? No news,

Cheers,
Bud

Radji Beach, Bangka Island

16 February 1942, pre-dawn

Second night on the beach. Again the bonfire blazes, its flames incandescent thanks to the oil-soaked wood. Bud has been on duty for the latter half of the night while searchlights cut the darkness. Japanese boats, she assumes. Where are the Allies? Despite the nurses' efforts, their patients are getting weaker by the hour – as are the nurses. Children cry and grizzle, their mothers unable to soothe them. Bud is all too aware that the beach will become a mass grave if they don't get help soon. She feels dizzy and unbalanced, as though she could topple over at any moment. Her body, particularly her ribs, aches as though it has been battered with fists. What she would do for a cigarette, and food – she's trying not to think about either. She has taken to holding her right hand like a claw, since it hurts to straighten it, and she can still use it that way – as a prop – if she's careful. The underside of her chin is still gashed from the lifejacket rubbing and now has an itchy sting. She tries to ignore the dull pain of her ribs and the bites which cover her, and gives Mr Betteridge a drink of water from the canteen.

As she lays his head back down, the sea lights up like a firecracker. Those who were asleep startle and wake, and turn to face the sea. Bud watches, horrified, as a ship is caught by searchlights and smashed by gunfire. She can feel her heart-rate quicken. A whip sound bounces over the water, up the beach and smacks her ears, a cruel soundtrack to a lopsided battle. Pulses of light flare in the sky and no one is in any doubt what the outcome will be. Then the flashes disappear and only columns of smoke remain, puffing in the sky. Is the ship sinking after the attack? Flashbacks to shards of glass, shouts, the *Vyner Brooke* tipping, and children grasping for their mothers. Her head pounds and she makes fists to massage it, digging knuckles into bony bits.

'How far away d'you think they are?' Bud asks Clarice. 'Poor bastards. Hope some of them make it to land.'

'Same distance as we were? Hardly heard the planes,' Clarice replies. 'Fingers crossed any sharks have been scared away.'

Rosetta calls out, she needs help to turn and toilet. Bud hurries, an urgency to her work now, as she resumes her rounds, one eye firmly on the sea, from where she hopes survivors will emerge. The waves swish in and out, the bonfire crackles and the stars glint, but there is an unmistakable menace in the air.

Just before dawn Bud sees a dark shape moving near the shore. Like an apparition, it emerges from the sea. Who is it? Bud stands.

'Someone's here!' A voice yells. A lifeboat and several life rafts have beached.

'Who's there?' Sedgeman asks, holding the others back and peering into the dark.

'Lieutenant Martin, captain of the *Pulo Soegi*,' comes the response in a Kiwi accent. 'Can you help us? Our boat has sunk and we are wounded. We are mainly Royal Army Ordnance Corps, plus crew.'

They haul twenty or so men ashore – a mix of British and New Zealanders. Matron and the nurses triage the injured and hand the most serious to Dr Tay for further assessment. Matron instructs the sisters to provide whatever treatment they can. Bud and Mona lie one Private Cecil Kinsley on a great-coat arranged on the beach, careful to clear any sand away. He has most of the upper part of his left arm and shoulder blown away and the bone is visible. They check to see the extent of the damage, note a deep, soft tissue injury to both bicep and rotator cuff muscles, with profuse bleeding. Bud and Mona work fast, squatting beside him, to clean the wound and stop the haemorrhaging – which has been temporarily dammed with a ripped-up shirt – or he could become hypovolaemic and, down the track, risk septic shock.

Mona moves off to help another. Bud gives Kinsley a shot of morphia, knowing their treatment is inadequate. He needs surgery and intravenous help. To distract him she asks, 'How did you get into this mess?'

'Arrived just in time.'

'What d'you mean?' She lifts his arm and slides a bandage

underneath. Kinsley recoils and Bud can tell by the caged look in his eyes how much this hurts.

'Part of the eighteenth reinforcements – came to Singapore in time to surrender.'

She makes a face in sympathy. 'Hold still. Where are you from?'

'East Yorkshire.' He clenches his teeth, accentuating the tendons in his neck. 'You?' he spits out the word.

'Cheshunt, country Victoria.' Bud sits beside him as she bandages him up. 'It's a dot of a place.' She waits to see the morphia kick in and the tension slide out of his body.

The nurses work through the night, keeping up a brave face. In their quiet moments they whisper to each other, 'What are we going to do? So many who need serious attention.'

A couple of patients babble in their sleep. Whimpers are suspended in sea air.

Daybreak. Sedgeman stands on the sand and sweats. Hoists himself straight to address the group. Remnants of the bonfire they had overnight glow and hiss as the sun rises.

'Today we must make our decision.' He clears his throat and tries to project calm through his wide-legged stance. Earlier, Bud watched him grind the ground. In front of him, in the early morning haze, are those with ruptures, burns, hernias and deep shrapnel wounds. Up close, when Bud is doing the rounds of the patients, their vacant, listless faces make her want to weep. The nurses are trying their best to keep up fluids and prevent bugs and green-backed flies from gorging on wounds.

'There are now many critically ill among us who will not last more than forty-eight hours, if that,' Sedgeman stresses. Must be nearly a hundred of us here, all up, Bud estimates.

'We've heard they aren't taking prisoners,' a sailor from the *Pulo Soegi* interjects. Most of the new arrivals nod in agreement. So, they've heard that too.

Mrs Langdon-Williams, a middle-aged member of Singapore society, disagrees. 'Half of us are women and children. Surely they'll respect that.'

'Doubt it,' another soldier retorts.

'We'll put it to a vote,' Sedgeman says. 'Let me remind you that if we decide to escape, we'll have to leave the wounded behind, which neither the nurses nor I are prepared to do.' He looks around to see how this lands. 'Those who think we should hand ourselves in under the Geneva Convention, raise your hands.'

Bud looks beyond the group to two pathetic mounds of sand – another man has just been buried, having only made it ashore a few hours prior. These two men lie in shallow sand, a long way from home. No one to bring flowers. Will tides and monsoonal rain obliterate their graves? Thoughts bounce back and forth in her mind like tennis balls, and Bud can see no other choice but the one Sedgeman is proposing. She delays a second – attempts to halt time – to see what others have decided. Inch by inch they raise their hands. Her gut wrenches. Up goes her hand, despondent. The vote is reluctant but unanimous.

Things start to move fast now as a plan is formulated. Sedgeman consults with Jimmy Miller and Matron. He volunteers to walk into Muntok, where they know the Japanese have headquartered themselves – he will not make others do what he won't do himself. A couple of sailors, originally from the *Prince of Wales*, say they will accompany him.

Bud gets up to move to Florence, whose dressing must need changing.

'We need to make more stretchers in case the Japs don't bring enough back for everyone who needs one,' Matron says to Miller, who nominates some of the sailors and soldiers for the job.

'Use anything you can find,' Miller tells them.

'Once they're made, start transferring the patients from their makeshift beds,' Matron adds. 'Don't forget those in the fisherman's hut.'

Before anyone can argue *No! Stop!* Sedgeman and the others are winding their way along the path. Bud sees the tops of their heads bob, disembodied, above the foliage until they disappear from view.

Out of our hands now, Bud thinks, trying not to get too far ahead of herself but also reminding herself to hydrate for the trip when Sedgeman returns for them. Tonight we will be sleeping under guard, in a prison. Will we have a pillow? Perhaps a sack stuffed with dry grass. Bud's head drops any time she sits for longer than a few minutes.

Mrs Hutchings steps forward. 'The children are suffering – they've hardly eaten for days.'

'Let's send you ahead to Muntok,' Matron replies. 'Any children, women and wounded who can walk, prepare yourself to go now. If you get a head start you'll be closer to a meal – and there won't be so many walking on the jungle path later on.'

An elderly Australian mining engineer, Mr Dominguez, volunteers to lead the party with Able Seaman Cake and Leading Seaman Noble, both of whom were crew on the *Vyner Brooke* and have shrapnel wounds. 'We won't be much use carrying stretchers,' they point out.

Dr Tay also volunteers to go. Not much love lost between him and Matron, thinks Bud.

Some of the men urge the nurses to go too.

'No,' says Matron, 'we stay here with our patients. We're not making that mistake again.'

'I'm not going anywhere,' agrees Bud to Florence, while checking her wound, 'not after Singapore.' Florence nods, too frail to talk – she has lost a lot of blood and is drifting in and out of consciousness. 'Can't leave you behind.' Bud pulls a couple of stray hairs from her face and slides them behind her ears.

About eight women and three children set off, bidding a quick goodbye: Mrs Hutchings, Mrs Langdon-Williams, Mrs Dominguez, Miss Louise Beeston, and others whose names Bud does not know. Izzy and his mum follow them, walking hand in hand off the beach, with Alice close by on Izzy's other side. It must be eight-thirty or nine by now, Bud estimates.

But Mrs Betteridge is going nowhere. She fiddles with her wedding band and insists, 'I've never been separated from my husband in all these years and I'm not going to start today.'

She lies down beside him and will not budge.

Radji Beach, Bangka Island

16 February 1942, around 10 a.m.

The sun turns its rays to bear down on raw skin. The water shimmers. Bud sits cross-legged under the palm trees near the edge of the sand, a momentary reprieve. Beads of sweat drip down her neck and onto her limp collar, now stained a yellowish-brown. Her thoughts are jumbled and she can't focus on much else apart from the gnawing hunger in her stomach and her physical discomfort. Others construct rudimentary stretchers out of driftwood, belts and spars. Console each other in hushed tones. Sedgeman and the others have been gone a while now. Surely they will return soon. Bud turns her head repeatedly to the jungle track. Looks up to the sun, wonders what time it is. Eventually she hauls herself up to inspect the Red Cross flag they have fashioned, now flying on a stick. Has to be visible from different vantage points. Clear that we pose no threat. For the fifth time this morning she adjusts the Red Cross armband on her sleeve and fidgets with the edge. Her foot jiggles.

Army photo of Bud, *c.* 1941

The Elmes family: Mummum, Jean, Bud and Dadee

Jean and Bud at Karouda in Cheshunt – Bud's grandparent's home

Studio shot of Bud, undated

Bud outside Corowa Hospital, *c.* 1940

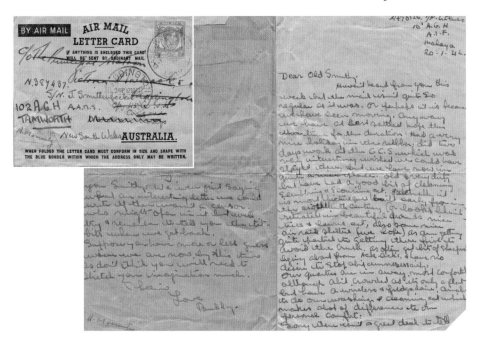

One of Bud's letters to her friend Jean 'Smithy' Smithenbecker, 20 January 1942

(AWM PR88108)

Bud and her friend Marjorie 'Schuey' Schuman. Both were stationed with the 2/10th Australian General Hospital in Malacca, Malaya.

Schuey, Bud and two Australian Army officers on leave

Staff of 2/10th Australian General Hospital, Malacca, Malaya, 1941. *Left to right, back row*: Sisters Joy Bell, Dorothy 'Bud' Elmes, Pat Gunther. *Front row*: Sisters Beryl Woodbridge, Betty Pyman, Nell Keats. All are holding air raid equipment including steel helmets and respirators. (AWM P01180.004)

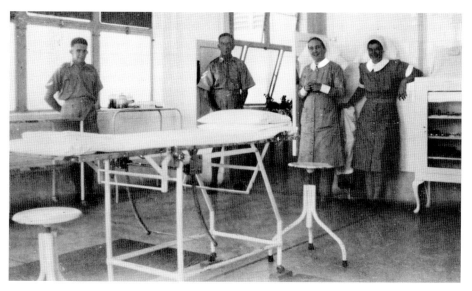

Staff of 2/10th Australian General Hospital in an operating theatre, *c.* 1941. Identified (*far left*) Lance Corporal Raymond Benjamin Beckman, who became a prisoner-of-war after the fall of Singapore, and, *far right*, Bud. (AWM PO1180.005)

Group portrait of Australian Army Nursing Service sisters who were among those attached to the 2/10th Australian General Hospital. *Left to right, back row*: Miss Winsome Zouch (physiotherapist), Sisters Nan Drover, Pat Gunther, Miss Thelma Jean Gibson (physiotherapist), Sister Winnie May Davis, Miss Bonnie Howgate (physiotherapist), Sisters Kathleen Margaret Neuss, Jess Doyle, Kath Blake. *Front row*: Sisters Margaret May Olliffe, Joyce Lockhart Bell, Veronica Taylor, Veronica Jean Taprell, Violet Haig, Marjorie Schuman, Claugh, Bud, Helen Jacobs, Blanch Moriarty. (AWM P01180.002)

The *Vyner Brooke*. The ship, originally a cargo vessel, was built in 1928 and named after the third rajah of Sarawak, Sir Charles Vyner Brooke.

A relative found and lost on the same day: Mrs Sally Alsop reflects on letters written from Singapore by her late aunt.

Old letters unearth a wartime nursing hero

By VICTORIA GURVICH

Vivian Bullwinkel was with fellow nurse Gwendoline Elmes in February 1942 when they were ordered by Japanese soldiers to walk into the sea before being shot.

Matron Bullwinkel, now Mrs Statham, was the only survivor of the Banka Strait massacre in which 21 Australian nurses were killed.

Dorothy Gwendoline Elmes, who was known as Gwen or Bud, was 28 when she died.

Her niece, Mrs Sally Alsop, cherishes a treasure-trove of letters written by her aunt that she now hopes will be collated and published as a book.

In 1995, the 50th-anniversary year of the end of the war in the Pacific, Mrs Alsop decided that the letters should become an official part of Australia's history.

In the last letter Nurse Elmes wrote to her parents, dated 8 February 1942, she spoke of her hopes of receiving mail from her family. She

died eight days later, not having received a letter sent by her mother saying how proud she was of her daughter.

Several days before the massacre off Sumatra, nearly 300 men, women, children and nurses, including Nurse Elmes and Matron Bullwinkel, were evacuated from Singapore on the Vyner Brooke, a ship designed to carry 12 people. The steamer was one of many ships sunk by Japanese bombers in the Banka Strait. Many passengers

drowned, some made it to shore to become prisoners of war, others were shot.

Mrs Alsop said she grew up knowing little about her aunt, although her picture was always on the wall. Ten years ago, when her mother was ill, she heard about the letters.

She found the letters, many written on rice paper, in a cupboard — all were stamped with "Passed by Censor" — and spent the night reading them. "I just got to know her and I lost her at the same

time," Mrs Alsop said. In 1944, the family received two letters from the Australian Red Cross. The first said Nurse Elmes was "officially believed to have been killed". The next day, an apologetic letter arrived saying Nurse Elmes was "missing, believed killed".

Mrs Alsop said it was important to treasure the letters as they helped show the impact of war on families, the horrors of wartime and the selfless bravery of the Australian nurses.

In a 1996 newspaper article in *The Age* the author's aunt, Sally Alsop, reflects on letters written from Singapore by Bud in the early 1940s.

The seventy-fifth memorial service of the Radji Beach massacre, 16 February 2017, laying wreaths on the beach: Philippa Dickson (Matron Drummond's niece), the author, Kate and Eve (Laney Balfour-Ogilvy's nieces), Lorraine (Clarice Halligan's niece), Australian Defence nurses and members of the Muntok History Volunteers Group (AAP/Lauren Farrow)

The walk into the water, at the seventy-fifth memorial service, by Australian Defence nurses (Michael Noyce)

The Walk for Humanity, February 2019 (Michael Noyce)

Blessing the Radji Beach memorial, February 2019 (Michael Noyce)

'Think they'll bring enough stretchers?' asks Kath, who rests nearby and traces a leaf pattern in the sand with a twig.

'Hope so, I don't think we could carry them far.' Bud inspects her palms, peeking under bandages. 'Though I doubt the soldiers will carry the stretchers themselves.' An ulcer is starting to form on her right hand, from the tell-tale swelling and pus around the blotch of red. Please don't let it get infected. Needs another bath in saltwater.

'How long till we make it back, d'you think?' Kath traces 'Home?' in the sand. Then swipes it away with her hand.

'Soon as this bloody war is over,' replies Bud, 'whenever that is.' She heads down to the water and takes off the bandage. Back and forth she swishes her hand in the shallows. Saltwater stings her skin and her nostrils fill with the stench of tepid, rank seaweed. It's a strange thing to anticipate your captors' arrival. She does, however, feel relieved that she'll be able to write to her parents and Jean, tell them she's alive – might leave out some of the more harrowing details though, Mum is such a worrier. Bud starts to compose the letter in her mind. *Dear old Tumpy and Dad, we are alive and safe in captivity on Bangka Island – that's a small, tropical island in the Dutch East Indies. Don't worry about me, I am fine, being treated well and at least have rice to eat and medical supplies.* Something like that. Fill them in but don't alarm them – and no mention of Schuey or Matron Paschke.

Bud shakes droplets of water from her hand, walks back up the beach and grabs a clean bandage made from a torn-up shirt. The dirty one she throws on the to-be-washed pile. She remembers her mother's relief on receiving a letter from a friend saying her son was a POW. 'At least he's safe now,' she had said.

Bud squats back down beside Kath, who nods at the bandage.

'Sure.' Bud holds out her hand. 'Thanks.' Kath wraps it around Bud's palm. Firm, but not too tight – there is no give in this shirt-bandage – she ties the ends together.

'I've definitely heard they're not taking prisoners.' Kath is now scratching the sand with her twig.

Jolted from her letter composition, Bud responds. 'Look at us … Mainly nurses, wounded, civilians.'

Kath widens her eyes, as if to say, don't be naïve. Bud continues, agitated. 'Even the soldiers and sailors aren't armed. Or are in no state to fight, anyway.' She points to the prominent Red Cross. 'Pretty clear we're surrendering.' Her heart is racing. Kath looks down and keeps her counsel.

Matron Drummond summons them all for a final briefing before the Japanese arrive, up near the tree line, where the stretcher cases are lying at the back of the beach. Not far from Bud and Kath, Matron stands, heaves herself up to full height and adjusts her spectacles. 'They'll most likely be here soon,' she starts resolutely. 'I expect they'll come on the same track Sedgeman set off on.' She twists her neck to indicate dense jungle behind her. 'It's important that you go about what you are doing in an orderly manner. Remain calm.' They nod in agreement. 'Don't make any sudden moves, or do anything to cause alarm … And God bless.' Matron looks out to sea for a brief instant, crosses herself. Bud feels her insides constrict as she prepares for her last round on the beach. The air is dense, ponderous, absolutely no movement.

'Doing okay?' She sits beside Kinsley.

'My shoulder … where the shrapnel hit.'

'I know.' Bud dabs his face clean with a wet torn-up shirt-cloth. 'Least you'll get proper treatment soon.' She glances past his hair, matted with coagulated blood, towards the track. 'Maybe even a cup of tea.'

'Hate surrendering to the Japs, Sister.'

'Don't we all.' She frowns. 'Think about Elsie.' Bud has heard him mention his wife back home.

She moves to her next patient, Mr Ernest Charles Watson, the retired magistrate, who Bud thinks must be around seventy and the eldest on the beach. Mr Watson lies impassive on a stretcher, face up, staring at the sky.

Finally, around 10 a.m., they hear voices in the jungle. Exactly as Matron predicted, Sedgeman walks hurriedly along the track. Directly behind him are a group of Japanese soldiers, fifteen or so of them, plus one small, well-dressed officer with a sword, who is clearly in charge. Bud reels back, stumbles and sits with a thud. They don't have any stretchers. The officer barks orders at his men. His voice is pitiless and his face is devoid of emotion.

Sedgeman approaches the officer. 'These are the people I told you about,' he gestures to the group. 'They want to become prisoners-of-war.' Sedgeman points to the Red Cross – at pains to make it clear that there are protocols here.

The officer looks through him and shoves him aside. Legs astride, blank-eyed, he stands and assesses the group. Bud can feel her sternum rise and fall, its twinge, and time stretch like elastic.

Post-calculation, the officer snaps at his men, who pick up their rifles and cock them, with a metallic click. Then they level their guns. Bud's stomach spasms and her mind blanks. The officer shouts a direction to his soldiers, who point with bayonet tips at the men gathered near Matron Drummond. It seems the soldiers are telling them to stand behind Sedgeman.

Those who are able to line up. About twenty-five of them who can stand, do so. A similar number can't walk, are on stretchers, or are still lying incapacitated in the fishing hut. They are counted off.

'*Ichi, ni, san, shi* ...' The staccato sounds harsh in Bud's ears.

Perhaps we're going to different camps, thinks Bud. But I didn't get a chance to say goodbye. She tries to make eye contact with some of the men, catches Eric Germann's gaze for a millisecond. His face is blanched and peaky.

Guns point at Bud and the nurses, motioning them to line up too.

Bud places her hand on Mr Watson's collarbone to quieten his protest and can feel her muscles tighten as she pushes against sand, rises to her feet and steps into line. The soldiers stand like sentries on either flank.

'*Ichi, ni, san, shi* ...' They count the women off too.

Bud looks down at her dirty, roughed-up feet. Wishes she had Smithy's shoes – which by now will be lying on the seabed – to stop her skin from being shredded by the time they reach camp. They stand in line in the sun for what feels like a very long time. Bud sways on her feet, she hopes she will not faint or fall over. Why aren't they moving? She's burning hot and her guts are heaving – is she going to vomit? Some of the men break from the line and resume fixing stretchers.

The Japanese officer confers with another soldier, nods and indicates for half the men to move. Six soldiers at their back usher them along the beach. But they're not heading on the track towards Muntok. They are going in the wrong direction. A soldier motions the rest of the men to sit. Bud, giddy, also lowers herself to the ground. Sand kicks up behind guards who are pushing the first group of men down the beach with bayonets. One guard carries a machinegun. Around the rocky headland the men climb – their figures outlined against the backdrop of the sun as they disappear from sight at the southern end of the beach, about a hundred yards from where Bud and the others are sitting.

About ten minutes later, the soldiers return without the men. Where are they? Have the Japanese moved them to another beach? And that cracking sound …? Bud cranes her neck, shifts her position – her legs are getting pins and needles. Soldiers approach, gesture to the second group of men, which includes Sedgeman and Miller.

'Kiritsu shiro!' one of them barks.

Sedgeman and Miller point to their epaulettes. With a flick of his gloved hand, the officer shouts down their protest. He indicates for them to carry Mr Watson, who was earlier prone on his stretcher, rasping, but is now sitting up. Eric Germann and Sedgeman lift him, grunt and start their reluctant procession down the beach towards the headland. They stop halfway there, putting Mr Watson down. Bud can hear shouts. Eric hands the officer something, who throws it on the ground, picks up a plank of driftwood and swings. Eric is still standing, though, after the swing. Did he block it with his hand?

Now they are moving again, with Mr Watson, but they stop at the outcrop, where it appears they are labouring to lift him. From what Bud can see, the officer gestures and they place Mr Watson down again and leave him there, propped. Up and over the rocks and driftwood they go, like figurines. As they disappear from sight Bud wraps her good hand around a leaf and squashes it.

Minutes pass. The women are silent.

A sound pierces the silence. The sound Bud heard before. The cracking sound. Like when she used to shoot rabbits on the farm. One single bead of sweat rolls along her profile and drops a long way to the sand.

After a hiatus the Japanese soldiers appear again, back from around the headland. They walk towards them, holding their rifles, laughing. Bud sees them wiping their bayonets with small cloths or handkerchiefs. Two groups of men have now been led beyond the headland and none have returned. She thinks she might pass out.

'So it's true – they aren't taking prisoners,' Nancy Harris whispers.

An eternity passes right there on the sand. Horror-struck, Bud gauges her options, glancing around ever so slightly. I could run, she thinks, sprint for the sea – I'm a good swimmer. Or into the jungle ... villagers might take pity on me. Or up the beach – but I'd have to sprint like the wind, there's no cover.

Jenny Kerr turns to Vivian. 'Bully they've murdered them all.'

Laney whispers Bud's thoughts: 'We could try to make a run for it.'

Matron reminds them of the injured behind them: 'They are relying on us for support and comfort.'

Bud looks down at her bandaged, lacerated palm, and everything in her training tells her to stay, but everything in her instincts tells her to run.

'We have run away once before.' Matron's words bore into her. 'We are nurses ... while there is life there is hope.'

Soldiers come closer, squat down in front of them and start to clean and reload their rifles. They take their time to do it well. Meticulously. Bud imagines blood, red, glistening on metal. A wave of nausea engulfs her but she will not gratify them. She sits erect, hoping to impede the moment. Fixes her gaze on a kingfisher that's fossicking nearby, magnificent in orange, royal blue and black. Rather than rotate their entire heads, these birds move their eyes within their eye sockets.

She trains her eyes back on to the Japanese soldiers, observes the jodhpur-style trousers of their uniforms and caps with gold stars. Three gold balls joined with a chord, like insignia, adorn the breast of their jackets. Their black boots have a curious pocket for the big toe. Made for the wet, she supposes – their feet look webbed like amphibians. The one in charge is wearing a smart suit, which looks tailored. His sword hangs by his side. Bud looks away, her mouth bone-dry.

Out of her periphery, she sees the soldiers move towards them, form a semi-circle, and motion them to stand. '*Kiritsu shiro!*'

This could be my moment, my last chance, and Bud prepares

to take it, but at least a dozen Japanese eyes are fixed on her. The kingfisher will stab its prey, either with the bill closed or open, depending on the size.

No one speaks but Bud imagines matron instructing them, *Straighten your uniform.*

The familiar command is tinged today with a different hue. Bud runs her hand along her tunic, smooths out the creases and dusts the sand away. She presses the crumpled, stained collar back where it belongs. Movements she has made many times a day.

She rises to her feet. She feels as vital as when she enlisted but full of disbelief. The officer and his men point, exchange comments in Japanese, and direct the women towards the water. One of the soldiers sets up a machinegun at the back of the beach, about twenty yards away. Bud plants one foot on the sand, wobbles, and begins to walk across the beach. The soldiers circle, she cannot see a way to make a break. Without a word – as if in a trance – the nurses find each other and link arms. Bud is near the middle. Time seems to be distending. She sees Rosetta, Clarice and Flo – struggling to walk – pulled, propped and carried, next to Matron Drummond at the right-hand end of the line. Straight ahead towards the Bangka Strait they continue, one step after another.

If I am to run I have to do it now, Bud thinks. In and out, she breathes, in and out, her chest coiled, ready to spring. Alert to opportunity, she glances sideways at Kath and Laney. Will they make a break too? They are halfway down the beach now, in a line, facing the sea. Twenty-two Australian Army nursing sisters and one elderly civilian, Mrs Betteridge, who didn't want to leave her husband. Bud thinks of Jean and her young nephew, Rowley.

He must be almost four by now. She sees her parents' faces seated at their dining table in Cheshunt. Eating their midday meal of meat and three veg.

Have to time this right, she thinks. Looking behind her to see where the soldiers are, she catches a glimpse of Florence and Private Kinsley's outlines, just visible at the back of the beach, immobile on stretchers. Patients she has left behind come back to her: the soldier from the 8th in Singapore, the elderly man on the *Vyner Brooke*.

She hears Matron Drummond's voice. 'Chin up, girls, I'm proud of you and I love you all.'

Down the other end of the line Alma Beard speaks up. 'There are two things I've always hated in my life, the Japanese and the sea, and today I've ended up with both.'

Bud's will to run collapses. A guard is right behind her, shoving her to move. She rams her foot into the sand. I will *not* run! In front of her, a current surges and swirls. Courses through her and into the arms of her sisters. As if this line is charged: duty, service, country, blood.

Another soldier jabs her in the back, forces her forward. Metal against flesh, the bayonet almost pierces her skin. Bud wants to slap him, to spit and fight back. Lungs spasm, claustrophobic. She's got to get some air. Could bend down, grab handfuls of sand. Throw them in his face. But now the bayonet is gone; it seems the guard has retreated.

'Girls, take it, don't squeal,' yells Esther Stewart.

Crack. The sound breaks the silence. Bud turns to her right and sees Matron Drummond crumple. Her face hits the sand

and her glasses land in front of her – Matron stretches her arm to reach for them. Bud wants to pick them up and place them back on for her. One bullet, two. Matron now still, down on the sand. More sisters are falling: Flo, Rosetta, Clarice, knocked forward and slumping. Soldiers laugh in high-pitched tones. Bud and the others keep walking forwards till they reach the foamy water churned up by bullets. They step in. Up to their ankles, now their knees. The sea is foreign, tepid, as it touches Bud's hamstrings. Flashes of Cheshunt; alpine country, water that trickles from unblemished creeks. She clutches the arms on either side of her. Each time someone falls, she can feel the jerk of the machinegun, a tug on her arm, and the water kick up.

Bud wades straight ahead, her eyes stuck on the horizon. She can hear the Lord's Prayer, Hail Marys, and the cry of a loved one's name.

As soon as she is up to her thighs, the whack of a bullet hits her in the middle of her back. The last thing Bud feels is a burning sensation, and her body falling.

The kingfisher flees.

The tide catches and lifts Bud.

Her blood flows out into the sea.

And her mother's voice cries out. 'My darling little Bud, oh dear, I wish I knew where you are in the world.'

Military Hospital, Heidelberg, Melbourne, 18 April 1942

Letter from the Australian Red Cross to Dorothy Jean Elmes

Australian Red Cross Society.
Incorporated by Royal Charter 1941.

FOR SAFETY.
IN YOUR LETTERS DO NOT REFER TO:—
The name of your ship or other ships in the convoy or its escorts;
The date of sailing, ports of call, or probable destination;
The description of troops aboard, any other information which, if intercepted, would be of value to the enemy.

(UNOFFICIAL)

Military Hospital
Heidelberg
18/4/42.

Dear Mrs Elmes,

Excuse my belated reply to your enquiry. My addresses have been many in the last few weeks & your letter took some time to find me

Unfortunately, Mrs Elmes, I am unable to add any more to the news you already have of the girls — General Bennett told us that they all definitely left the island, (Singapore) and where they went from there is what he is endeavouring to find out.

I know how very worried all the girls' parents must be and we are hoping that they will sail in one day out of the blue as some ships from that direction still seem to be doing.

I shall never cease to be amazed at the fact that I am safely back here again. The girls who are not with us are continually with us in thought & I do so hope that you will receive some news very soon.

Sincerely yours

Kathleen Forsyth

159

Records Office, Sydney, 3 July 1942

Letter from Officer in Charge of Records to Dorothy Jean Elmes

AUSTRALIAN MILITARY FORCES

Records Office,
N.S.W. Lines of Communication Area,
R.A.S. Showground,
SYDNEY.

3 JUL 1942

Dear   Madam,

With reference to my recent letter informing you of the absence of news concerning your Daughter Number NX70526 Staff Nurse Dorothy Gwendoline Howard ELMES. 10th Australian General Hospital A.I.F. I am directed by the Minister for the Army to advise you that he must now be posted as Missing, and to again convey to you the Minister's sincere sympathy.

Your natural anxiety at the non receipt of further particulars is appreciated and you are assured that everything possible is being done by the Department and through the International Red Cross to obtain further news of him. On receipt of such news you will be immediately notified by telegram.

Yours faithfully,

Major
Officer in Charge Records

Mrs. Dorothy. J. Elmes.
Cheshunt,
Via WANGARATTA. VICT.

Australian Army Nursing Service, Melbourne, 21 April 1943

Letter from the Principal Matron to Dolly

TELEPHONE

AUSTRALIAN MILITARY FORCES.—VIC. L. OF C. AREA.

IN REPLY PLEASE QUOTE
No.

AANS OFFICE
AAMC DRILL HALL
WILLIAM STREET
MELBOURNE.

21st April 1943.

Lieutenant Commander A R Banks, R.N.
Naval Officer in Charge,
WHYALLA

In reply to your enquiry re NFX 70526, Sister Elmes, G. it is advised that some members of the Australian Army Nursing Service are missing in Singapore. No correspondence has been received, but news of some of the Sisters has been received over the wireless, - this is believed to be authentic.

It is regretted that no further information is available.

G P Field

Principal Matron
AANS, Vic L of C Area

161

Australian Red Cross Society, Melbourne, 23 June 1944

Letter from Red Cross Bureau for Missing, Wounded and Prisoners of War to Dorothy Jean Elmes

Australian Red Cross Society

OS/CK   VICTORIAN DIVISION

RED CROSS HOUSE
289-293 SWANSTON STREET, MELBOURNE, C.1

Telegraphic Address:
"Aurecrom"

Telephone:
F 9151

23rd June, 1944.

Mrs. Dorothy Elmes,

CHESHUNT. Vic.

Dear Mrs. Elmes,

It was with the deepest regret that we heard that your daughter -

NXF70526 S/Nurse G. Elmes

is now officially believed to have been killed on or after the 11th February 1942. This very tragic end to your hopes and fears will be very hard to bear and we offer you our deepest and truest sympathy.

The courage and heroism of these fine women who went abroad gladly to attend our sick and wounded men, facing as they did many known and unknown dangers, fills us with humble pride and admiration. There is little we can say to bring you comfort in your loss, but we hope that later on when the edge of your grief has softened a little, you will be helped by the knowledge that Sister Elmes and the other nurses who offered their lives in similar circumstances, will always be honoured by their friends and country.

Yours faithfully,

Vera Deakin White

(Mrs. T. W. White)
Director - Red Cross Bureau for Missing,
Wounded and Prisoners of War.

Australian Red Cross Society, Melbourne, 24 June 1944

Letter from Red Cross Bureau for Missing, Wounded and Prisoners of War to Dorothy Jean Elmes

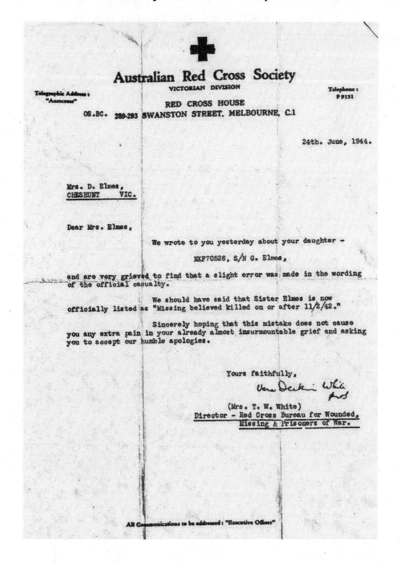

Australian Army Nursing Service, 29 June 1944

Letter from Matron-in-Chief to Dorothy Jean Elmes

Australian Army Nursing Service.

DEPARTMENT OF THE ARMY

29th June, 1944.

Dear Mrs. Elmes,

I was very grieved to learn the latest information conveyed to you regarding your daughter, Dorothy.

I realise the strain of the past two and a half years and the shock of the news that we can no longer hope for her return.

Every member of the A.A.N.S. pays tribute to her outstanding bravery and devotion to duty.

May I, on behalf of the Sisters in the Army, offer their deepest sympathy and assure you of their desire to make the Service worthy of such gallant members.

Yours sincerely,

Anne M. Sage

Colonel

Matron-in-Chief A.A.N.S.

Cheshunt, Victoria, 2 March 1942

Letter to Bud from her mother, marked
'Delivery Impracticable Return to Sender'

My darling little Bud.

Oh! dear I wish I knew where you are in the world. I suppose we will hear soon. It seems that some nurses have returned to Australia. I can't help wishing you were amongst them. As long as you are safe it is alright. The last letter we got from you was written on the 8th? of Feb: just a month ago ...

... I had a letter from Marge a few days ago asking for news of you. Everyone is thinking of you – she said Bennett who was in Singapore just after leaving Johore said the men and the nurses were marvellous and never complained under very trying circumstances. I feel proud of you darling as you were one of them. Don't know if he ever got out. I don't seem to have much to write about, we hope to get a cow this month it will be a big help if we can.

Goodbye darling no news.

With all my love from Mum

PART TWO
AFTERMATH

Radji Beach, Bangka Island

16 February 2017

Finally we headed to Radji Beach. Dismounting the four-wheel drive, I shook my bones back into place and hurried down the track to the shore. I wanted to spend some time here alone, take everything in ahead of the others.

The jungle track ended where the brown mud met sand and the trees opened up to the heavens. I stopped. Took a step. Placed one foot onto the sand. My skin touched Radji and I paused, waited for a feeling to hit me. I was sure the place would possess an aura that betrayed its brutal past. But I didn't feel it. Nothing. Instead, I saw a pretty, crescent-shaped beach fringed by jungle and palms. A rocky outcrop punctuated the southern end.

My nervous system turned up high, I took a second step, still surprised I could feel nothing. Not a sense of them. Had we waited too long? Brackish, choppy water was the only sign of disturbance. Rain must have stirred it up. The sun was trying to emerge, to push its face forward past pillows of grey. Ramshackle fishing huts sat at the edge of the sand, and wooden pastel boats, painted yellow, pink and green, rested alongside. There was some tar on the beach, sticky like goo, from an oil spill, I assumed, or the tin mines nearby, which scarified the landscape.

Once the others had arrived we moved quickly to retrace our relatives' footsteps and recreate events of that day, starting with the spot where the two groups of men were led around the headland. Vivian Bullwinkel said it was about 100 yards from where the nurses and wounded were sheltering at the back of the beach, under the trees and vines.[1] Amanda and I tried to locate the spot. No vines there now, just jungle, a tangle of green. Palm oil plantations, which whizzed by on the way in, gave way to pandanus, coconut and other verdant varietals. I pictured the nurses up there. A sea of grey tending the wounded: Florence Salmon, with the ripped-off breast; Mr Betteridge, half the South African couple who had never been separated before February 1942; Private Cecil Kinsley, with shrapnel wounds; Mr Watson, the elderly magistrate.

Where was Bud when the nurses heard the first shots? Bending down, I grabbed a fistful of sand, let it strain through my hands. A couple of granules stuck to my skin; I rubbed them between my thumb and forefinger, held my fingertips near my cheek. Now I could feel the vibrations.

Sarah and Helen, sisters from Wales, led the way around the headland at the southern end of the beach. They had come to retrace the steps of their grandfather, Stoker Ernest Lloyd, who had somehow got away from the Japanese soldiers on this beach; dodged the bullets, survived the camps, and made it back to Wales.

I nearly cheered when I met the sisters. Stoker Lloyd had only just died. One of only three male survivors of the massacre, he never came back to this place. Scrambling after them over large boulders, I asked the grand-daughters, 'What would he have thought of you coming?'

They eyed each other, then replied in unison, 'That we were mad!'

'"Why'd you want to go back there?"' The sisters channelled Stoker Lloyd, exaggerating his Welsh accent. 'He was very matter-of-fact about it. Showed us the scars on his ankle and head. "I ran into the sea, I survived," and he was *very* keen to make sure we could swim.' Sarah added, 'As a little girl I was afraid of Daleks and Japanese soldiers.'

I laughed, but it was bitter. Feeling an urge to be alone, I continued around the headland. Out of sight, I leant back against a rocky outcrop – *the* rocky outcrop – took a breath and the muggy air inflated my lungs. I conjured the men in my mind's eye, wanted to get it all straight, go through it step by step. Separated into two groups, the men were marched around this headland; behind them Japanese rifles cocked and bayonets attached. Three small gold balls, or insignia, adorned the uniforms of this battalion. Only visible when up close. My lungs squeezed out air, like bellows, deflated. The men thought they were walking to Muntok, to an internment camp – the first group, that is. The second group would have seen the bodies, lying in fresh pools of blood. Forced to rip up their shirts, tie blindfolds around their eyes – by then there would have been no doubt. Then came the sound of machinegun fire and the stab of bayonets. Down in the cove in front of me, blood spilt and spread like mercury. Stoker Lloyd made a run for it, chopped up the water. Able Seaman Jock McGlurg beside him muttered, 'This is where you get it, Ernie, right in the back.'

'Not for me, Jock,' he replied.[2]

Survivor of both the *Prince of Wales* and *Vyner Brooke* sinking, Lloyd had nine lives – or three. Before the Japanese soldiers had time to react, he, Jock and another unnamed man sprinted off and dived into the sea, which was deep enough for them to start swimming. Caught off-guard, the soldiers responded with a volley of bullets. Did they fire from behind where I was sitting? I turned around; my heart hammered. The other two were killed but Stoker Lloyd was not. His scalp was grazed by a bullet, another went right through his shoulder and leg. He was knocked unconscious. Drifting, half-submerged, he washed up on a sand spit and passed out – down there to my left somewhere, past where I was sitting and on the way to Muntok. I twisted my neck to see the body floating in the slaty-blue sea. My tongue felt frizzy and thick. The Japanese soldiers assumed he was dead and turned their attention to the nurses. Swallowing, I tried to expel the taste but couldn't. The jagged edges of the rocky outcrop pushed against my palm. My hand recoiled and I stood up.

We arranged ourselves on the sand, dignitaries at the front, in a horseshoe shape, relatives clustered together, staring straight ahead. Michael Noyce cradled the plaque he had brought, and I put on my sunglasses. Army chaplain Troy White read John 15:13: 'There is no greater love than to lay down one's life for one's friend.'

'I want you to imagine what was here when dawn broke on the sixteenth of February, nineteen forty-two,' Michael Noyce said. 'The nurses were somewhere down there, with the wounded, under those trees, on makeshift stretchers. There was a fisherman's hut ... and there were some more badly wounded inside that hut. When dawn broke there were about a hundred people here.'

I looked around at solemn faces. The starchy white of naval uniforms was stark against the backdrop of the sea.

Michael continued, 'Over the last two days there'd been a lot of people ... coming from various boats that had been sunk out there. Some had been in the water for many hours ... There were at least three lifeboats up and down this beach, many rafts, and lots of debris from the sunken boats.'

Lauren was filming the speech for posterity and Michael was going to post it on Facebook. I wondered how Sally and Dad would respond, so many years later, to see the beach that had cast such a long shadow.

I refocused on Michael. 'Over there were the remains of the bonfire that the first boat under Sedgeman had built as a beacon, to attract people from out at sea. In one sense it was a scene of chaos and in another there was complete control ... under the great leadership of Matron Irene Drummond.'

I looked over at the niece of the iconic matron, Philippa Dixon, whose broad shoulders suggested the same take-chargeability. A late arrival, Philippa was affable, 'up for things', and, like me, was getting up to speed on these family and historical events. Like me, she had never met her aunt. None of us here had met our relatives. We were all born after they were killed.

Michael went on: 'Overnight, ships were sunk out there and a whole lot more wounded and survivors came to the beach.'[3]

A hundred or so people here, wounded, fleeing sinking ships – it was hard to imagine. The straits and sea a battlefield, later a mass grave. Biopic war movies rehashed in my mind, *Dunkirk*, *Gallipoli*. Michael outlined the story we all knew, and I tuned in and out, lost in my conjuring. Did they *really* believe the Geneva Convention would protect them? They placed their hope in Article 9. 'The personnel engaged exclusively in the collection, transport and treatment of the wounded and sick ... shall be respected and protected under all circumstances. If they fall into the hands of the enemy they shall not be treated as prisoners of war.'[4] Japan had signed but not ratified the convention.

The roll call of honour commenced. Philippa was reading it. 'I hope I get the names right,' she whispered.

'Better get mine right,' I whispered back, trying to lighten the moment.

After the roll call we moved in unison to pick up the wreaths and lay them in the sea. I held Bud's, full of chrysanthemums, braced myself to go in. I'd said before that I couldn't possibly stand in this water. That it was sacrilegious, macabre even. But I couldn't lay the wreath if I didn't. Side by side I stood, with Philippa, Eve, Kate and Lorraine. Michael Noyce and his family were at the other end of the line. We started to walk. There was comfort being shoulder to shoulder, floating our offerings. I wished my father, aunt, grandmother and great-grandparents could stand on this sand. Steeling myself at the edge, I dug my toes into the shallows. Water touched my ankles and I winced.

Deeper we waded into the sea, which lapped lukewarm against our calves. I hoped the wreaths would float freely, unhindered by currents, not wash back to shore as the nurses' bodies had. One of the volunteers kept trying to take Bud's wreath from me, but I tightened my grip. Finally, with a push, I released it. Backwards and forwards on the currents, the wreaths drifted.

And as they were let go, I felt the sadness of my family, heavy in my bones.

Knee-deep, the hem of my dress now wet, I turned to look back at the shore. Twenty-two contemporary army nurses stood in a line, wrapped in brown uniforms. Linking arms, they started to walk towards the horizon. At the shoreline they stopped, their black shoes lapped by Bangka water.

I blinked and could see my grandmother Jean reach for her sister, Bud.

'Sweetie,' she said, and stretched out her arm.

I could see the nurses on 16 February 1942; their grey uniforms, their Red Cross armbands, their looks of utter dis-belief. Shots rang in my ears, the sea turned to red, and one by one, the nurses fell.

Sister Elaine Lenore Balfour-Ogilvy
Sister Alma May Beard
Sister Ada Joyce Bridge
Sister Florence Rebecca Casson
Sister Mary Elizabeth Cuthbertson
Matron Irene Melville Drummond
Sister Dorothy Gwendoline Howard Elmes (Bud)
Sister Lorna Florence Fairweather
Sister Peggy Everett Farmaner
Sister Clarice Isobel Halligan
Sister Nancy Harris
Sister Minnie Ivy Hodgson
Sister Ellen Louisa Keats
Sister Janet Kerr
Sister Mary Eleanor McGlade
Sister Kathleen Margaret Neuss
Sister Florence Aubin Salmon
Sister Esther Sarah Jean Stewart
Sister Mona Margaret Anderson Tait
Sister Rosetta Joan Wight
Sister Bessie Wilmott
&
Mrs Betteridge

I repeated Vivian's words to myself. 'How could anything as obscene as this happen in such a beautiful place?'[5]

*

Afterwards, I noticed a group of young Indonesians hovering on the edge of the beach, observing proceedings. The women wore white dresses, with white or coloured hijabs. The men were in uniforms, white and maroon. All stood with an elegant ease. Julie explained, 'They are local Indonesian nurses and doctors. They would like to conduct their own service in honour of the Australian nurses.'

They gathered in a circle and spoke in Bahasa. We formed an outer ring. In their arms were wooden baskets filled with petals – chrysanthemums and roses; pink, yellow and white. When their service had finished, they moved to the water's edge and with fluid gestures their arms arced and they scattered petals into the sea – pink, yellow, white, pink, yellow, white, pink, yellow, white. The colours streaked the sky in the afternoon light. I stood humbled on the sand. Later, I found out, they had bought new hijabs for the occasion.

Melbourne

February 2017

Farewells were made to the other relatives and promises to Michael Noyce that we would keep the service going, maintain the momentum. 'We could re-enact the spontaneous walk into the water,' we said in the back of the minivan, 'call it the Walk for Humanity, a symbol of peace.'

When I got home to Melbourne, I rang Sally to recount my trip. She picked up straight away and sharply inhaled when she heard it was me.

'How was it, George?'

'Where do I start?'

My dog Lola sat on my lap and balled up into my arm – sensed she'd be there a while – her black curls velvety as I twirled them round my finger.

'I want to know *everything*.'

Determined to bridge the gap between Muntok and Melbourne, I launched in. When I reached the bit about the contemporary nurses walking into the water, my voice faltered. This was the image that had haunted Jean, Mummum and Dadee's world, that was pinned on their mental screensaver. The one Vivian had told over and over to the press, and to the Tokyo War Crimes Tribunal (the International Military Tribunal for the Far East) in 1946.

'They linked arms in their uniforms,' I said, 'and started to walk towards the water ... spontaneously, like Bud and the nurses did ... all those years ago.' I tried to convey the poignancy of the moment, push it down the phone line to Sally in Warragul. Lola licked me on the face. 'Tears streamed down their faces. It was as if they were in a trance.'

'Oh, that's giving me shivers,' Sally said. 'So moving.'

'You can watch it on Facebook, I'll send you the link,' I added, pleased I had something tangible to offer. Something she could keep, as well as the poppy scarf, which she could wear close to her skin. The footage would transport her. What would it be like though, I wondered, for Sally to see *that* beach for the first time? Confronting, probably. But it would fill in some gaps, questions she'd had for years, with no answers.

'But I'm not on Facebook.'

'You don't need to be.' I could hear the same patronising tone in my voice that my children directed towards my one-fingered texting. No doubt I would have the same conversation with my parents later on.

'Thank you for going, George,' Sally sighed. 'Now I feel a sense of peace and can put it to rest. It was always this place so far away, over *there* somewhere, but no one knew where it was.'

I could feel a tremble as I imagined Jean and Mummum sitting at the kitchen table in Cheshunt, wondering about the beach where Bud was taken. Somewhere 'over there'. It didn't seem right that I'd flown to Muntok and back within a week. Of course, people rarely went overseas in those days. 'The chance of a lifetime,' Bud wrote, in a letter to Smithy.

But no beach, no body, no Bud to say goodbye to, to cradle and to hold. The body with no breath is the tangible evidence of finality. I wanted to know what happened to the bodies. The remnants must be around that beach somewhere, or out at sea.

It was cold in Melbourne, autumn was coming. Pulling my jumper around me, I moved away from the draught, kept my gruesome thoughts to myself.

'Did Mummum and Dadee ever talk about her?' I asked Sally. Now that I had been to Muntok and was deep into Bud's story I had all these questions I hadn't voiced. It was all so real: as if the past, 1942, was right here, present in 2017.

'No,' Sally replied, 'but we were never allowed to speak during the twelve-thirty news.'

'Why?'

'Because she was missing for so long. Every time the news was on, they were listening out for something, anything about her or the nurses. It was an ingrained habit.'

How odd we are as humans, our contorted efforts to cope, what our instincts are for survival. No psychology textbooks in those days, no Beyond Blue to get best-practice advice, no free counselling hotlines. *Put it behind you, get on with your life* were the best they could do. And maybe that worked, in some way, for some time. They might say we are too soft now, too psychological. Doesn't bring the person back.

I looked out at our garden; the red gumnuts had flowered on the silver princess gum, like wispy starbursts. 'Was there a funeral service?'

'Maybe a memorial service,' Sally replied. 'Um … but I think the dedication of a plaque at the Wangaratta Hospital would have been it. I'll send you the faded report from the *Chronicle.*' Sally really was the archivist of all things Bud. 'If there *was* another service it would have been reported in the *Chronicle*, I'm sure, but I've never seen any mention of it.'

How suspended the death must have felt, how surreal. Maybe *not* having the service kept Bud alive, the possibility of her coming home. Rewind. *We made a mistake, Mrs Elmes, she's not dead after all. Here she is, back in time for dinner, put the spuds on.* Or, perhaps it was the telegram Mummum received from the Red Cross on 24 June 1944, changing the wording from 'officially believed to have been killed', which they had written the day before, to '*missing* believed killed'. The possibilities for hope the word 'missing' opened up.

'Did Jean ever talk about her around that time?'

'I wasn't born when Bud was killed.'

'Oh, of course.' I corrected myself. 'And later?' I looked outside again – the princess gum was leaning at a precarious angle. Have to straighten it up, so it doesn't lean so far it breaks. An old stocking, which had lost its elastic, was all that held it together.

'No,' Sally replied. 'All I knew was a sepia photo of a woman in uniform that hung on the wall. Somehow I knew that I shouldn't mention her or ask any questions. There was a triangle raffia basket in the sideboard, no doubt sent from Singapore, which I eventually realised was full of Bud's letters, which I also knew I shouldn't touch. That was it.'

That was it? My throat ached. Sally continued, 'When I found and read her letters years later, after Jean died, I felt I was discovering my aunt – who I never knew – and losing her at the same time. No, hang on, I think I waited till Jean was in hospital to read them. I couldn't talk to her about it.' Sally was definite about that.

Something I hadn't thought about for a long time came back to me. I hadn't been to Jean's funeral either. Why not? Probably because we didn't have much money, too disruptive to drive all that way, better if Dad just went by himself. On hearing the news about Jean, as a teenager, I remember that I stood on the stairs, looked up at Dad, and demanded, 'Aren't you upset? Your mother has died. Why can't you cry?'

I was eighteen and had never met grief.

It wasn't till years later, when I did a drive-by of Jean's house in Dixon Street, Wangaratta, which was by now shabby, and to the Wangaratta library where Jean had been a librarian, that it hit me she was gone.

How strong the silence was, so that Sally waited till her mother was in hospital before she retrieved Bud's letters.

Later, Sally told me that the death of their father, Dolly, was likewise never mentioned. He became a mystical figure – she began to wonder if he'd even existed. She had searched, unsuccessfully, for his grave at both Kew and Wangaratta cemeteries. Why did our family respond like that?

Jean lost her only sister and her husband within a few years: the grief encircled her like a fog. Bereft, alone and with no qualifications or support from her in-laws in the UK, she had to *get on with it* as best she could, moving back to Cheshunt to live with her parents. Later, she ran the VIP guesthouse at the Zinc Corporation mine in Broken Hill and my father was sent to boarding school in Adelaide, aged ten. No wonder Jean valued education for women and was bloody-minded about it. Determined to be an actress, I used to stonewall her when she tried to convince me otherwise. Jean locked up her grief, threw out the key. Got on. Tall and thin like a eucalypt, I remember her straight spine, the way she stood up erect, and how her clothes hung off her.

I rang my father next, not sure how he would respond. There was a lot of loss in his young life. The scar tissue was knitted tight.

My parents were there together. 'Wait, I'll put you on speaker,' Mum said. I was relieved she was there as a buffer. She fussed around, tried to get it to work.

'Can you hear me? I asked. This routine was familiar, comforting.

'Wait a minute … just turning up the volume.' I could hear scratches and mumbles on the other end. 'Okay, George, we're both here now,' Dad said.

I recounted my adventures for the second time, glad to have had the first run with Sally. Again, I paid attention to the service on the beach. Tried hard to stuff my emotions down. I should be good at that; stoicism runs in my veins.

The end of the line was silent, Dad didn't say much, bar the occasional 'hmm', but I could tell he was taking it in. At the last minute before I'd left, he had told me, 'I'd like to pay for the wreath.'

I sent him a bunch of photos, including one of the wreath, plus the link to the speech and the walk into the water – which I noticed had had fifteen thousand views on Facebook. Fifteen thousand! It had hit a chord. Dad could watch it in his own time – he liked to stay up late and watch things on his iPad; British comedy and American politics usually – when, and if, he wanted to.

'Good job, George,' Dad emailed back.

Family business was done now: memorialising and retracing. The trip to the beach.

Melbourne

February 2017

Not long after I returned home, Michael Noyce sent me an article: 'Vivian Bullwinkel, the Bangka Island massacre and the guilt of the survivor'. It was by Tess Lawrence, an ethicist and writer for the Independent Australia online news site, and had been released three days after the seventy-fifth anniversary. 'You are not going to like this,' Michael said. The byline to one passage screamed at me: 'Vivian Bullwinkel tortured by two awful secrets'.[6]

The article reported that Tess had met Vivian on several occasions in Melbourne at both the Hotel Windsor and the now defunct Naval and Military Club on Little Collins Street. They had spoken of the massacre and Vivian had told Tess that she felt 'she was allowed to live so that she could be a messenger'. She then confided in Tess about 'two things she was keeping secret for the time being' – but said 'there would be a time she was going to speak publicly about them'. Tess said Vivian was tortured by keeping the secrets and that it offended her sense of justice to do so.

Firstly, she told Tess, 'Before the massacre on Bangka Island, Japanese raped nurses': in Vivian's words 'most of us' had been 'violated'. Secondly, she said that she was ordered by the government not to speak of any of it, which caused her much distress as she had wanted to put it in her statement at the War Crimes Tribunal, where she had testified in Tokyo in 1946.

Tess commented that in her mind the tribunal – adjourned in 1948 – was 'a less than honest affair', further stating that 'the Americans did not want to overly antagonise Japan and jeopardise political, strategic and economic opportunities'.

Every line punctured another hole in my heart. I shut my computer, *snap*, went into my room and lay on the bed. I stared at the cracks in the bedroom wall. Cracks we had been trying to repair, but which kept opening up. What if we injected silicone, taped over them, or even gyprocked the whole thing? Put a wall inside a wall. But our house was built on a swamp, so this would be a futile exercise. 'Reclaimed land,' Kingsley kept telling me. 'You have to learn to deal with it,' but I didn't want to. No.

Was it true? I tried to dismiss it. Dismiss Tess's report. Why would Vivian have told her, a journalist? Vivian had never made any public mention of this before. But a cry formed deep within me, jammed against my ribs. This was too much, sickening. There were no words I could find. The massacre had become a symbol of women's sacrifice – the twenty-two holding hands, walking nobly into the water. It had a place in history and a heroic narrative – as if the women had somehow transcended the event. But a rape brought that day into my world, now. As if I was experiencing the violence and grief in the present. I felt the soft focus sharpen into jagged edges and I couldn't bring myself to look but nor could I look away. My insides twisted, and I sobbed. Not a sob of sadness, but of horror.

I jumped up, grabbed books from the bookshelf – I had started to collect a few about Bangka Island. Found the one I wanted: *On Radji Beach* by Ian Shaw. Tearing through page after page till I found it. I must not have read this far the first time, but it now stood out. Right at the end, in the postscript, Shaw said it was a possibility – apparently there were rumours at the time – that this *may* have happened.[7] I ran into my study, opened the cupboard and pulled out the folder of Bud's letters. Scanned them for evidence or denial. I found one from Frank Statham, Vivian's husband, responding to a letter Sally had sent Vivian in 1996. It asked Vivian if she had any personal recollections of Bud. Frank had replied on 5 March 1996 on Vivian's behalf, saying that she was sorry she couldn't reply herself but since she had suffered a stroke her right arm was 'incapacitated'. He went on to say that Vivian couldn't provide any more personal comments about Buddy, as since they were in different units they didn't serve or work together. Of course, he acknowledged, they were both on the *Vyner Brooke* and 'finally were with the group shot on the beach'. He finished by saying, 'Viv says she was wonderfully brave – like her colleagues when they were ordered into the sea. None cried out or called for mercy.'[8]

That's what I wanted to hear: 'she was wonderfully brave – like her colleagues when they were ordered into the sea'. That's how it plays in my mind, how the tape goes – heads held high, 'none cried out or called for mercy'. That's the memorial anthem and long may we sing it, antidote to dismay. I sat on the floor and held the thin letter in my hands.

Vivian visited my great-grandparents after the war, as she did many of the nurses' parents. Dad remembers the visit and the sadness, though he was a young boy. He told me he had a 'vague memory of Mummum and Vivian sitting at the dining table having afternoon tea and talking, and of course I wasn't part of the conversation. As far as I can remember, Dadee wasn't there, which in retrospect seems strange, but I may be mistaken. I can remember a general sense of worry about Bud's welfare and whereabouts.' They hadn't heard anything from her, or of her, for a couple of years until the bad news arrived.

How many times did Vivian recount her tale, each time perfecting the narrative of bravery and heads held high? And at what cost to her, who'd lain floating in her sisters' blood? Every time she sat and had tea with bereft and disbelieving parents, she must have felt the guilt of the survivor and the weight of her calling as the messenger. How did she choose which narrative to tell? The real one? The one that would protect the families from further suffering? Or the one she was instructed to relay? And as she was asked, 'Would you like milk with that, dear?' there might have been a moment when she was tempted to slip between the pages of history and speak an uglier truth. But as Mummum passed her homemade scones with clotted cream and plum jam, it would have been hard enough for Vivian to tell of the bullets and the blood of their daughter, Bud, spilt in the water. And if she had seen the hollow eyes of Dadee, no doubt she would have shifted on the sofa and recounted how brave the nurses were, how dignified. Who could blame her, given the stigma at the time, the shame, and – if this was true – the pressure not to speak. Offering a better version of the deaths may have been her ultimate gift to relatives.

Or maybe Vivian was seething inside; incensed she had been silenced. Distressed that the course of justice had been perverted by the omission she was ordered to make.

I lay back down, shaken, slammed into the wall.

'I am the great-niece of Dorothy Gwendoline Howard Elmes, who was killed in the Radji Beach Massacre,' I started my request to the National Archives. 'A few of us, who are all family members, are interested in finding out if there are any embargoed documents from Vivian Bullwinkel's war crime trial statements that have not already been released.' It felt strange to write something so personal to an anonymous recipient, but I put on my researcher hat and tried to ring-fence my emotions.

'Dear Ms. Banks,' was the response I got, 'thank you for your inquiry ... I identified the following records potentially including army nurse Vivian Bullwinkel's statements and testimony.' There was a list of all the entries and records:

War crimes – Banka [sic] Island – Massacre of 21 Australian nurses ...
Access status: Open. Location: Melbourne
Access status: Open. Location: Canberra

Not really what I was asking for. I was hoping for something more personal, specific. Pointers in the right direction. Some help. I wrote back. 'Can I assume from your search that this means that there are no documents that have been embargoed? Is there anywhere else I should be looking?'

'Dear Georgina,' came the reply from the information access officer, who was not sure what I meant by 'embargoed' but wished to inform me that all the records identified were 'OPEN' – meaning that none of the contents had been withheld under the Archives Act. The access officer advised me to check what sources other writers had cited – otherwise the claims might just be 'conjecture based on what is generally understood about the behaviour of the Japanese forces at the time'.

OPEN. Got it. So we'd have to trawl through them ourselves, find the strands, knit them together. I imagined a mountain of archival material in front of me, and me standing at the bottom looking up. Michael Pether said he'd seen most of the documents in Melbourne. I wanted to see them with my own eyes, though, look again through a different lens.

Michael Noyce emailed Tess Lawrence saying that she had raised some controversial issues that he thought should now be more widely canvassed. Tess responded thanking him for his advocacy on behalf of the nurses, saying how moving the ceremony on the beach must have been and that he made the world a better place. She wanted to know if he had found anything in his aunt's papers – such as family discussions on rape, hints or codas, and asked what she could do to help. Michael emailed Tess again to find out exactly what Vivian had said. He didn't hear back.

Months later I decided to contact Tess myself. 'I would like to talk to you about your conversations with Vivian if you are open to that.' No reply. I sent a follow-up email, still no reply. I kept refreshing my emails. Why would she respond to Michael – at least to his first email – but not me? Was she getting my emails? Perhaps she'd been burnt in the past by upset relatives. *Tess, I wanted to say, tell me more about your conversations with Vivian; what else she said, how it came about, anything. Your notes, recollections, scrawlings. I am not here to accuse or besmirch you. I just need to know. Do you not understand what this opens up for us now?*

I decided not to mention anything to Sally or Dad. This was distressing news and I pressed pause till we had more evidence one way or the other.

Judy Balcombe, Michael Noyce and Michael Pether started sending me things, asking me, to 'read this, and this'. 'There are other accounts.' Turned out that Yuki Tanaka, a retired professor of Japanese wartime history, had in 1993 at an international conference on Japanese identity raised the possibility of the nurses having been raped.[9] Tanaka thought it was significant that the men were separated from the women. And marching them into the sea, whereas the men's bodies were left where they were killed – was that to hide evidence of rape, he wondered?[10]

James MacKay's 1996 book *Betrayal in High Places* included a section on the Bangka Island atrocities, based on a supposed cache of files from one Captain James Godwin, one of the investigators with 2 Australian War Crimes Section (AWCS) stationed in Tokyo. MacKay said these files were given to him by Godwin, and that they were originally 'spirited out of SCAP's [Supreme Commander Allied Powers] jurisdiction in 1950'.[11] The only problem was, when I consulted the two Michaels and Judy, they had never seen them. Odd. 'The other original Godwin files are housed in the National Australian Archives in Melbourne,' Michael Pether told me.

In his narrative about the massacre, MacKay quoted interrogation file number 152, 'Bangka Island atrocities', recording the reinterrogation of a Leading Private Tanemura Kiyoshi (also called Hiyoshi) of the 2nd Platoon, 2nd Company, Orita Battalion.* They were from the regiment responsible for the massacre and rapes in Hong Kong at St Stephens College (Hospital) on Christmas Day.

According to MacKay, Tanemura recounted in his reinterrogation:

> hearing screams coming from nearby houses situated between
> groves of paw-paw and mango trees, and was told by platoon
> members that some officers and NCOs were pleasuring
> themselves (raping) some Australian nurses … Pressed as to
> the fate of the nurses, he volunteered the information that the
> following morning after the nurses had been raped incessantly

---

*   The 1 Battalion was also known as the Orita Battalion after its commander, Captain Orita Masaru.

he heard that they had been herded down to the beach and there forced to bathe (ostensibly) whereupon a machine gun opened fire and disposed (executed) them.[12]

I pushed the book away. It was so matter-of-fact, dispassion-ate, while I felt fever in my veins. And yet MacKay's account didn't seem to add up. As far as I knew there weren't houses by the beach at the time – only a fisherman's hut. The nearest houses were about four kilometres away up in the village (they would have been huts too but bigger than a fisherman's hut), or in Muntok, which was even further. And the time frame was wrong. According to Vivian, the group on the beach had handed themselves in and were killed on the same morning, 16 February. There was no overnight. Unless Tanemura was confused – he had had malaria.

Vivian had said, 'At about ten o'clock in the morning, Mr Sedgman [sic], the ship's officer, returned with a party of fifteen Japanese in [the] charge of an officer.'[13] They were killed shortly after.

I consulted Michael Pether again. Captain James G. Godwin and Sergeant Arthur H. Weston, both investigating officers with 2 AWCS, in their 'Weekly Investigation Reports' in the National Archives, did summarise the progression of file 152, among others, and they also mentioned Tanemura, but only in reference to him naming other Japanese suspects, not in regards to a statement of rape.[14] Godwin said (in the week ending 13 January 1950) that Tanemura was called for reinterrogation and that the results would be reported in Weston's weekly investigation reports. However, when you consult Weston's reports for that week, he gives a general summary and says that a 'copy of Tanemura's report appeared on file 152.' But it is not with these documents. If Godwin *had* taken it out of the official files, why hadn't he shown it to anyone? As proof. My jaw was tight. I tried to unclench it. The dentist said I was grinding my teeth.

Another article landed in my inbox: 'MacKay's Betrayal'.

Greg Hadley, a professor of applied linguistics and cultural studies at Niigata University in Japan, and James Oglethorpe, an industrial engineer with an interest in Second World War historical research, in a 2007 article for the *Journal of Military History* analysed the font and typeface of one of the cache of files in MacKay's book – not file 152 – in comparison to the original Godwin files. They claimed the files were manufactured.[15]

Cupping my head in my hands, I stared at a photo of the two files. They did look different. Since MacKay is dead now he could not speak for himself. We were interested just too late to speak to those who were there. We had come at the wrong end of history.

The dishwasher beeped and I got up to unpack it. As I put away plates, I remembered, deep in my email trail, encouragement to look at Barbara Angell's website. A former nurse herself, Barbara Angell was the author of *A Woman's War*, the biography of Wilma Oram Young, one of the *Vyner Brooke* nurses who was in the women's camps with Vivian and survived the war. Barbara's website contained 'Appendix B. A hypothesis, concerning the Banka [*sic*] Island Massacres'. She wrote:

Interestingly, Wilma Oram Young deliberately drew my attention to this particular book [*Betrayal in High Places*] without commenting on the contents, but making sure that I would read it for myself.[16]

I read on past this silent endorsement. Next, Barbara proposed the uniform clue. Based on forensic analysis of the position of the bullet holes, Barbara hypothesised that the nurses were raped, because the holes in the uniform did not match the wounds on Vivian's body.* However, if the uniform was open at the front down to the waist, because soldiers had ripped it open, and was trailing behind Vivian in the water, then the holes in the uniform were consistent with those on Vivian's body.

Closing my screen, I sat back in my chair. I felt torn. Torn between maintaining the nurses' memory as Vivian had told it, the official story, and finding out the truth. Some of the relatives of the nurses were adamant that we shouldn't talk about it. Vivian and the other nurses who'd survived the camps clearly didn't want to, took their secrets to the grave. During the writing of *A Woman's War*, a friend of Barbara Angell was driving Wilma and another *Vyner Brooke* nurse and camp survivor, Betty Jeffrey, to a function. 'You won't tell our story, will you?' Betty had said to Wilma, who replied, 'No.'[17]

Jessie Elizabeth Simons, also a *Vyner Brooke* nurse who'd survived the camps, had written in the preface of her book

---

* John Hilton, then associate professor of forensic pathology for NSW Institute of Forensic Medicine, assisted Barbara Angell in her research.

While History Passed, 'There are many things about which I have kept silence in this book. For one thing, I cannot recall everything in its right setting; there are other things I have left out intentionally.'[18]

And Vivian? After digging through the relevant books on my shelf, I found that Vivian herself had said to author Patsy Adam-Smith, in the book *Prisoners of War*, 'Mind you, there are things that I haven't talked about.'[19]

'Can't we just remember them as they were,' one of the relatives said to me, 'heads held high walking into the water?'

Another relative of one of the nurses in the camps said that the hypothesis that the nurses were raped that morning was, in their opinion, based on 'multiple erroneous assumptions'.

I stood up. I needed to move. I did not wish to bruise their memory either, was desperate for it not to be true. But it is already out, I thought, whether we like it or not. Journalists, historians, PhD students, they weren't going to stop theorising if they were interested in the story. The lid was well and truly off. *Look around*, I felt like yelling, *we have royal commissions, #MeToo, Harvey Weinstein in the dock*. Does staying silent protect the victims or the perpetrators? Especially all these years later, when social mores regarding rape have changed: the stain of shame – a fate worse than death – no longer on the victims.

Or was it ourselves we needed to protect? I was a generation further on, I reminded myself, from the most involved relatives of the nurses. Had not lived through the primary grief and trauma of a sister who left, a child not returned, an aunt gone missing. Did not have quite the same conditioning around *things that are better not spoken of.* Would not feel as sharply the cuts inflicted with each additional piece of news. I had extra decades of buffering. Nonetheless, I was churned up – felt the pull in equal measure: to stay silent and live with what was starting to appear as the comfort of a lie or pursue truth at all costs.

I massaged my throbbing temples. Who owned this information anyway, these stories of the past? The nurses, relatives, historians, the public? This was not just a family event. If we sanitised history, remembered only what was convenient, palatable, then we were on a slippery slope. And where would it end but in a pit of grainy partial truths?

My breathing felt short, as though my alveoli were trapping not releasing air. Reaching for the handle on the back door, I turned the key, yanked it open and walked outside to stare up at the stars. Covered by light pollution in the city, the sparkles were obscured.

I felt as though I was falling.

Melbourne

February 2018

I had just arrived home from my second trip to Radji, where, as hoped, we had established a yearly memorial service and the Walk for Humanity, which re-enacts the nurses' last walk towards the water – our gesture of peace and positive defiance – when Michael Noyce sent me an email. He was forwarding a message, which he described as 'An interesting if not disturbing email from Judy [Balcombe].'

Apparently Radji Beach was not, in fact, Radji Beach. Just prior to us leaving this last time, there had been a few rumblings from Mr Abubakar Fakhrizal, historian and director of the Tinwinning Museum, and other local officials, that it might not be the right beach.

What? I shook my head, couldn't believe it. Judy had written:

After you had left Muntok, we became aware that Radji Beach may indeed be further South. But I think it is quite OK for the

Memorial built by MHVG [Muntok History Volunteers Group] to stay where it is placed as it overlooks the area to the left and is accessible by road.

There is a Dutch map from the early 1940s … which shows the area 2 coves South of the Memorial. The bay is called Teluk Menggeris and some references on Google also call this place Teluk Inggris (English Bay).* A river or stream leads inland from the bay to [the] Kampong … The road to Muntok is just beyond the kampong. The area was identified by elderly residents who had been alive at the time of the massacre … Our plaque is at Tanjung Betumpak.** It is believed the women were killed on Teluk Menggeris and that the men were killed around the cape of Tanjung Sebajau [sic].

We may have the wrong beach. I sat gawping at the news.

A month later Judy and I took a trip to Melbourne's National Archives to search for evidence and information on which beach was the real Radji, and anything we could find out about the possible rape of the nurses.

The tram stopped outside the children's hospital and I took a left onto Abbotsford Street, past rows and rows of well-preserved Victorian terraces. I walked along the wide autumnal streets, drank in the pale yellow light that filtered through the shedding

---

*   Teluk is the Indonesian word for a bay.
** Tanjung is the Indonesian word for a cape.

trees. Out of my normal routine, I felt like a visitor in my own city. The maps app on my phone directed me to Shiel Street, and as I turned the corner, the National Archives of Australia appeared in front of me – a contemporary building with brutalist overtones, a popular architectural style in Melbourne. Handsome, with an angular, concrete façade, it presided over its neighbours. Protectionist rather than welcoming, which wasn't a bad thing given what was inside.

While I waited for Judy I greeted the woman at the front desk. 'Have you been to the Archives before?' she inquired, observing me through her square-rimmed glasses as if to ascertain my archive worthiness.

'No, this is my first visit,' I replied, straightening up, hoping to convey researcher bona fides.

'Welcome' – it must be working – 'you are my first researcher of the day.' I was pleased to be officially in the club. 'Here's the list of items you are allowed and not allowed to take into the reading room.' She passed over a typed list of prohibitions. On the permitted list was a pencil, laptop or recording device (without case), and a small notepad. Designed to keep our national history intact, I suppose; to avoid marks, blemishes and stealing. Once I ticked 'yes' to the conditions, I was given a locker key and security pass.

'Sorry I'm late,' Judy turned up as I was going through the process, 'I had to drive my husband somewhere on the way.' Judy had an air of endless patience. 'I have muffins,' she continued, 'since the café is closed for renovations and we might be here all day.'

We entered the Reading Room and saw heads bowed over documents at sparsely occupied tables as we requested our items. Despite lowering our voices, our anticipation was audible. Two large plastic tubs full of documents were brought out for us: 'War Crimes – Banka [*sic*] island – Massacre of 21 Australian Nurses MP742/1, 336/1/1976 & 1965'.

We started with the 336/1/1976 tub. I couldn't believe we had our hands on these documents. Surely we should be wearing gloves? Judy looked flushed. On the other side of the spacious desk was a serious-looking woman and her assistant, punching codes and references into a computer program. An academic, I thought. I wished I had her skills, her dispassionate detachment. I took a breath, whispered to Judy, 'Ready?'

She was, her face scrunched up, expectant. Stretching my fingers, I reminded myself that in one of these tubs could be file 152 – some of it at least – and the original statements made by Vivian Bullwinkel, Stoker Ernest Lloyd and American civilian Eric Germann, all of whom had survived the massacre. Pulling manila folders out of the tub, I doled them out between us – we'd have to comb through every one.

Vivian had survived the massacre because the bullet from the machinegun, presumably intended for the middle of her back, struck her 'in the back at about waist level and passed straight through'.[20] It had missed her vital organs. The force of impact knocked her over and she feigned death. Waves carried her to the edge of the water. She lay in the shallows controlling her breathing for about fifteen minutes till she thought the Japanese soldiers had disappeared. Then she sat up and fled into the jungle, where she passed out for about two days. As she came to, she narrowly escaped being spotted by the same Japanese soldiers, who walked right by her hiding spot. When she was certain they had gone, she returned to the beach to get a drink from the stream. A voice called out, 'Where have you been, nurse?'[21]

The voice belonged to Private Cecil Kinsley, the fourth survivor of the massacre. Bayoneted in his chest while he lay on a stretcher at the back of the beach, he told Vivian, 'I saw what they did to you girls; then they came back to put the bayonet into us wounded.'

He and Vivian hid in the jungle for twelve days. Vivian made a couple of forays to the village to ask for food and was given rice, fish and pineapple wrapped in banana leaves by the women. She dressed Kinsley's wounds with coconut fibre tied with bits of vines. After he had celebrated his thirty-ninth birthday a free man, they agreed they must hand themselves in, or starve. Vivian washed their uniforms to erase traces of blood and covered her bullet wound with a water canteen slung over her shoulder, before they started on the path to Muntok. On the way they were picked up by a patrol car. By way of explanation, they pretended they had been wandering in the jungle since making their way ashore. Did not mention the massacre. Kinsley died shortly after in the camp hospital.

As far as I was aware there was no official statement from Kinsley, and I would not find one in the large pile of manila folders on the table in front of me. Much later, when I was looking over scanned documents at home one night, I noticed in Stoker Lloyd's statement, right at the end, the comment, 'Apparently

Pte Kinsley C. J. ROC died at Muntok in Feb 42. He is reported to have made a statement.'[22] How I wish I could have found and read it – if he did ever make it – one has never been recovered. He was right there, an eyewitness lying on a stretcher at the back of the beach.

The papers were in good shape, but as I opened the first cardboard folder, I was shocked to see they had big metal clips skewered right through them, in some sort of act of archival brutality. A few of the more fragile ones, such as Vivian's official statements, were at least filed in plastic sleeves, embalming her testimony in time. I started to delve and realised I'd read some of these statements before, digitised and passed around by relatives of those on the beach that day.

Judy nudged me, whispered, 'I've found a clue about the rapes.'

She pushed a file towards me. Leading Seaman William Dick Wilding – whose ship, HMS *Li Wo*, had sunk – had made it ashore and saw the aftermath of the massacre. I looked at his statement, now right in front of me, Judy's finger underlining it. 'We found a lifeboat and about a dozen bodies, all women except two. Some were scantily dressed possibly as civilians, some in nurses' uniform and one naked.'[23]

Judy and I looked at each other. Wilding was there on the morning of the seventeenth – the day after the massacre. This backed up what Stoker Lloyd said in 1970, in John Smyth's book *The Will to Live* (about British military nurse Margot Turner, who was a prisoner in the women's camps in Muntok and Sumatra). After surviving the shooting himself, 'a few days' later Lloyd found the bodies of the Australian nurses and other women.[24]

'They lay at intervals of a few yards – in different positions and in various stages of undress.'[25] But where was Stoker Lloyd's official statement from 1945? It should be here in this file. I rifled through the pages … and there it was. *Look*, I elbowed Judy. It said, 'Further along the beach where we had left them I came across the bodies of the nurses (about 10) and after that the civilians. All appeared to have been bayoneted or shot.'[26]

That was all he said in his statement.

And then I found Eric Germann's affidavit from 1945, which also didn't mention the state of undress, or the bodies at all. Only: 'I received a bayonet stroke that went through my body, coming out below my right breast. I played "Possum" until the Japs left, then escaped to the jungle. I hid out in the jungle for 3 days then walked into Muntauk [*sic*] to surrender.'[27] We know Germann saw the bodies of the nurses because he is mentioned in Wilding's statement: 'We were joined on the beach by an American civilian.'[28] Yet Germann has omitted to mention them in his affidavit. Why?

Frenzied, I started to scan, to collect the evidence, but the documents filed in plastic were difficult to see. Big white patches from the overhead lights blotched the pages. Judy tilted them for me at different angles but still they were obscured. To block the light out completely, I ducked under the table. It was dark under here and in these pages.

New names to follow up were found, and a few other crumbs, which Judy recorded meticulously in pencil on her sheet of paper. No mention of the name Radji, though, in any of these statements taken by Lt K. M. Dixon Interrogating Officer 2 Aust

PW Contact & Inquiry and conducted in Palembang (except for Germann's, which was conducted in Calcutta) and dated September 1945.[29] Instead, the tragedy was referred to as 'the Massacre at Banka [sic] Island', or, 'the beach'.

Judy had theories as to where the name Radji could have come from because it turned out that the Indonesians didn't use the name at all, except for our benefit.[30] One theory was that 'Radji' was a misspelling of the name Karang Hadjie, which is a coral reef just off the coast near Tanjung Kelian – the lighthouse closest to Muntok. This geographical feature may have been used to identify the beach. A capital H can easily look like an R when handwritten. Radji could have sprung from a mis-hearing of Hadjie. When the Indonesians say 'Hadjie', it can sound like Radji in English. (Judy has recorded an Indonesian colleague doing this at different speeds.)

The earliest trace of the name Radji Beach we found was on 8 November 1945 in the *Newcastle Morning Herald and Miners' Advocate*, which reported the dedication of a flag in Newcastle that had once flown over the 2/4th Casualty Clearing Station in Malaya (though the article mistakenly refers to a prisoner-of-war camp in Burma). The article observed that, 'Repairs to be seen in the flag were the work of some of the nurses who were murdered on Radji Beach, Banka [sic] Island.'

Subsequently, in *Soldier Surgeon in Malaya* – a book by the commander of the 2/4th Casualty Clearing Station, Newcastle doctor Lieutenant Colonel Thomas Hamilton, published in 1957 – Hamilton refers to a statement he was given some months prior to September 1945, by a Lieutenant Colonel Miller, who had been a prisoner in Sumatra. Hamilton wrote that Miller's statement read, 'They were found by a Japanese patrol on Radji Beach.'[31]

Two o'clock, my phone said, and we hadn't moved from our corner of the Reading Room, or the mass of files, since about ten-thirty. The muffins lay uneaten in the locker. You could get lost in here, scratching around in history, picking at threads.

Judy stuck her head up. 'I'm going to have to go now, Georgina,' she said, though she was a reluctant leaver.

'I *really* should get going too,' I replied. But the finisher in me wouldn't leave – I couldn't resist flicking through the final pages in the folder, though I knew it would mean extra time jammed in traffic.

Lots of duplicates in here – I was getting déjà vu. An account from the Australian War Graves Commission caught my eye. Post-war, the commission had travelled to Muntok to investigate grave sites. I skimmed the document. I'd seen part of this report by one Captain Yemm before. Michael Pether had emailed it around since we'd started to question the location of Radji Beach. It backed up where Judy and Mr Fakhrizal thought Radji Beach was. Yas Sin, a local fisherman, who had lived in Kampong Menjelang during the war, took investigators from the Australian War Graves Commission (40 Australian War Graves Unit) along the jungle path from his village to the beach site of the massacre in 1946. This part of the report, signed by a C. H. Field S/Sgt, stated:

This man YAS SIN, told us that many ships were sunk on that part of the coast and when the Japs came he and his family made for the jungle, there was much shooting. Returning after two (?) days he found on the beach many bodies of white men and women mostly in decomposed state.[32]

And then I saw them. A series of maps, hand-drawn in blue ink by Sergeant Yemm to accompany these accounts. One in particular drew my attention: 'Plan 4: Muntok – Banka [*sic*] Island women's internment camp and cemetery'.

It identified 'Kampoeng Mendjelong' [Menjelang], from which two paths of 4 kilometres led to the coast. At the top left-hand corner of the map there was a box that said, 'Vicinity in which Australian nurses murdered.'

Three arrows pointed to the coast. My adrenaline surged. But I couldn't see the name of the beach because of the way the maps had been filed – with a metal filing clip stuck right through the middle. There was no way I was leaving without seeing what was under that clip. Looking around to check who was observing, or if anyone would be upset with what I was about to do, I started to remove each item from the history-piercing skewer. I was precise, placing the papers in order so that later I could repeat the process in reverse. When I reached the bottom I glanced around once more, though I had by now bonded with the woman at the counter over our fascination with papery things of the past. Every cell ready to pounce, I peeled off the last page, and there it was. The massacre was identified on the map as having taken place between two headlands: Tanjung Besayap and Tanjung Sabajau.

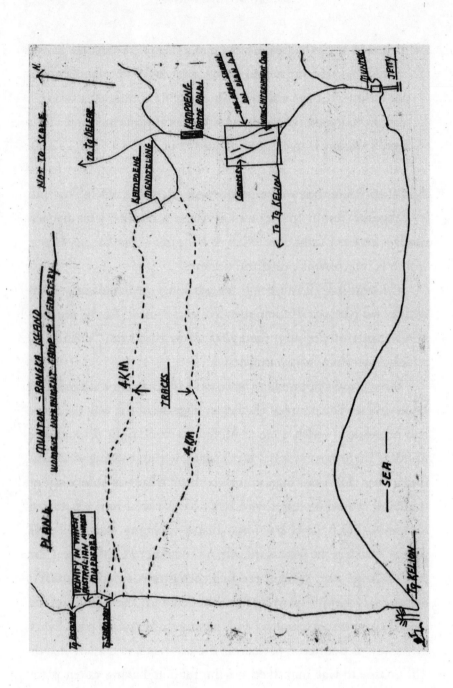

PLAN A   MUNTOK – BANGKA ISLAND
Women's Internment Camp & Cemetery

Not to Scale

N.

To Tg DELLER

KAMPONG Batoe BALAU

7th AGH Closed, Dr. PLAN No B

Women's Internment Camp

MUNTOK JETTY

To Tg KELION

KAMPONG MENDELIANG

Connecting Track

TRACK

4 KM

4 KM

SEA

Vicinity in which Australian nurses murdered

To BAKAU

To KAMPONG

To KELION

Which meant Radji Beach was surely Teluk Menggeris. It was two bays south of our memorial on Tanjung Betumpak. Exactly as Mr Fakhrizal had said to Judy.

Outside, the afternoon sun cast an orange glow on northern streets. I wandered through North Melbourne, my dubious sense of direction guiding me instead of the maps app, and called Michael Noyce to give him the news.

'Guess what? I found a map that seems to confirm where Radji Beach really is.'

'You're a regular Sherlock Holmes. I've never heard you so excited.' He proceeded to tell me his idea to campaign for posthumous medals for the nurses.

Definitely lost now, I weaved my way to a main street, hoping to find a tram that would take me in the general direction of the city. Though I probably walked in circles, my steps skipped. I jumped on a tram and texted Judy the map.

At three in the morning one Sunday, my phone beeped. Who was sending me messages at this time? Was Dad sending WhatsApps from England? He and Mum were on their last trip to the UK to see my mother's sisters – one of whom was turning eighty and hosting a party in Devon. Scrolling through a number of messages, I saw a bunch of family pics from Dad, and a Facebook message from Stoker Lloyd's grand-daughter, Sarah. I went to tap on them but restrained myself – if I looked at them now I'd be up all night. I rolled over in my half-sleep state and tried to keep my dreams secure.

Around eight I sat up, pushed back into my pillows and took in Sarah's message: 'Mum says that what she knows about the massacre is really what is in the book "The Will to Live".[33] I have to say though, that she was always convinced that the nurses had been raped. Whether that was from my grandad saying something or his comment that the nurses were "in a state of undress" I can't say. Apologies that we haven't been able to give you a more definite answer.'

I put my glasses on, tapped out a reply, pushed a bit further: 'Do you mind asking your mum one more thing from me, why she always thought they were raped? Did her father say something else? Or did he infer it? What specifically was it that made her think that? Hope you don't mind being the message transferor! I could call your mum if she was open to that and ask her these questions myself.'

Sarah messaged back and said she would try, but it was 'really difficult to get my mum to talk about Grandad's experience'.

'I understand,' I texted back. 'I don't mean to pressure you, I am just very aware of the responsibility of writing about these issues and basing them on facts … I really appreciate all you are both doing.'

It was like looking through a fogged-up glass. Half-answers. Older generations not wanting to talk. If I could just reach further through time.

I put on the coffee. Ground the beans in the grinder, tamped it down in the Bialetti. It was something tangible I could grab hold of.

Melbourne

July 2018

I decided to visit my supervisor. Usually I went to reflect on the psychological aspects of my consulting work in organisations and to ensure good practice. Today I needed to discuss the nurses. We had an informal, collegiate arrangement that veered between the professional and the personal.

Opening the wrought-iron gate I stepped into a secret garden; green buffer to congested, concrete streets. An elderly woman was planting in one of the beds. She gave me a nod, pulled her gloved hands from the soil, then rested a moment on her shovel. It was a sunny winter's day and the sky was full of promise.

It was a while since I'd seen my supervisor. Her door was open and as I peered in, I could see she'd cut her hair in a short grey crop, abandoning dyed hair with confidence. Dressed in wintry shades – aubergine turtleneck, black fitted skirt and suede boots – she looked entirely at ease. Last time I'd seen her she was hovering between decades: one foot in pre-fifty, one foot in post. Now she had shed her skin and settled.

Taking my usual seat, I looked out of the window and was comforted by the solidity of the old stone wall I could see. Perhaps I could just sit here and breathe, take a pause from life. However, I had things on my mind.

'Remember when I told you about Bud and the nurses?' I said. We'd had previous conversations about the impact of the grief.

'Yes.' She leaned forward.

'And you said it was dark. That it would help to balance it with lighter things.'

'Yes.'

'Well, that's why I'm here.'

'Go on ...'

I picked at my cuticles, not wanting to confess. 'It's starting to get to me.' I picked again, brought my fingers to my teeth. 'I feel like I've become obsessed with finding out whether the nurses were raped or not.' There, I'd said it, blurted it out.

Silence.

I chewed my thumb, tried to stay with the thread. 'Should I just leave it be ... let it go?' I could see through the window that the day was already losing its winter sun. 'Am I just stirring up agony for the surviving relatives? How will I find out what really happened, anyway?' I faltered. 'And why am I so consumed by this?'

It was a relief to verbalise the questions that were swirling around in my mind, ruminations churning me up. But my supervisor didn't intervene. 'Is it because I have two daughters?

Because the #MeToo movement is in full force? Or because of the injustice I feel? That women have been silenced throughout history when atrocities like this occur.'

'Let's start today,' said my supervisor, 'not by working with the personal psychology of why you are drawn to this, but taking it to another level.' She gestured, her hands up high. Relieved to be off the hook in discussing my personal psychology, but not sure where she was going with this, I stayed silent. She continued, 'Let's consider that you are drawn to this because it sits in what Jung calls "the collective unconscious".'

I paused, let that land. This was unexpected.

'You need to surrender to it. It is speaking through you.'

I stopped chewing my fingers and looked up. That was a weighty idea, it settled on my chest, threatening to burrow.

'But I don't know how to find answers,' I countered. 'Eye-witnesses are dead, the primary sources don't say definitively, and secondary sources are elusive. Anytime I get close, the answers slip away like shadows. Perhaps I should hire a historian, an investigative journalist, or a detective.' I could feel my voice rising.

'Have you considered visiting a psychic?'

My mouth smacked open. Did she really say that? I eyed her; she knew this was an 'out of supervision' suggestion. I shifted in my seat, my mother's voice loud in my ear, warning me about the dangers of the occult. My insides churned and I wanted to scream, I need *evidence*, real historical answers – typed, signed and official. *PROOF!* That the War Memorial and people who write history books would accept.

I steered the conversation towards more stable ground. 'What I do is pray and meditate.'

I was unsure if she had heard that but we chatted a bit more about suburban psychics, me with other things on my mind. When the session finished I panicked at how late it was – I had a meeting on the other side of town. Heart racing, I rushed out the door and down the stairwell.

Inevitably, I ended up sitting in traffic. Fidgeting with the radio, I searched for something loud to blow off some steam. Beyoncé, circa the late 2000s. 'Halo'. I belted the lyrics out loud, sang at the top of my voice. Eventually the traffic started to move and so did my dark mood. I was going to make the meeting.

The collective unconscious had hit a chord.

I didn't want to talk to the dead. I did, however, want to uncover the truth.

I got out of the car, clicked the door shut and shuddered.

Melbourne en route to Brisbane

October 2018

Judy and I were flying to Brisbane to meet ninety-year-old Ralph Armstrong, author of *Short Cruise on the* Vyner Brooke, and survivor of the camps, and his wife, Verna, who was ninety-six. When Judy suggested the trip I was quick to say yes to the opportunity to meet one of the few living survivors of the *Vyner Brooke* sinking. To hear, hopefully, his recollections of the nurses. Ralph was only thirteen when he was interned with his mother, sisters and the other women in Muntok, until, just over a year later – by this stage in a camp in Palembang, Sumatra – the Japanese examined his genitals, deemed him a man and moved him to the men's camp.

Released at the end of the war – now at Belalau, Sumatra – Ralph hurried to the women's camp, also at Belalau, anticipating his reunion with his mother and sisters. Instead, his young nephew, who hadn't yet reached adolescence so was still interned with the women, told him they hadn't survived. Ralph thought he was an orphan till he arrived in Singapore, where his father was waiting.

Our hotel in Fortitude Valley was opposite the Brisbane Showgrounds and a Food Truck Park, where there seemed to be a type of Oktoberfest on. Young and fleshy, the party-goers were wearing corsets and lederhosen. The girls had plaits and the boys tidy hair, slicked back and parted in the middle. Four in the afternoon and they bounced along café-lined streets, full of vim and vigour. No doubt they would be messier later, after das bier.

In my room I flicked the television on to a twenty-four-hour news channel and half-listened as I unpacked. The Nobel Peace Prize had just been announced, and the words 'combat war crimes', and 'end the use of sexual violence as a weapon of war' grabbed my attention. I logged on to the hotel wi-fi, sat cross-legged on the bed and clicked on to the Nobel Prize website. This year's peace prize had been awarded to Denis Mukwege and Nadia Murad. Denis was a gynaecologist and founder of the Panzi Hospital in the Democratic Republic of Congo, where he and his staff treated thousands of victims violated during the civil war. He had been critical of the Congolese and other govern-ments for not doing enough to combat sexual violence towards women as a strategy and weapon of war. Nadia Murad was a Yazidi woman from northern Iraq, a survivor of sexual violence and now an advocate for women in conflict settings facing, or having suffered, this kind of brutality.

I pressed a link to the ceremony. The screen buffered and came to life as Denis stood at the podium in the Oslo City Hall. My gaze followed him, transfixed. He spoke in French and I read along with the English subtitles. Part way in, he said, 'We prayed in silence – *mon dieu*, tell us what we are seeing is not true.'[34] A flicker of horror passed across faces in the audience. He continued, 'It is to all victims of sexual violence across the world that I dedicate this prize. It is with humility that I come before you to raise the voice of the victims of sexual violence in armed conflicts.'[35]

A group of Congolese men and women stood, like a congregation, and started to holler. Their bodies swayed as though joyful for the recognition of their suffering. Palpable and fervent, their response was a stark contrast to the cool tone of the event. A woman dressed in Liputa covered her eyes with her hands. From beside the bed, I took a fistful of tissues.

Nadia Murad was kidnapped by Islamic State and held as a sex slave when she was nineteen. The Nobel committee said she had shown 'uncommon courage in recounting her own sufferings and speaking up on behalf of other victims'; that she had refused to bow to social norms that require women to stay 'silent and ashamed'.[36] The power of those two words, now and back through time.

She took to the stage next and spoke in an unguarded voice. 'I want to talk to you from the bottom of my heart,' she said. 'I do not seek more sympathy; I want to translate those feelings into action.'[37] The audience sat motionless. So did I, the air pressed out of me.

After I'd watched her speech I forced myself back to my unpacking, but unbelievably the newsreader embarked on another story, as though speaking directly to me. A new monument had been unveiled in San Francisco to Japanese 'comfort women' (sexual military slaves), which had caused the sister city of Osaka to uncouple the arrangement as its authorities were offended by the statue.*

Yuki Tanaka had written that about 100,000 women were held as 'comfort women' – sexual military slaves – during the war (including the Second Sino-Japanese War from 1937 to 1945), though it is impossible to say exactly how many as a significant number of records were destroyed by Japan after it surrendered in August 1945.[38] Yoshimi Yoshiaki, one of the preeminent researchers on the topic, says it was between 50,000 and 200,000.[39] It is the largest case of sexual slavery, as well as government-sponsored human trafficking, in modern times.[40] The women were primarily Korean and Chinese, as well as some Taiwanese, Indonesian, Malaysian, Filipina, Japanese, other South-East Asian women, and some Europeans (mainly from the Dutch East Indies).

The Women's Active Museum on War and Peace in Tokyo, conceived by the late Yayori Matsui, a women's rights activist, has mapped the comfort stations. If these women were still alive, would they feel erased today? I say out loud the names I know, whose testimonies I have read: Maria Rosa Henson, the first Filipina to break the silence, and Jan Ruff-O'Herne, a Dutch-Australian woman imprisoned by Japanese Imperial forces and kept for three months as a sexual slave.

---

*   There are over forty such 'statues of peace' around the world, in South Korea, the US, China, Australia, Germany and Canada. They have often been accompanied by requests from Japan to remove them.

Denis's words rang in my ears: 'Justice is everyone's business.' My supervisor's talk of the collective unconscious. I was incensed by this weaponising, this silencing of women in war. But when I thought of Bud and her family waiting at home, I felt a heaviness that threatened to drag me down. To fold in on itself and solidify into inertia.

Seventy-six years after Bud's death, what did it mean to turn my feelings into action? I could feel the scream of generations mounting. What hope for justice now, years after Vivian had already testified about the massacre at the War Crimes trials? Though if she was ordered not to tell the truth, her voice, the voices of the other nurses, and Bud's, had not fully spoken and were not fully heard. If her testifying was censored, then what had been inscribed in history, kept in archives and in war crimes transcripts was a partial truth-telling. Perhaps justice now was rewriting, reinserting what had been taken out, or was never included in the first place. Did I have the nerve or the skills? Who knew if definitive evidence even existed?

I lay down and sought solace under the doona.

Mount Gravatt East, on the south side of Brisbane, was a leafy middle-class suburb, its weatherboard houses slowly being superseded by brick and concrete ones. Young families came here to spread out. To place trampolines, pools and basketball hoops on their quarter acre blocks. Ralph and Verna lived in an older-style house almost at the top of the hill.

Verna opened the door. Looking lean and agile for a ninety-six-year-old, with a head of cropped, white curls, she was upset.

'He's fallen!' she said as she turned and scurried down the hall. The white lace curtains were drawn and the blinds half-down. 'He was getting up to see you and he fell. Can you help me? I can't lift him by myself.'

We followed her, at a pace, into the bedroom. Ralph was on his knees, moaning in the corner, his body upright, elbows jammed on his walker.

'Ralph, are you okay? Let's try to get you up,' Judy said, in calming GP tones. We placed our arms under his shoulders. I followed Judy's lead. 'One ... two ... *three*!' We grunted with the strain. Ralph's hands trembled on the walker as he pushed against it, but he didn't budge.

'I can't, I can't,' said Ralph, 'just let me fall.'

'You mean onto the ground?' I asked, alarmed.

'Yes,' he winced. 'Let me fall!'

Judy nodded. 'Slowly,' she said. We pushed the walker forwards and leaned back to counterbalance Ralph's weight. He let himself down, rolled onto his side and I placed a pillow under his head.

'You okay?'

Ralph looked at me with half-shut eyes. 'Yes, but I feel giddy.'

'I'll call an ambulance to get him up,' Verna grabbed the phone.

'Ralph, this is Georgina.' Judy said.

'Who?'

'Georgina,' I repeated louder, knowing that Judy had explained who I was. He had forgotten with the fright. He stared up at me from the floor. He had warm features and an impish face.

'You have a lot of hair,' he said.

'Yes,' I replied, taken aback. 'When I go to Muntok they take lots of photos.' Ralph half-smiled.

'I feel like an idiot stuck here, like glue on the carpet,' Ralph said.

'Georgina's great-aunt was one of the nurses shot on Radji Beach.' Judy stroked his arm – unsurprisingly, she was at ease in such situations; I felt uncomfortable even mentioning the subject with Ralph lying incapacitated on the ground and someone he didn't know bringing up distant memories of trauma.

'The bloody beach at Bangka. I don't remember much; I was a child,' he replied.

The paramedics arrived pronto and we left the room. From the living room we could hear one of them talking to Ralph in the bedroom. 'You should really go to hospital, you know, after a fall ... get checked out.'

'I'd rather die than go to hospital,' Ralph replied.

'He won't go,' said Verna with a tut as she sat on the floral sofa. She didn't seem perturbed – it was clear she had been through this many times before. While we waited for Ralph she chatted, pointed out tropical plants through the window, and showed us the local newspaper, which featured a photo of her, Ralph and their archbishop.

'He came last week – here,' she said proudly, 'to bless our marriage. Sixty years,' Verna proclaimed. An achievement in any circumstances.

'I'll do a deal with you,' the paramedic was saying to Ralph in the bedroom. 'If you fall again today, you *must* go to hospital.'

Ralph agreed, but I think we all knew he had no such intention.

A few minutes later he shuffled in with his walker to join us in the living room. We stood to cheer. Ralph sat down on the sofa, dropped his weight with a thud. The paramedics left, off to rescue someone else. Should we leave too? I made noises to Judy and Verna.

Verna dismissed my concern with a wave of her arm.

'Once he's up, he's okay.'

We gave him a moment to catch his breath, then I asked, apologetic, 'Ralph, could I talk to you about the nurses?'

He nodded, as though he had remembered why I was there.

'Do you mind if I record you?'

He nodded again. Verna chimed in now, while I checked my phone was recording, 'He didn't meet any of the nurses anyway ...'

'I was a boy,' he said.

'You were very young,' I agreed, hoping he remembered something, though whatever he could or couldn't recall, I was sitting opposite one of the few living survivors of the *Vyner Brooke*, I reminded myself.

'Do you remember the nurses at all, on the *Vyner Brooke*?'

'I remember them to the extent that when ... we ... had no dinner and then all of a sudden there was a cheerful sound, they were singing "Waltzing Matilda".'

'Ahh,' I sighed. Ralph chuckled. I remembered reading in *A Woman's War* that a group of the nurses had sung 'We're Off to See the Wizard' as they clung to a length of wood after the *Vyner Brooke* was sunk. Such determination to be upbeat.[41]

Ralph continued. 'We were expecting a ship's dinner but ... they gave us some of their rations – I remember that.'

'Aaah,' I said again, like a chorus, grateful for the scraps he was retrieving.

'That was very nice of them,' Ralph said. 'You'd think that on a ship you'd have everything, but no, nothing. Hopeless!' He batted his hand away, dismissive of the lack of planning for the evacuation of Singapore. Singapore's Dunkirk, it has been dubbed.

Behind the well-loved sofa, wood panelling framed his face. Ralph still had all his hair. Pure white, it was parted on the side and combed forward, as if his hair, like him, pushed against the odds.

'When you left Singapore, were people hopeful you'd make it to Jakarta?' I had always wondered how many of those on the ship really thought they would get through the Bangka Strait.

'Yes,' he replied with certainty. 'We thought we would go straight to Australia ... go right through like big ships. But when it came to February it was too late, they were already hiding between the islands and dodging around, you know.' Ralph smiled, as if to acknowledge Japan's superior tactics. 'They were already there before us; we had no chance.'

Ralph continued with his recollections, 'From memory and from reality, the coordination between the two ...' as he put it, 'I'm not sure what it was, whether I'm right or wrong. I can't remember ...'

Some things stood out, were burnt in his mind (the in-between was hazy): moving along the ship's passage after the bomb, dead bodies falling, water spouting, someone pulling him

223

aside – 'Don't stand there you'll get shrapnel!' A Malay man on the raft with burns, his sister wrapping the man's legs and arms with sheets, till the man drank so much seawater he went mad and went 'downstairs' into the sea.

Ralph remembered, through the distance of time, and the protection of a safe suburban life in Mount Gravatt, and Verna. And yet he had lost his mother and his two sisters in the camps. His nephew, who also survived, 'has never been the same since'.

'Was there a lot of chaos and panic when the *Vyner Brooke* was bombed?' Some accounts said yes and others that most were calm.

'Yeah, there was chaos. The first officers were trying to guide us into line, saying go up these stairs this way and that ... they were quite good trying to coordinate the people.'

'Ralph, do you remember what the nurses were doing?'

'I can't remember, no. All I remember was they were singing "Waltzing Matilda".'

'That's funny.' I paused. 'And when did you first hear about the massacre on Radji Beach?'

Silence. Ralph looked around, thinking, searching; trying to decipher what he remembered and what he had since been told. 'Coordinating between the two,' as he put it.

'I'm not quite sure. But you hear these stories going around while you are in the camp. But I'm not quite sure, was it before or after, you know?' He looked into mid-distance. 'And you are told to keep quiet about some things.'

Yes, I get that, I thought. I forged on.

'In your book – because one of the mysteries is what happened to the bodies – you say that someone told you they were made to put all the bodies of the nurses in a pile and then they were burnt. Do you remember who told you that?'

Ralph looked blank. Then, 'Ahh, I remember. They said, "All men work, all men work and come and clean the place and bury the bodies or burn them … or something …"' His voice trailed off and he had a filmy look in his eyes.

Verna spoke up, intervening in Ralph's ponderings, she had been sitting there silent, staring at me for a while. 'You look like someone,' she said, 'I'm sitting here trying to work out who it is.'

I shrugged; we didn't know anyone in common apart from Judy. We kept chatting for a bit, but Ralph was tired after his fall, the paramedics and recounting his past. Judy and I looked at each other. We should go.

'Gabrielle, the homecare nurse! That's who it is,' Verna said with emphasis, pleased at her recollection. I may look like a nurse, I thought, but, unlike Bud, I have few practical bones and no stomach for bodily fluids. We said goodbye, effusive in our thanks, and wished Ralph a happy birthday in advance of his ninetieth, which was imminent.

Back at the hotel, I dug out *Short Cruise on the* Vyner Brooke, which I had carried from Melbourne. Ralph had written it more than fifteen years before, when he was in his early seventies and his memories were clearer. In the passage I'd asked him about he'd written:

A little-known ending to this horror is described by another survivor, who said a group of Australian soldiers were rounded up by the Japanese and ordered to carry the bodies of the massacred men and nurses from the beach to be burned. They had to collect all the wood and debris that they could find, build a large funeral pyre and then place all the bodies one by one on this pyre until only ashes remained.[42]

This account has never been verified by anyone else.

Later that night, hunting around through the files I had accumulated on my laptop, I found a transcript of an interview with Mavis Hannah, one of the nurses who'd been taken prisoner in Muntok, conducted by a Dr Amy McGrath, who had undertaken a series of oral history interviews in the early 1980s. Mavis recalled:

A sailor and survivor on [the] beach, 3rd man to survive came up to me and he pulled my uniform and said 'Good God, what have you got on'. I told him. He said 'I have just buried some bodies on the beach dressed in that uniform and they'd been shot'.[43]

Many of the local villagers believe the bodies were washed out to sea by the tides. Mr Fakhrizal had interviewed a Mr Idris, a resident of Old Kampong Menjelang – the village nearest the beach. Mr Idris recalled what his parents had told him:

At the time of shooting on the beach, the people of the village no one knows, let alone Idris, who was 8 years old. After a few days of incident, there are 1–2 villagers who want to [go] fishing and just learned that there are many corpses on the beach. They told the people of the village. But not many want to see for fear of Japan. The villagers did not dare to bury the bodies, only a few corpses were buried, it [*the bodies?*] was located in their hut. They are afraid of Japan. The corpses were carried by ocean currents and eventually drifted away. Not visible again after a few days later.[44]

Vivian Bullwinkel's accounts varied – as she herself said: 'I am sorry I am hazy about some of this. I have tried hard to forget.'[45]

In some accounts she said the bodies were washed out to sea on the tides, or were washed out on the tides and then back in, and in others that they were still lying on the beach. An account in the *Adelaide Advertiser* in September 1945 detailed:

[Vivian] lived in a daze for two or three days until she recovered strength to go from body to body, seeking signs of life and noting names.[46]

Alternatively, in *Bullwinkel*, Vivian said that having been shot, when she came to she was still lying in the water, and then 'she searched the sea and its shoreline only to confirm that the bodies of her friends were not here.'[47]

When Vivian awoke from her semi-conscious state while hiding in the jungle for a couple of days after the massacre, some Japanese soldiers walked straight past her hiding spot and onto the beach. It is possible they were there to push the bodies out on the tides.

Another loose thread, seventy-five years on. We have several plausible explanations as to what had happened to the bodies of the nurses: burnt, buried, washed out to sea, or pushed.

History, memory and the gaps left in between. I shuffled and reshuffled my papers and the multiple endings came over me like a wave till sleep took over.

Melbourne

November 2018

There was enough distance now, it was time: seventy-six years since the bombing of Darwin on 19 February 1942, Shinzo Abe was making a visit to the city to honour those who had been killed in the raids. It was the worst wartime loss suffered in Australia, and Abe was the first Japanese prime minister to visit the city since the Second World War.

Turning on ABC TV, I grabbed a coffee, pulled up a chair. A highly 'symbolic gesture', the newsreader kept saying. At least 243 people were killed when the Japanese Imperial forces launched the air attacks, three days after the Radji Beach massacre. Over 260 bombers carried out two raids.[48]

Scott Morrison and Shinzo Abe moved in unison – heads bowed, in matching dark suits, at the Darwin cenotaph. The furious click of cameras underscored the event. Kneeling, they laid wreaths bright with yellow flowers – chrysanthemums, I think, like the wreaths at Radji. 'The Last Post' rang out, wobbled on a couple of notes but found its bugle call. Cameras zoomed in on Abe, whose face had a crumpled, lined look – he had only just got off the plane. He closed his eyes, then cast a side glance to Morrison, who was sombre with a half-smile. Dignitaries stood rigid, hands by their sides, in respect. One man just behind Morrison clasped an Akubra to his chest.

Later that afternoon, speaking through a translator, Abe said:

> It is a great pleasure for me to be visiting Darwin for the first
> time as the prime minister of Japan ... Darwin was once a
> place where the former Japanese forces conducted their first
> air bombing against Australia, leading to much sacrifice ...
> I extended my condolences in honour of all the fallen soldiers
> and renewed my vow towards peace.[49]

Would Abe ever make a trip to Bangka Island, I wondered? To acknowledge the war crime on Radji Beach and the deaths of those in the camps and the straits. Michael Pether's ongoing research estimated that about eighty of the hundred or so vessels that left Singapore between 11 and 14 February, as it fell to the Japanese, were bombed and sunk, or captured. The straits and the beaches were one mass grave. About 1133 had died around Bangka Island, by his estimates, and a similar number further north between Singapore and Singkep Island. Overall, it is thought there might have been four to five thousand casualties. Vessel by vessel, Pether's painstaking research found, named and numbered the dead. Mainly British and Australian men, women and children, with some New Zealanders, Malaysians and Chinese.[50]

Though it happened in the past, the past is still with us, as unfinished business. If we could only have an acknowledge-ment of what happened, specifically, to our relatives, it would make a difference, in some way. As salve to a wound. As a line in history. Though I cannot reach back in time and hand it to my grandmother and great-grandparents. The Germans call it *Vergangenheitsaufarbeitung*. It means 'working off the past'.[51]

I could write to the Japanese ambassador and ask for an acknowledgement. Kingsley's cousin was a former federal senator and a current state MP – he would know how to approach this. I decided to ask him what he thought as I mentally laid my own wreath for the Japanese people killed and wounded in the bombings of Hiroshima and Nagasaki. Around 225,000, accord-ing to the Children of the Atomic Bomb Project.[52]

A month later Kingsley and I hosted a country lunch for my mother-in-law Wendy's ninetieth birthday, taking her out of the nursing home in Kew, where she lived, with the 'inmates' as she called them. Three long trestle tables were placed down the centre of our dining room and covered with tablecloths. Though Wendy was getting forgetful, she liked things to 'look nice'.

Chauffeured by her grand-daughters, she arrived in a pink dress and matching pink feather boa. Miraculously, they had got her here on time and away from her beloved *Pride and Prejudice*, which she watched on high rotation.

She giggled as I wished her happy birthday, and took my hand, then sat at the head of the table, like the grand dame we hoped she felt she was. 'I think I'll just sit quietly and gather my thoughts till they come.' Placing a glass of sweet white wine in her hand I continued the preparations. Her breathing sounded off-kilter, as though she were sucking it in and out of a straw.

'You okay, Mum?' Kingsley asked.

'Yes,' she replied, 'just takes me a while to get going in the morning.' My sister-in-law Amanda frowned and came to take her pulse, sat down beside her and held her hand.

'Isn't life wonderful?' Wendy said. 'I wake up every morning wondering what the day will bring.' I nodded as I sailed past. She went on, 'Somehow, I always seem to be looking up.'

'That's because you can't find the remote for your bed and you're lying on your back,' Kingsley retorted, in his laconic mumble. The three of them erupted.

We had set up hay bales down by the creek, which in December was almost dry, under the boughs of the oak tree. The plan to have a drink down there before lunch was over-turned when it decided to rain heavily, creating rivulets of mud in the otherwise hard ground, so we remained inside, squishy but content. It was, after all, an achievement to reach this age and, despite dementia, still enjoy life. Relatives and friends had flown in from Sydney and Tasmania. Around the table we were telling 'Wendy tales' – there were plenty. Wendy recited a poem about Peter Rabbit, word perfect; I had heard it before – it came out on special occasions. When she got to the bit about his nose, she did a little twitch.

'She should have been an actress,' we said and stood to clap.

My thoughts drifted to Bud and the milestones she'd missed, the birthdays not celebrated, the meals not shared – she was born only fourteen years before Wendy. Our wonky weatherboard, built in 1910, was not dissimilar, I imagined, to where Mummum and Dadee had lived in Cheshunt. Charging up the hill, dog at heel, trailing Dadee – I could see Bud here. Shotgun slung across her shoulder. Sitting by the fire at night as an older woman with Jean, reading or playing pick-up sticks, spillikins, chess and charades. Recalling this and that and arguing, Banks style, about who was right.

During a lull after the main meal, when the formalities were over and the poem recited, I decided that now was a good time to talk to Kingsley's cousin, the politician. Most people didn't know the story of Bangka Island, had a vague recollection at best. They'd falter, say, 'I *think* I've heard of this before.' We chatted first about family, what our kids were doing. When he asked about me, I told him about the nurses, my trips to Radji and the one planned for February next year. His eyes darkened, flickered; thoughtful, disturbed.

'I'm very interested in World War Two history,' he said, digesting what I had told him. Now that I thought of it, I remembered he had walked the Kokoda Trail, and campaigned for a Victoria Cross for Teddy Sheean.

'What's your advice on how we might go about getting some sort of acknowledgement, like they did in Darwin?' I asked, growing more confident in my request with his obvious interest. Though I really wanted to use the other 'a' word, 'apology',

I thought 'acknowledgement' was probably more realistic. No doubt a lot of attention would be given to wordsmithing. Others had said 'good luck' when I mentioned my plan. I was trying to decipher the politics.

'Should a request like this come from the families?'

'You need help at the political level,' he said. 'I'd like to help you.'

'Would you? For the families?'

He looked at me directly. 'Healing,' he said, 'you need healing.'

My stomach roiled. How did he know? I tried to read his expression, which followed me with alarming compassion. Was it intuition, experience with other families, or something I radiated? Before I could ask, at the other end of the table, Wendy piped up, 'I've had enough now, that was lovely, dear. I'd like to go home.'

Melbourne

December 2018

I was eating scones with Betty Jeffrey's great-niece, Emily, at the Australian Nurses Memorial Centre. Betty survived the internment camps on Bangka Island, and those on Sumatra at Palembang and Belalau, made famous in her book *White Coolies* and later the film *Paradise Road*.

Cups, saucers and plates were laid out with bright baubles on clustered tables – it was the Christmas fundraiser. Royal Doulton, Wedgwood, Spode – as if the afternoon tea service at the Hotel Windsor had been relocated to St Kilda Road. There were mince pies, scones, cakes, chicken or cucumber sandwiches and copious cups of tea that brimmed over porcelain.

What a shame Vivian and Betty weren't here. They helped establish this place, raised the funds post-war. Criss-crossed Victoria in Betty's little Austin, and visited every hospital of twenty beds or more. They would have needed a cup of good strong tea. Thousands of kilometres they drove to create a living memorial for nursing sisters lost in the war, at Radji Beach, the camps and from the *Centaur* – the hospital ship sunk off Australia in May 1943 by a Japanese submarine.

'I've just read an order,' Emily told me, 'broadcast to POWs in the Far East.' Her usual infectiousness was curtailed by a sober tone. 'It told them what they could and couldn't say when they came home from war.'

'Could you send it to me?'

Emily nodded, sipped her tea.

It was a letter of silence.

This is a personal message from H.Q. ALFSEA [Headquarters, Allied Land Forces South East Asia] to all newly released Allied Prisoners of War.

You are news now and anything you say in public or to press reports is liable to be published in the press of the whole world. You will have direct or indirect knowledge of the fate of many of your comrades who died in enemy hands as a result of brutality or neglect. Your story if published in the more lurid and sensational press will cause much unnecessary unhappiness to relatives and friends. If you had not been lucky enough to have been recovered and had died any form of unpleasant death at the hands of the Japanese you would not have wished your family and friends to have been harrowed by lurid details of that death in the sensational press. That is just what will happen to the families of your comrades who died in that way if you

236

start talking to all and sundry about your experiences. It is felt certain that now you know the reason for this order you will take pains to spare the feelings of others. Arrangements have been made for you to tell your story to interrogating officers who will get you to write it down. You are not to say anything to anyone until after you have written out your statement and handed it in.[53]

Relatives of the nurses to whom I'd spoken, including Dad and Sally, said their parents and grandparents weren't told much by officials. The 'lurid press' and whispers of what might or might not have happened were all they had. Telegrams were received advising that loved ones were missing in July 1942, and then two years later, in June 1944, that they were 'believed to have been killed'. Two years of waiting with no news; of being hyper-alert to the radio, the postman, whispers and suggestions.

As for the nurses who survived those years and were rescued from the camps in Sumatra, army authorities asked them to hand over their personal belongings for routine fumigation. Diaries, notes, music and recipe books, as well as personal items, carefully hidden during captivity, were destroyed in the process. (Though some, like Betty, refused to part with them.)[54]

It wasn't just silence in my family, there was a blanket of official silence too. Though how long this edict lasted I do not know. There is no indication from Betty's family that she was silenced after the war.

During the war an ongoing debate unfolded about censorship among the Allies, as journalist Norman Abjorensen discussed in his 1995 article 'Biting the lip on war crime' in the *Canberra Times*: the authorities oscillated and repeatedly shifted position between releasing details of atrocities for 'propaganda value' and withholding them because of their 'harmful effect on morale in the Far East', the 'further anxiety' they created for relatives, and 'the hope of securing better treatment for prisoners still held by the Japanese', which, it was felt, reports of atrocities might jeopardise.[55]

Senior Allied officers in Singapore also felt a sense of guilt for not evacuating the nurses well before the island had fallen – especially when they'd known about the attacks on nurses in Hong Kong and of the Rape of Nanjing.

Furthermore, military nurses occupied an uncomfortable place in terms of gender norms at the time. These women were present on the battlefront, traditionally a male domain, rather than safe at home, where the customs of the 1940s dictated they should be. Their being in the midst of war, unarmed and in a caring role, created an ambiguity that did not sit easily with societal or military expectations. Yuki Tanaka calls them 'boundary-crossers'.[56]

As academic Christina Twomey has explained in her article 'Australian nurse POWs: Gender, war and captivity', 'Imprisonment by the nation's military enemy confounded popular and symbolic notions in Australia about men's duty to shield or protect women from the worst horrors of war. They were also white women who had been captives at the mercy of men long constructed as racially and culturally alien and, therefore, a danger to them.'[57]

These entwined, complex issues of gender, race and national identity may explain the silence of these women, with many of them acknowledging there were things that they hadn't spoken of. Whether they were officially silenced long term – beyond this edict – or chose silence, we may never know.

If Vivian was silenced, as Tess Lawrence claimed, at the War Crimes Tribunal, then no doubt these issues were at play, and potentially complex political issues as well, related to General MacArthur wanting to rebuild Japan quickly post-war, and defend against the spread of Communism. Other factors likely included the Allies' decision not to prosecute Emperor Hirohito as a war criminal, as well as their wanting to take advantage of economic opportunities. Powerful forces, in other words, may have contributed to the pressure on these women to remain silent about their various ordeals.

Melbourne

January 2019

I hadn't heard back from Kingsley's cousin, the politician, which I thought was surprising given his obvious support at Wendy's birthday lunch. Just before Christmas I'd sent him details about the massacre and links to various sites. Maybe he hadn't received my email, or a government firewall had spammed me out.

I texted him; he replied straight away: 'Sorry, I wrote a letter to the minister for Veterans Affairs on your behalf, thought I'd copied you in.' The letter asked for support from the minister and the Australian government for an acknowledgement from the Japanese government for the eightieth memorial service in 2022. A possibility was opening. I wondered what the other families would think. Both the ones I knew and the many I didn't.

'They were so young, they were so young.' The lament cried off the wall as I passed photo after photo of men, and a few women, in their prime, lining the entry corridor to the Australian War Memorial. Relieved to be inside, I paused to feel the cool in these air-conditioned halls of war. Forty degrees in Canberra all week. This heat sucked you dry, took out every bit of moisture. Even the gum trees looked parched, frizzled in the sun, and the grass was tinder-box brown. Fire signs read 'High Alert'. It was a relief to arrive at the Research Centre and have time to think there each day, to piece things together, not knowing what I'd find.

Guarding the entrance to the Research Centre was a Ben Quilty painting of a naked soldier, prostrate and writhing. Paint, in tones of skin and earth, layered on thick, heaved up off the canvas. Up close, on the plaque, Quilty's subject said:

> [Ben] was after ... the raw soldier who's [come] home ... I guess he wanted to paint their soul and not just a captured image from another place.

Late in the afternoon, I went outside and stood on my toes to place a poppy beside D. G. H. Elmes on the Roll of Honour, which overlooked the pool of reflection. Bud's name was underneath the great Matron Drummond's and slightly out of reach. After a few attempts standing on tiptoes I had to settle for the general vicinity. There was a sea of poppies here anyway, to the left and to the right. Presumably someone would come in from time to time with a ladder to 'poppy' the names that couldn't be reached. There were 102,000 names overall on that roll.

In the Research Centre, I trawled through Vivian Bullwinkel's private correspondence. There were metres of it, in spidery handwriting.

'How do I decipher these?' I asked one of the volunteers.

'I'll give you a tip,' she replied. 'Take a photo, then trace over the writing with a pen and you'll start to get a feel for their style.'

'Thank you,' I whispered and went back to the boxes.

A couple of days later, buried in archives, I found something. A letter, written to Vivian by Bud's aunt, Evie. No longer lulled into slumber by the soporific, sober air, I sat up straight. *Thank you, Vivian, for keeping it safe all those years*, I wanted to yell, but this wasn't the place for exuberance.

Dated 5 November 1945, it read:

Dear Sister Bullwinkel,

You will no doubt be pestered with letters from friends and relatives of those nurses who did not survive that terrible massacre. I am an aunt of Sister Elmes. It was providential that you survived to tell the dreadful tale. In one account it was reported that Sister Elmes was one of those who was bayoneted, her parents did not see this and I am hoping it will never reach their ears. They heard that you might be going to Wangaratta and Mrs Elmes may see you there. I heard that one of my nieces took you to see Mrs Banks – Benda's sister.

I trust that you are getting back to usual health after your terrible ordeal. I wish you could report to me that Benda was not bayoneted. Apologising for worrying you.

I am

Sincerely yours
(Mrs) Eva C Macknight[58]

I searched Trove to try to find this 'account' of the bayoneting. Among others, these quotes came up:

The Japanese then bayoneted those about whose fate they were uncertain.

Townsville Bulletin, 18 September 1945

Some of the nurses lying half dead on the beach were finished off with the bayonet.

Evening Advocate Queensland, 17 September 1945

Further digging around in archival records now scanned and stored on my laptop, I found that the information in these articles was based on a report by Major Tebbutt, compiled by him in Changi from interviews he had done three years earlier with witnesses and survivors, both verbal and written, when he was in the camps on Bangka Island. He'd destroyed the written statements for fear of being caught with them, so his report was compiled from memory. It was leaked to journalists though he asked it not be.

It said, 'After the shooting the Japanese bayoneted any bodies of whose deaths they were not certain.'[59]

Additional research found the most likely candidate for the 'account' Aunt Evie may have seen: Sydney's *Daily Telegraph* from 17 September 1945. In bold titles on page 1, it reported that: 'The killed on Banka [*sic*] Island were bayonetted and machine-gunned.'

Underneath it went on to say: 'Of the 21 nurses massacred, nine were from New South Wales. They were …' and then a list of nine nurses, one of whom was Sister Elmes (she worked at Corowa Hospital in New South Wales). By inference you associate the nine names with those who had been bayoneted.

In this cardboard crib of Vivian's personal papers were letters of dismay, similar to Evie's, from other parents, including Michael Noyce's grandfather, who wrote in November 1945, searching for answers: 'I have had no advice from army of what actually happened. Or any advice of her death.'[60]

Vivian's letter in response to Evie's was not here; I checked a couple of times. Aunt Evie's second letter was, though, towards the back of this box of polite desperation, this thinly veiled anguish. From what Aunt Evie wrote the second time, it seemed that Vivian had probably written back and said Bud wasn't bayoneted, or that she'd died quickly. You could feel the subtle pressure to do so in Aunt Evie's words, 'I wish you could report to me that Benda was not bayoneted.'

Dear Sister Bullwinkel,

Thank you very much for your letter written about a month ago.
I have been ill for the last weeks and I cannot remember if I
acknowledged it. It was comforting to hear that dear Buddy was
spared prolonged suffering.

I trust that you and the other survivors will soon be restored
to your natural health.

Mrs. Elmes did get your letter and if you are in Wangaratta
she would love to see you. She and Mr. Elmes full of sorrow but
very brave.

May the New Year bring you health and happiness.

I am Sincerely yours,
Eva C. Macknight[61]

'It was comforting to hear,' and who wouldn't want to offer
comfort? I could feel my own inclination to reach for a pen and
scribble some balm to the broken-hearted. All the shooting, the
bayoneting, the waiting. It was hard to keep reading. The chasm
on the page between being 'restored to your natural health' and
the talk of killing. The hope implicit in 'Dear Sister Bullwinkel',
as the one – the custodian – who could tell them what they
needed to know, and keep them from what they didn't.

I ploughed on, shuffled my notes and sharpened my pencil.

Vivian wasn't bayoneted herself, only shot, as her wounds
and uniform testified. I had now laid eyes on her uniform, spied
it through the glass cabinet upstairs, in the Second World War

gallery, where Henry, a kind volunteer, had taken me on a personal tour. Beside the uniform were the rolling faces of the nurses, on a screen that turned around and around on rotation.

'Look, that's her.' I spotted Bud through the glass, the same photo I had found on Facebook, with the rakish smile.

Vivian always maintained that they walked into the water arm in arm and were machine-gunned from behind. There was no mention of bayonets in her official statements. To the Board of Inquiry (Australian War Crimes), she said: 'We went towards the sea and kept walking in and when we got up to our waists they started firing up and down the line with a machine gun.'[62]

Mainly, she gave simple accounts and avoided talk of bayonets, but in a couple of unofficial accounts she says the women were *not* bayoneted. On 18 September 1945, she told the *Sydney Morning Herald*: 'The Japanese bayoneted the men's bodies but left the women's alone.'[63]

Corporal Robert Henry Seddon, a Royal Marine, gives quite a different account, however, in his official statement. He had been swimming for twenty-four hours after the sinking of the *Yin Ping* and saw the massacre unfold before him:

> 2 ... I was about a hundred yards from the shore. I was in a slightly delirious condition but was fit enough to swim without a life belt ... 4. The Japs appeared to be rounding them up and were pushing them with rifles with fixed bayonets ... 10. The Japs started from my right to bayonet the women one by one from behind their backs ... 11. A Jap wearing a sword and with a revolver in his hand shot one or two of the women who

had started screaming … 14. By this time the remaining men and women were trying to escape. They were being bayoneted and shot.[64]

One hundred yards. I wondered how clearly you would see from that distance. He did say 'appeared to' and acknowledged that he was slightly delirious. And he didn't mention them being machine-gunned, as the official story went. Surely he would have heard that clearly enough.

Others who walked on the beach after the massacre were Stoker Lloyd, Eric Germann and Leading Seaman Wilding. In his statement Wilding said, 'We found a life boat and about a dozen bodies, all women except two … Of the only two women I examined one had been shot and bayoneted and one killed by a sword.'[65]

Stoker Lloyd said that a few days after his own survival, 'Further along the beach where we had left them I came upon the bodies of the nurses (about 10) and after that the civilians. All appeared to have been bayoneted or shot.'[66] In *The Will to Live*, published in 1970, Lloyd gave a slightly different variation, saying, 'They had been shot and then bayoneted. It was a shocking sight.'[67] And finally, in another statement, reported by Major Gideon Jacobs of the British Royal Marines, whose assignment was to take control of Sumatra from Japanese troops and to oversee the liberation of prisoner-of-war camps, Lloyd said that when he saw the nurses three days later, they were 'scattered in terrible attitudes and many must have been killed as they were tending the wounded men'.[68]

Eric Germann, who doesn't mention seeing the bodies at all in his affadavit from 1945, in the 1949 book *By Eastern Windows* is described as having found the nurses the next morning:

> However, they had been shot, not bayoneted. The bodies he examined had single bullet holes at the base of the skulls. Rifle shots. He wondered at no evidence of machine-gunning. He presumed, from the way they were widely scattered along the water's edge, that some bodies had floated away when the tide went out. Four bodies lay huddled in one group and three in another. A red-haired nurse was lying higher on the beach than the others. Her skull had been crushed but the sea had washed it clean.[69]

Tilting backwards in the chair, I closed my eyes. Records I had not absorbed now shrieked back at me like banshees. It seemed that death had come more violently than had been portrayed upstairs in the Second World War gallery. Agitated, I grabbed the boxes and dumped them on the counter. Brushed quickly through the doors to flee these files of war. Beware, I wanted to inscribe at the entrance, in big red letters, horror lives here! Do not be deceived by these air-conditioned halls of war.

The heat hit me like a furnace as I opened the door. Back in the hotel, cold water from the shower spilt over my shoulders, dropped to the bathroom floor and spun clockwise down the drain. The fan on full, I lay on the bed with wet skin but soon it was pushing around warm recycled air.

When I was a kid, celebrating Christmas at Jean's house in baking hot Wangaratta, my sister, brother and I would put wet flannels on our foreheads. Taking one from the shower now, I soaked it and placed it across my temples. It had a momentary cooling, if not nostalgic, effect. I could almost smell the peppercorn trees and see the real candles on Jean's neighbours' Christmas tree.

A few people drew my attention to an article from Sydney's *Sun* newspaper on 8 September 1946 titled 'The Japanese leopard with unchanging spots'. I could hardly bear to read it and when I had finished it, wished to rip it up. I hadn't bargained on finding worse again. The first few times I read it I had a type of temporary amnesia and buried it beyond consciousness. Dismissed it in favour of the official story. But now I looked again in the cold, hard light.

It was a chaotic and violent account of what had happened, written by Hal Richardson, who was ex-8th Division AIF and a journalist. While Richardson was a prisoner-of-war in the Muntok and Palembang (Sumatra) camps, he was directed by the British senior officer to conduct interviews about internees' war experiences – including the massacre of Australian nurses. He kept the shorthand notes in the soles of his boot to avoid detection.[70]

In the article Richardson quoted Wilding as saying, 'I saw the Australian nurses. One was nearly naked. Another had three bayonet wounds in the back. Footprints showed where women ran up the beach. At the end of the footsteps they lay – heads cleaved.'[71]

249

I thought I'd wanted to know, but what is known can't be unknown, and what is seen can't be unseen. This was an impossible dilemma.

I engaged a historian – Dr Janet Butler from La Trobe University in Melbourne – to do a comprehensive search of newspaper articles at the time. She said that when Richardson's article was published in the *Sun* in 1946, claiming to tell the full story for the first time, the next day no other newspapers picked it up or even commented on it. This is despite the high degree of repetition of previous stories across newspapers, which suggests a level of consistent syndication.[72] I wondered if he and the newspapers were told to shut up.

There seems to be evidence for this in that Richardson himself, in his book *Into the Fire* – published much later, in 2000, and based on the same interviews he had done in the camps – gives a very different, sanitised account, consistent with the official story:

> then the gloved hand signalled and the combined firing dropped
> them, almost in unison, into the gentle waves. The firing went
> on and on, then dwindled and the Japanese ventured into the
> water, stabbing with bayonet as they selected bodies in the
> tinctured water.[73]

I wanted to cut out Richardson's brutal newspaper account and paste over it with his narrative softened by 'gentle waves'. Whisper Aunt Evie's words: 'I wish you could report to me that Benda was not bayoneted.'

Melbourne and Indonesia

February 2019

'I'm going back again,' I said to Sally tentatively on the other end of the phone.

'To Indonesia?'

'Yes.'

The trip had come around so fast I hadn't told many people. To be honest, I worried Dad and Sally might feel it was over the top – I was sure Dad would – so I wasn't exactly proactive in my telling.

'That's great, George.'

'Really?' I was alert for any kind of a *that's a bit intense* tone. 'Wish you could come.'

'No, I can't,' she replied. 'With my legs ... I couldn't.'

'Tim and I were talking about how we could get you there. Maybe we could bring you by boat, so you wouldn't have to walk.' Tim, my cousin, had even mentioned a helicopter, he *was* in the air force after all. 'For the eightieth?' But Sally was losing mobility and might be worse by then. The opportunity for her to come was closing.

'No ... be too hard with the beach and the heat,' she said, hosing down my plans. 'I'm just so grateful that you are doing all this ... all the things I should've done.' Sally sighed and I felt my chest constrict. On top of everything else it seemed she felt guilty. I wanted to weave my arms around her in Warragul.

'It was probably too traumatic for you ... being second generation,' I stammered. 'When I started looking into it ... I ...' Digging my fingernail firmly into the ribbed arm of the sofa, I traced the weave along the arm rest.

Sally jumped in, 'Yes, but now I feel okay about it. That it's being addressed, I suppose.' Before I could say how grief-stricken I felt, how the sadness of the years had sunk into me, she went on. 'It affected my whole life really.'

I wanted to ask more, to go deeper, but the habit of not intruding was ingrained. The moment passed and she was off the phone before I could think of how to respond, how to navigate the conversation into uncharted places.

If only I could speak to my grandmother, Jean, hear what she would have offered by way of account. Perhaps everyone had shut down at once, suspended in shock. Taken cues from each other to leave it be, just get on as best you could. Then, when Dolly died in January 1948, stoicism seemed to have solidified like concrete.

Ian Shaw had warned me, when I'd emailed him to introduce myself, that he had come out the other end of writing *On Radji Beach* a slightly different person. He had used an exclamation mark and predicted laughs, tears and introspection. Ian said he loved Bud's sass and sense of humour. He wished me luck, saying he was glad I was telling her story, and glad too that the nurses' broader story was 'finally creeping ever so slowly into the public consciousness'.

How would I come out? With vicarious trauma? No wonder Dad didn't want to open old wounds – though I had been critical of him for it, I was starting to understand this impulse for defensive self-protection. Sometimes it felt as though the grief had erupted right though me, bits of molten rock coursing through my veins. So, yes, I was starting to want to shut down too. I placed my head on the velvet cushion on the sofa and let it stroke my face.

Jean and Dolly must have talked about Bud's murder with Vivian, at least in a roundabout way, when Vivian had visited. What intimate conversations might Jean and she have had, side by side on the sofa? No fanfare, no parents, no need to be heroic, and no one hanging over her telling her what she was and wasn't allowed to say. Perhaps Jean had turned, head straight, hair back in a bun and leant in towards her: 'Vivian, please tell me what really happened to my sister. I want to know it all.'

This third trip to Bangka Island came around fast. Michael Noyce said we had to keep the momentum going till the eightieth and he was most persuasive. Beside me on the flight out sat Major Tebbutt's daughter, Joan. Aged eighty-four, she had decided to come spontaneously when she'd heard about the trip a few weeks before. She wished to immerse herself in the same water that her father had traversed as he swam ashore to Bangka Island after the *Vyner Brooke* sunk.

'I think we each need to have our own trolley,' she said when I tried to carry her bags at the airport, 'if we are to get along.' Pulled from her bottomless duffle bag, beside the bottle of scotch, she passed me a spare pair of compression stockings – she'd promised her daughters she'd wear them on the plane. White nylon stretched to opaque as I pushed my toes in tight.

The roll call of attendees was impressive this year: Joan; the governor of Bangka Island; representatives from the Australian embassy and the Dutch War Graves Commission; the Australian assistant defence attaché, the New Zealand defence attaché; Bruce Bird, ex-naval lieutenant commander, interested in running historical tours of Muntok; plus relatives and friends. Michael and Val Noyce were coming, and Michael's cousin Kate, for the second time. Matron Drummond's niece Philippa was returning with her son, James; Michael and Lesley Pether would also be there.

Hopefully, we would set foot on the *right* Radji Beach.

As I opened the doors to the balcony of my lake-view room at the Bandara International Hotel, Jakarta looked fine this evening, and I sank back into a wooden chair dressed with an orange batik throw and breathed in deeply. Then I noticed the smog veiling the view and coughed before it filled my lungs.

Judy Balcombe couldn't make the trip this year so she and Arlene were visiting separately with Emily, Betty Jeffrey's niece, in a few months' time when Emily had a break from teaching.

But Judy messaged me as I sat down. 'Ralph Armstrong has died.' I drew in a sharp breath of surprise.

'Is it a coincidence,' she wrote, 'that Ralph has died seventy-seven years to the day that his family boarded the *Vyner Brooke*?'

The lake below was perfectly still, like the dank air, which had a tinge of floral fragrance right at the end of your inhale. No stars were visible – Jakarta smog. I thought of Ralph; his exchange with the paramedic, his bright white hair, refusal to go to hospital, and his wobbly shuffle of triumph into the living room after they got him to his feet using a sheet to haul him up. The inscription on his tombstone might say 'Ralph Armstrong: husband, father, grandfather, son. Faithful, stubborn. Survivor.' I reread Judy's text and subsided into the sturdy chair, grateful to have met him, because now another survivor was gone.

During the war, the men and women who died in the camps were buried by their friends in fields or jungle nearby. Warding off bugs and rats, their companions dug graves, carried their bodies – the stench must've been unbearable – and provided what dignity they could. Exacting records were kept by the internees as to who lay where. Post-war, as time went by, the graves started to deteriorate and the land was repurposed. Villages sprang up on top. In the early 1980s, to make way for a new petrol station, it is thought that the women who died in the Muntok camp were reburied in three communal graves in the Muntok Catholic Cemetery, and it was right there, shortly after we'd arrived in Muntok, that we now stood. Only civilian women were reburied here, though. Any Australian Army nurse or other military personnel who died in the camps was moved to the Jakarta War Cemetery.

Tiled in pale colours – blue, green, grey and cream – crosses sat on top of the graves. Local women were paying their respects; they dusted, cleared, made good and kept some reverence for the dead. Staring at the tombstones in front of me, I searched for Ralph's mother and two sisters. It didn't take long. Armstrong was at the top, with his mother, Theresia, listed first, followed by his sister, Dixie.

Mrs Theresia 'Resie' Armstrong (51), 7 February 1945
Miss Dixie Armstrong (32), 5 April 1945

My finger traced the grooved inscription but halted on the last letter as I noticed Ralph's sister Gracie was missing. Then I remembered. Gracie died near the end of the war, when she and Ralph were moved to Belalau in Sumatra.

Flowers should be placed here, but I had only thought to order them for the memorial service. Foraging in the grass nearby, I found a few purple wildflowers that resembled lavender and hurriedly assembled a roadside bouquet.

'For Ralph, for Verna, their children and grandchildren.' I placed my improvised offering on the gravestone.

'Can someone take a photo so I can send it to Verna?' The abandoned graves of Muntok were a long way from Mount Gravatt.

*

The next day we were to search for the real Radji. Mr Fakhrizal had found Yas Sin's son-in-law, Siman, who had lived in Kampong Menjelang, the village inland where the party walked to seek help during the war. Yas Sin had previously identified Teluk Menggeris as the site of the nurses' massacre and had taken the Australian War Graves Commission (40 Australian War Graves Unit) there in 1946.[74] Siman would be walking with us today.

'Pleased to meet you.' We nodded in deference to the man who may hold the key to our questions. Wiry, no doubt from a life lived outdoors, he was of indeterminate age. Brown trousers, a black and tan long-sleeved t-shirt and a red baseball cap shielded him from the sun. Mr Fakhrizal translated and we established that when Siman was a boy, Yas Sin had shown him where the bodies had lain. One day peaceful subsistence by the coast, the next, invasion and the aftermath of a massacre. Death all around – on the beach and in the sea, contaminating water and food. The villagers had feared retribution if they offered help. Shortly after the massacre, they moved away and wouldn't eat fish from the area for years.

Though we generally accepted Yas Sin's testimony, Michael Pether pointed out that bodies had been washed ashore up and down the coast from the many ships sunk by Japanese Imperial forces, including the *Vyner Brooke*. When Vivian came back in 1993 with other survivors of the women's camps and their families to unveil a memorial plaque near the lighthouse, she couldn't identify the beach either – no wonder we were having so much trouble now.[75] Seventy-seven years on; tides, erosion, tin mining, deforestation, palm oil plantations, and the vagaries of memory had all left their mark.

We banged and lurched our way in four-wheel drives down the rough washed-away track to the headland of Tanjung Betumpak, where the memorial plaque was. Not so nervous as in past years, but as uncomfortable as ever. Michael beamed, a manuscript in his hand. Fifteen years of research, he told me, into the boats captured or sunk after they left Singapore as it fell and made their way down through Bomb Alley, as the straits became known. It was a meticulous historical document, a tome of dedication. Michael had tucked the hundreds of bound foolscap pages under his arm, and was seeing for the first time the coastline he had pored over in documents, via satellite, and in his mind.

He had a list of criteria to locate the 'real' Radji Beach. His was the sharpest of minds, capable of catching and categorising clues. Most likely, he thought, was the beach just north of Tanjung Betumpak (and this beach didn't have a name that we were aware of), rather than Teluk Menggeris, as Yas Sin had said. This made it one bay north of where we now stood on the 'original' Radji Beach. Despite my attachment to the scanned map in my bag – the one I had found at the archives – I tried to keep my mind open.

Philippa, Michael and I started walking north and around a headland, till we saw extending before us, as Ian Shaw wrote, 'a sandy beach that stretched into the distance in the north and was about 20 m wide at high tide'.[76] When Vivian had landed in the second lifeboat, it seemed she landed on the same beach as the bonfire. There is no mention in her accounts of navigating headlands or rocky outcrops to get to the fire, which on any other beach, apart from this one just north of Tanjung Betumpak, you would have to do. The trip from the lifeboat to the bonfire was made twice – once to get help, the other to carry the injured. Vivian's exact words were, 'about two miles further down the coast there was a fire that had been lit by a previous boat that had come in'.[77] Eric Germann described the injured as being 'on the beach about a mile away'.[78]

So, criteria number one – tick. This was definitely the longest stretch of uninterrupted beach along this coast. I peered into the distance, tried to see the end, the sun biting my eyes.

Criteria number two was that the beach should be the midway point between two lighthouses, Tanjung Kelian to the south and Tanjung Ular to the north. Eric Germann said they saw 'flashings from two lighthouses about five miles apart on the coast. Midway between them burned a large bonfire.'[79] Philippa and I stood with our backs to the beach, turned our heads to the right and the left. Lighthouses blinked on either side.

'Equidistant?'

We gave each other a nod. Michael looked flushed, pleased to match maps, records and testimonies to the actual landscape.

Criteria number three was that there was 'a small promontory of rocks and driftwood about two hundred feet away' that the men had to 'climb over'[80] before they were killed at the southern end of the beach – Vivian had called it a 'headland'.[81] That got a tick here too.

And criteria number four was another tick: on the other side of the headland where the men were taken to be killed, there was a 'small cove', according to Eric Germann.[82] Stoker Lloyd described it as a 'small bay with large rocks at the entrance'.[83]

So far this beach was fitting pretty well with what Michael had distilled from reports, though I wasn't sure about the stream. It had been described as 'bubbling out of the rocks behind the headland. This spring formed a small stream that flowed inland into the jungle, disappearing into a swampy area back from the beach.'[84] However, Vivian described it as being in the jungle near the track to the village: 'it was off this track that the freshwater stream was located'.[85] She also said there were 'two fresh water springs near the beach about a dozen yards from where I was shot'.[86] The stream we could see on the beach north of Tanjung Betumpak was in plain sight on the main part of the beach.

Thrown by the idea that it could be this beach – it was very exposed, not as pretty as the other, smaller beaches – I reminded myself again to keep an open mind. I knew the other relatives had also bonded with Yas Sin's beach, Teluk Menggeris, as I had since my map discovery at the archives. Scrunching my bag to check it was still there, I heard proof in the form of a rustle.

'I'm going to have to bow out now, I'm afraid,' Michael apologised, as we started our trek south to Teluk Menggeris. 'Meet you at the other end.' Those who didn't want, or who would struggle, to walk the distance were being transported in four-wheel drives to the other end, where Mr Fakhrizal's family lived in a beach-side village and had invited us for barbecued fish. What a shame, we needed Michael's historical brainpower. But it was hot and he had to be careful. Last year he'd had a cardiac arrest; his wife Lesley had brought him back to life. A defibrillator had been surgically embedded. The three of us were red like lobsters, blotches marked our skin. Passing around the sunscreen – fifty plus,

I handed Philippa my umbrella since she didn't have a hat. Her décolletage was burning.

Back we walked around the headland, past our starting point, feet squeaking the sand on our way south. Past the memorial, the fishing huts; past the jungle and rocky outcrops. About half an hour in, the sand turned spongy and we started to sink. Like quicksand, but mud. You put your foot on it and it descended ever so slowly. Took a bit of force, a bit of suction, when you had to pull it out – like a plunger to unclog a sink. I couldn't believe I had encountered quicksand – I'd never thought it really existed.

Mr Fakhrizal's leg had sunk almost up to his knee and when he tried to pull himself out he fell over and started to laugh. 'Give him a hand, before he sinks further,' Michael Noyce yelled out, too far away to assist. Those on either side pulled him out. I kept an eye on Michael Pether's manuscript, which Mr Fakhrizal now clutched. Somehow, he'd managed to keep it unscathed. My bare feet resembled mud booties. Bruce Bird, who had started with fresh creases and polished boots, now had a white cotton hanky shielding his head, bare feet and trousers rolled up to his knees. Michael Noyce had come prepared – in Crocs and shorts with nothing to lose. 'This is a real adventure, Georgina.'

Philippa held her head back and laughed, deep and guttural.

Our chatter fell away when Siman indicated that we had arrived at Teluk Menggeris, or Inggris [English] Bay, the beach we had all quietly thought might be the right beach. It was more secluded than the others. Large rocks protruded from both the ocean and the sand, a distinctive sculptural feature. This was the sort of beach you could while away time on; soak up the sun, stare out to sea and stay until long shadows elongated bodies on the sand and the sun glinted red and pink with the last vestiges of light.

We started with Michael Pether's criteria. They sort of fitted and sort of didn't. There was a rocky outcrop to the south, at Tanjung Sabajau, and a cove of about sixty metres on the other side – could it be described as small, I wondered. The outcrop wasn't substantial either; not sure you would call it a headland.

'Here's the stream,' Michael Noyce called out. We moved to the back of the beach, where he had started to film. 'Radji Beach stream,' he was saying, 'this is now where we think the real Radji Beach is ...'

Wide and springing from a rock, it was a lovely stream. Squatting, I cupped my hand, dipped it under the surface of the translucent water and threw it up against my face. Droplets meandered their way down my neck.

Siman pointed out an area of the beach where, he said, the bodies were found. He and Mr Fakhrizal conferred a lot in Bahasa.

'Was there a fisherman's hut here?' I asked. 'And what about paths to Muntok and the village?'

The fisherman's hut was described in *On Radji Beach* as behind the headland, near where the stream 'flowed inland into the jungle, disappearing into a swampy area back from the beach' and 'among some palm trees that fringed the beach'.[87] Germann also spoke of the remnants of a second hut – 'the bones of a fishing hut', he said, 'higher up the beach, near the jungle edge', where he had slept, exhausted, on the very first night.[88]

'Yes, yes,' Mr Fakhrizal said, 'there was at least one hut. The villagers who lived in the jungle had a hut on the beach to fish.' (Months later, I notice in the War Graves report that there is the mention of a fisherman's hut on this beach 'just south of Cape Sabajau'[89], which is the right spot.)

Eager to lay hands on this sand, I crouched down and placed my palms flat. Rough grains met my skin. Turning my palms over I gazed at the remnants, the subtle gradients of tan and cream. Flakes of shell that once gave shelter to inhabitants long gone.

'There was a path ... about here.' Mr Fakhrizal pointed to the jungle beside him. Yas Sin's son-in-law nodded in agreement. My untrained eyes couldn't see a path. Overgrown, the jungle had reclaimed it.

'We can try to walk it next year,' Mr Fakhrizal said. He and some of his assistants had already done this. Photos of stone remnants from where the village once was had been emailed by Mr Fakhrizal to us in Australia.

Siman pointed north, towards where we had just come from. 'Up there, that is where they found all the bones.' I knew what he meant. When the Australian War Graves Commission came, Yas Sin took them to Tanjung Besayap, the headland at the north end of Teluk Menggeris. The War Graves report said, 'There were many bones. Some were lying amongst the rocks and others half buried in the half sand half earth on the edge of the water.'[90]

It didn't add up. If this was Radji Beach then you would expect the mass of bones to be at the headland at the southern end of the beach – Tanjung Sabajau. Vivian said that soldiers took 'half the men down the beach about a hundred yards behind the headland'; Stoker Lloyd that they were headed towards Muntok, which is south.[91] Not only was it in the wrong direction, Tanjung Besayap was more than a hundred yards away. Unless tides had played a role, or the bones were the remains of others washed ashore.

We stood in the shallows, which stretched out endlessly at low tide, Philippa, Michael Noyce, his cousin Kate and me, the water cool on our toes. You could walk out into the water a long way before the sand bar dropped off. We lingered, our figures outlined by the afternoon light, clutched red roses and tossed them into the sea.

'Feels like the right beach,' we muttered. We wanted it to be.

Sometime later, we broke our trance and resumed walking. Soon, we met Val coming the other way.

'Where've you been?' she looked at Michael. I averted my eyes and stared at the sun. We had been gone a long time. Did we say we'd only be an hour or so? It'd probably been more like three – not that we knew how long it would take. We were trying to piece the clues of history together, match them with the changing landscape. I looked down at my muddy feet, which now just looked dirty. Val continued, 'The drive in here was terrifying, worst we've done … narrow passes, four-wheel drives sliding through tin mines and steep drops on either side. It's going to be dark soon. We need to get out of here!'

The sun *was* dropping, the jungle pulling its curtains for the night, shadows passing in the dusk. I certainly wasn't sure I wanted to spend the night here, although Vivian and Kinsley had spent twelve. Camouflaged under the trees, injured, hungry, afraid. Kinsley with bayonet and shrapnel wounds, Vivian with a bullet that had gone right through her.

We walked faster as the colours of our surroundings changed to patches of deep green and black. Birds made squawking sounds as they found their spots for the night. Up ahead, we could see huts burrowed into jungle at the edge of the sand – presumably the village where Mr Fakhrizal's family lived. The smell of barbecued fish drifted through the trees that formed an overhead canopy.

Michael Pether stepped forward from the copse of trees. 'We need to get out of here.'

Barbecued fish, plated on leaves, teased my taste buds. 'Can't we just stay a while? Mr Fakhrizal's family have made all this especially.' But the others had already eaten and were antsy to go. 'Terima kasih,' they said, and got up to leave.

Two trips would be needed – there weren't enough vehicles to take us all out in one go. Through the mine, across deep water and large boulders – the way out was precarious, the group that had already travelled this route stressed. Plus, it was nearly dark. The drivers know what they are doing, I told myself, pushing aside the memory of the vehicle with dodgy brakes, and the driver who had placed a rock under the front tyre to assist the handbrake. The fish had lost its appeal.

'There's one more spot!' a voice yelled out.

'You go,' Philippa said.

Out along the shore shadows danced on the sand and I could hear the jungle switching to night.

'You go, I'll stay.' I tried to be brave and channel Bud. Shapes shifted around me.

'No, I'll stay,' Philippa reiterated. She really did have Matron Drummond's genes.

I piled into the back of the vehicle. A bird screeched in the dusk, and it was decided Philippa and Michael Noyce would stay for the second trip.

'This is a real adventure, Georgina,' Michael Noyce said again. I wasn't sure who he was trying to convince.

It was starting to feel like a strange re-enactment, Michael Noyce as Sedgeman and Philippa as Matron Drummond. I pushed away thoughts of them skidding over the side of the tin mine embankment.

I fixed my gaze backwards through the rear window rather than to the front, as we bumped out, my stomach lurching while the driver ground through gears, turned and slid, his high beams our hope of getting safely out.

Later that night, back in Muntok at D'Orange Café, our group mused that we may have found the *real* Radji. Most of the relatives thought that it was Teluk Menggeris, though we couldn't say for sure and Michael Pether still made a strong case for the beach north of Tanjung Betumpak.

'I expected it to feel eerie,' I said, 'but then I thought the same with the first Radji Beach and it didn't.' Others nodded their agreement. Michael Noyce – having returned safely – turned to Marc who was married to Yanni, the owner of the café. Marc and

Yanni had been instrumental in assisting us with our memorial plans. Michael had met them when he had first come to Bangka Island.

'That's not what you experienced, was it, Marc?'

'What do you mean?' I asked.

'Tell them your story,' Michael said.

Marc hesitated, sucked on a cigarette and looked at the ground to consider his options. 'Okay. One night, when I had lived here for about three years, I was invited by my friend Ferhad to go night-fishing on Teluk Menggeris. I didn't know of the terrible events that had taken place there and I needed to clear my head, so I jumped on my motorbike and headed there.'

Marc looked at us to see if we were with him. Tension, like heat, was building. 'It took us about forty minutes to get to this remote beach. It was a clear sky and it wasn't too dark because of the moon; the light was reflected over the bay.'

Thinking back to Menggeris, being there late this afternoon, I could not imagine going there at night voluntarily.

'When we got there, we were waited on by the owner of a small fisherman's hut and a few more friends of Ferhad. Because my Indonesian wasn't very good and I had an urge to go outside, I left the group to go onto the beach, where I found some drift-wood to sit on. As I sat there, I was suddenly slapped with what seemed like a wet towel. It wasn't painful but I was shaken. I looked around and could not see anybody.'

Nobody blinked. We were all alert. Marc stood as if to shake off the experience, his long frame unfurling. I took in a measured, slow breath. The others were quiet, but Marc hadn't finished. 'I could hear my friends talking inside the hut, but the whole situation – the light, the sea and the sound – had changed into a very spooky scene. Suddenly my whole body filled up with a sadness so deep, I had never felt anything like it before.'

As he spoke, I could feel the sadness creeping though his body and mine. It was what we had expected to feel; echoes of dark acts embedded in the sand.

'This experience lasted for some time. I was in a state of panic and I wanted to get out of that place as soon as I could. I walked back to the hut and called out to Ferhad. He came out and I told him to help me get back to the main road. Surprised, he asked me what was going on and I answered, "Never take me back to a place like this." I jumped on my motorcycle and when I turned the key, all its lights came on, and stayed on until the next day. I couldn't turn them off. Later, I found out that this is Radji Beach and learnt about its history.'

Marc paused, spent, stubbed his cigarette out on the ground.

Michael Noyce stepped in, sensing Marc had had enough. 'That's why we got the priest to bless it.'

Marc nodded. 'Radji Beach kept its dark personality to me until the beginning of 2018, when we built the monument and held a service remembering the victims of the massacre. It felt like a blanket was lifted off the coastline.'

Melbourne

March 2019

Historical documents were closing in on me. I pieced one recollection together with another and they differed, or didn't answer my questions about what had really happened on that day. I read over and over the same accounts, shuffled papers from pile to pile, and tried to hold them all in my mind. If only I were a historian, or an investigative journalist, had a steel-trap mind like Michael Pether. Mine felt more like a sieve. I had shaken the tree of history and only crumbs had fallen out, and more questions. My neck was sore from sitting for so long hunched over. My filing was voluminous; papers obscured the dining room table. I'd tried timelines, stick-it notes, whiteboards, electronic files, binders. This was just so damn hard. Glancing over, I saw other piles neglected on the kitchen bench – bills and tax, shoved in the 'when I get time' pile. Was this a form of mid-life madness? My business partner had told me I was a bit of a crusader when I wanted to be, and a relative of the nurses said that I should get my own private detective licence.

My youngest daughter and some friends pronounced my project was 'a good hobby for someone your age – better than a midlife crisis'.

Part of dealing with grief and trauma is to understand what happened to cause the grief. To tell the story until it is ordered in your mind, its pieces in place. Then you stop the ruminations, the imaginings you allow yourself in an attempt to fill in the blanks.

If I knew, could I then say 'case closed'? But this was not some cold case or true-crime podcast, though many of those don't find definitive answers either. This was my family. All the relatives' families. I wanted to believe that if I did know, then I could consider it, family business, put to rest. But what if I couldn't fill all the gaps?

Sally said that the grief had been passed to me. I was still recoiling from that comment. All these years later, what was I supposed to do with it? With this ambiguous loss that couldn't find closure and had ossified in time. I had been reading Pauline Boss, who coined the term. She used it to refer to loss that is unresolved or lacks clarity – like someone missing, presumed dead in war, or a loss with no body. Boss says that this ambiguity freezes the grief and the family processing.[92] When I sat still, I could feel it weighing me down, pushing me into the sofa. I wanted to move, to sprint up and down the hall, flail, and thrash it out of me.

Was I any closer to knowing Bud? I felt I had almost forgotten her in my quest to know the 'truth'. Was it really Bud I was trying to understand, or my family more broadly? I could feel the strain behind my eyes, beyond tears. If only I could say, 'Twenty-one Australian Army nurses were killed in a brutal manner by soldiers from the 1 and 2 Company, of 1 Battalion, of 229 Infantry Regiment, of 38 Division of the Japanese Imperial Army.'

Captain Orita Masaru, the commander of 1 Battalion, was to be interrogated and tried for war crimes in 1948, but suicided in Sugamo Prison, Tokyo, by severing his jugular vein with a sharp instrument smuggled into his cell from a 'screen repair detail' he was part of.[93] Many of the Orita Battalion were redeployed around the islands of New Guinea and died when their ships were sunk off the coast of New Georgia in the battle of Guadalcanal.[94] So no one was ever prosecuted for the Radji Beach massacre. On 3 February 1950, the minister for the army wrote to the Honourable Kent Hughes MP: 'It has not been possible to identify or arrest any other suspect in connection with the Banka [sic] Island murder.'[95]

We will never know the rest. Full stop. Then surely I could I give all of this up, focus on the living instead of the dead. But Bud's fate had got me by the throat and wouldn't let me go. I had prised open the lid of horror, closed many years ago in my family, and I couldn't put it back on.

I wanted the nurses known in the annals of history, with their own chapter heading. Truth told, no sanitising, no censoring. No shame.

Later on, historian Yuki Tanaka caused me to question whether Orita *was* the senior officer on the beach, when Tanaka stated in a lecture he gave: 'It is unlikely that the officer who led fifteen Japanese soldiers to Radjik [*sic*] beach was Orita himself.'[96] As commander, Orita was ultimately responsible for the massacre, but was he the actual officer on the beach?

I kept digging in the archival records till I found an examination of one of his platoon, Paymaster Captain Shibayama Sukezo, in which he described Orita as 'A tall handsome man with a big nose, he wore spectacles.'[97] In contrast, Vivian said that 'the one in charge was only a small fellow'.[98] Leading Private Tanemura Kiyoshi, in Arthur Weston's weekly reports as an investigator for 2 Australian War Crimes Section, identified Second Lieutenant Kohiyama Fumio as 'the leader of the platoon [2 Company] which massacred the nurses and other survivors on the S-W coast of Bangka Is'.[99] So Kohiyama may have been the officer on the beach. Kohiyama was killed in action in the Philippines on 1 March 1944.[100] Later on I find out author–historian Lynette Silver has come to the same conclusion.[101]

Sergeant Major Kato Taro, a sergeant major in 1 Company 1 Battalion, and Lieutenant Takeuchi Masayuki, leader of the 1 Company, have both been named by other researchers and writers as involved in the killings. As reported in the *Sun* newspaper in 1946, they were arrested in August 1946 and, according to the article, the evidence was to be heard in Singapore, but I have not found any interrogation reports from around that time.[102]

In Weston's weekly reports, three years later, on the week ending 25 November 1949, there is a summary of an interrogation of Kato Taro (in Tokyo) but it does not confirm that he was involved in the killing; it only refers to him providing information regarding 'the exact location of the units' on Bangka Island and related armaments.[103] As previously mentioned, after the suicide of Orita no one was ever tried or convicted for the massacre. I checked a list of 'accused Japanese war criminals', which included Australia's investigations and prosecutions in all courts.[104]

Though in some ways I felt compelled to find out who was culpable, really, I thought, how could I understand the collective forces, which author and historian John W. Dower writes of – Emperor-centred worship and indoctrination, the code of Bushido, rigid power structures, weak human-rights consciousness, socialisation, the Japanese brutalisation of their own soldiers, brainwashing, as well as individual choice – all of which must have converged on the beach that February day to unleash such brutality.[105]

I found particularly heartbreaking an excerpt from a letter from Orita Masaru, in one of the masses of pages detailing suspects, which showed a tender side. The letter was to his wife Sachujo before he was extradited to Tokyo, 'Are our parents well? Have our children returned home? I am well and now in the USSR.'[106]

Melbourne

April 2019

Eight a.m. and I'd just got back from a walk around local streets in the diffuse autumn light, anticipating my first coffee of the day, when there it was, a double page in *The Age*, sprawled on the dining room table. Kingsley had left the paper open for me, knowing I didn't always read it, preferring to listen to the news instead.

'Horrific truth about nurses' massacre finally told,' the headline blared at me. The piece opened:

> It is a secret that Australian army nurses from World War Two took to their graves. One was told by the Australian government to make no mention of violation by the Japanese in her statement before the war crimes tribunal. Now author Lynette Silver, known as 'the history detective', has pulled together all the evidence and says categorically that 22 nurses were raped before they were forced into the sea and machine-gunned.[107]

I placed my hand on the side of the table for support and stood there slack-jawed. I'd waited so long for this to be corroborated – or to be able to prove it myself – and there it was, casually laid out on the breakfast table, alongside the crumbs, the milk and the muesli.

I was shocked and not shocked. My instincts and research had left me thinking this was the case, but I couldn't prove it beyond the balance of probabilities. There was a photograph of Lynette Silver outside the Australian War Memorial staring down the reader's gaze. Was she steadying herself against potential detractors? Being a war historian, she must have had a few. I wondered how many would read this in print and online today.

'Horrific truth about nurses' massacre,' was so final, so public, so *published*. Approaching the paper with caution, I fought an urge to leave it be and picked it up. It existed, though I could tear it up if I wanted – and part of me did want to. The article was another horrible attestation of what I was still trying to accept, or what I was trying not to accept. And what some of the broader group of relatives might never accept, without one hundred per cent direct evidence.

Needing to move, I busied myself with chores: washing, tidying, wiping – putting things in their place. Then, when all was as it should be, I took a breath and settled to read the article slowly, steeling myself on the burnt orange velvet chairs, which provided some cushioning.

More and more claims were mounting: Yuki Tanaka, Barbara Angell, Ian Shaw, Tess Lawrence, Michael Pether, Lynette Silver. Each one adding their voice, like a Greek chorus chanting,

'Might have happened, may have happened ... probably happened ... *did* happen.'

The collective unconscious had awoken. The first sign had
been Tess's article. Reading it had knocked me horizontal, dried
out my tears, so today I don't have any left. Since then I had
been searching, scratching around for proof one way or the other.
Trying to plug holes in time, in manuscripts, in memory. Lynette
Silver had, it appeared, pulled the clues together; woven them
tight – like the buttons that had supposedly been ripped off
and resewn on the bodice of Vivian's uniform with the wrong-
coloured thread – aquamarine blue.[108]

What had Lynette found that I didn't already know? Quite
a few things. A document in the National Library in Canberra,
written by the wife of Major Harold Williams, Jean. Harold
Williams was a war crimes investigator with 2 AWCS. Lynette
had noticed, when reading Jean's account of her husband's investigation of the murder of the nurses, that 'the nurses' narrative
stopped mid-sentence ... there was nothing more on the next
page ... someone had crudely hacked off the top five centimetres
with a pair of scissors.'[109]

What had it said? We would never discover – it was gone,
destroyed. Maybe it was in a vault of discarded historical truths.

Lynette had also met Sergeant Arthur Weston when she'd sat
next to him at a Sydney RSL dinner back in 1999. She had raised
the massacre of the nurses at Bangka and he had said, 'There are
some things about that case that I had to keep secret and cannot
talk about.'[110] He did, however, endorse James MacKay's 1996
book *Betrayal in High Places* as pretty accurate on the whole.[111]

This was a turnaround given MacKay's critics, who had earlier seriously questioned his credibility.* Weston also didn't dispute the Tanemura reinterrogation, supposedly part of file 152, in which Tanemura reported that Japanese soldiers had raped the nurses. Lynette explained that the reason there is no official copy of Tanemura's reinterrogation in file 152 or Weston's weekly reports at the NAA is because in 1951 all files that didn't lead to a trial were culled when 2 AWCS closed down.[112]

A relative of one of the nurses who was killed on Radji Beach emailed me: 'All I can say is, at last! All the reading I have done left me with unanswered questions.' Another, a relative of the group of nurses who survived the camp, said they were sceptical: 'Is it just supposition, innuendo and circumstantial evidence?'

Sally texted. 'Have you seen *The Age*?'

'Yes', I replied. 'I've been on the same hunt trying to find out what happened. Scared to find the truth but at the same time determined to find out.' I probably should've told her earlier. Not acquiesced to my impulse to keep quiet, to protect.

'Pretty obvious when you think about it, I suppose,' she replied.

I'd spoken to Dad a while ago, warned him it may have happened and we were looking into it. He had sighed in response and hmm'd. I don't think he was surprised.

Sally, on the other hand, clearly was. 'Bit naïve of me,' she said.

---

* Because MacKay had passed off re-typed material as authentic, including file 152. The originals were damaged and falling apart. This caused him credibility problems in later years – as he did not disclose this.

'Not really,' I replied. 'It was a pretty well-kept secret.' And yet it wasn't at the same time. I told myself to slow down, give Sally time to take it in and not hit her with a summary of 'my research thus far'. 'Do you think Jean knew?' I asked her.

'How frustrating we can't ask her,' she replied. 'I think she might have had an inkling ... because it was a deeper grief she had. She didn't talk ... the shame of it.'

I felt a sudden need to get some air. Maybe that was it; why Jean could never even utter Bud's name. Dolly had enlisted in the navy during the war and was mainly stationed in Whyalla as Commodore of Convoys.* He surely would've heard murmurs of the types of atrocities being committed in the Pacific War.

'Mummum and Dadee?'

'No, they didn't know,' Sally said definitely. 'Ohhh,' her voice fell into a shudder, 'it would've killed them ... can't imagine my grandmother ... might've been worse for Dadee actually.' I pictured Dadee with the drip from his nose, sucking on his rollie and pacing the farm. His youngest daughter, his beloved Bud.

'How are you with this, Sally?' I asked, listening down the phone to hear her tone of voice, was it wavering, cracking ... signs of how she really was with this.

'I'm okay,' she said. 'Clive showed me the article this morning, said, "You're going to find this upsetting."'

'She would have been a virgin,' she continued, 'probably ... they were in those days, before they got married.'

---

* Lieutenant Commander RANER – Royal Australian Naval Emergency Reserve.

I felt queasy, couldn't think about this.

I sent the article to Mum and Dad. Thought it best to let Dad read it alone and let it sink in.

Dad replied straight away. 'I'd have thought that it was pretty obvious that it was deleted from the report to protect the sensibilities of the already grieving parents and siblings of the nurses involved.'

'Obvious to who?' I let my frustration spill over.

Did we not have the right to know? That a war crime was censored. Now the gatekeepers are dead. They'd taken the truth with them. Lynette had caught some vestiges just in time.

Another nurse's relative emailed: 'Thank goodness my grandparents didn't hear this.'

I checked my response, reminded myself that many of the relatives were from a different generation, with different conditioning and social norms. These were understandable reactions. I myself had been oscillating.

What about the nurses themselves – would they have wanted the world to know? Nineteen forty-two was a long way from where we are now with speaking up and truth-telling. Could they have imagined themselves out of the stigma and the shame? 'A fate worse than death' as it was commonly known. The nurses had literally been offered by an English officer in Singapore to be shot rather than fall into the hands of the Japanese Imperial forces.[113] Even now, though we have different sensibilities, there is still terror about speaking up. Certainly, you do not get rewarded for it and many do not psychologically survive media swarms, if it is a high-profile case, and online hatred, not to mention the barrage of interrogation if a case ever goes to court.

But this was not only rape at a personal level – though I did not wish to diminish that devastation. It was weaponised as a strategy of war, to dominate and demoralise the enemy.

Right now, in the war in the Ukraine, 'Women who are survivors of sexual assault during the war refrain from being identified due to fear of reprisal and shame. Sexual crimes that involve rape, torture, and sequestering often go 'underreported' during the military conflict.'[114]

Even now.

I stood up and screamed.

A few days later I emailed Lynette Silver. 'Can I talk to you?'

Yes, she replied, within a few hours. 'I did a double take when I saw the heading on your email. I have just this minute looked up the records of your great aunt to see where she was born, enlisted from and lived! I have not ever done it before – first time. I decided to record this as extra information. Your aunt must be wanting us to get together.'

'What other information do you think might be out there,' I asked her, 'and how do you think we could try to get it out?'

Kyneton, Victoria

April 2019

The drought was in full force in regional Victoria. There had been no rain for four months and we were having to buy in water. It was Easter and the family was gathering at our house in Kyneton. Mum and Dad were down from Sydney, my brother Oliver had come from Dubai and my sister Imogen from inner-city Melbourne. Our daughters had both had their wisdom teeth out, were housebound and on a diet of soup.

Mum and Dad had gifted us some legacy trees. The planting was taking place this weekend, despite the lack of water. We had decided on a chestnut, a cherry and a lemon-scented gum. Mum had got it into her head that she and Dad would like their ashes to be scattered under one of them. They were both in their eighties now and considering such things. Though I wasn't sure what Dad really wanted; wondered whether he was acquiescing to Mum's stronger desires.

'Put me anywhere, I'll be dead,' is what he'd say, I think.

Bushy, a local stonemason, had suggested the legacy trees for those who came after, as he gazed up high behind the house, where sheep grazed on hills of granite boulders, denuded from previous clearing and now cracking without water. Cracks would turn into crevasses if rain did not intervene soon. Already there was a cedar of Lebanon up there, on the hill, and a Californian redwood. On Black Saturday, as Victoria burnt, fire swept along Piper's Creek, scorched the eucalypts and raced up those hills, narrowly missing the house. The owner at the time climbed into the redwood to put out the sparks. Stayed up all night putting out embers to protect it. Now we were the beneficiaries. We had dreams to reforest some of this land, replant indigenous species to create an oasis for native animals, fence it off from rabbits, foxes and other marauders.

The drought was so bad that kangaroos had started chomping on the garden so the plants were stripped, half-eaten with bites and chunks taken out. Kingsley had erected chicken wire around one garden bed to give the tiny propagated plants a chance. He had tended these plants for months in our South Melbourne courtyard. Now they had been transplanted and had to go it alone. Two large bruisers of kangaroos sat on the lawn hemmed in by a stone wall. They weren't the 'aren't they gorgeous' black wallabies that bounced along the creek. More the 'keep your distance' types, the sort that tower above you when they stand up straight; bullies of the species. We kept our distance.

The creek had dried up, water tanks were empty and the dam was low. The landscape was a pale shade of wheat and the grass seed and burrs were barely hanging on – tough though they were. Still, there was beauty; shades of autumn – reds, browns and tones of ochre. Sinewy fallen trees where cockatoos rested, and hills of yellow in the long shadows of the afternoon.

Though winter would be a better time, our plan to plant proceeded – Mum and Dad wouldn't be here in winter. It would be too cold and they would stay in Sydney. We didn't have proper heating and the temperature was officially 'bloody freezing'.

'We can come up to water every weekend,' we said, convincing ourselves. 'Construct roo-proof wire fences around each tree and place ag-drain piping in the ground, so that when you water the saplings some of it shoots straight down the pipe and onto the roots.'

'Fingers crossed,' Imogen, Oliver and I said to each other, hopeful the legacy trees would survive.

Since we had a full house, Kingsley and I were sleeping in the bunkroom with the girls. We hadn't done this for a while, not since they were much younger when they wanted to sleep close by. Wooden venetians had just been put on the windows – a large wall of them – so you didn't get blinded by light. Seven a.m. on Easter Saturday I woke up, looked out the window and up the hill. Picking up my phone I checked the forecast – no rain today.

Stoker Lloyd's grand-daughter Sarah had sent me a link. 'Hello, you might like to know that the BBC website has a story about the massacre. They are considering the possibility that the nurses were raped and that this was kept a secret after the war.'

I jumped on the site and there it was, 'Bangka Island: The WW2 massacre and a "truth too awful to speak"'. The article's platform was Lynette's book and research. She pointed out as the piece began that 'It took a group of women to uncover this truth – and to finally speak it'. As I read, this caught my eye:

> An Australian Defence Force spokesperson says a decision on
> whether a new investigation into these sexual assault claims
> will commence is up to the government, but that 'new historic
> allegations can be reported by family' to a unit which investigates
> such crimes.[115]

Is that what I should do? Try and play my part as a family member to have these allegations officially investigated. How would I enlist the other relatives I knew?

I asked Lynette again, the walking war encyclopedia: 'What's the likelihood if we ask for an investigation into the rape allegations and subsequent cover-up that they will find anything we haven't already?' She thought it unlikely. If Vivian was told not to tell, it was probably not written down.

Later that day, I looked out at the eucalypts fringing the creek, their trunks long and exposed, stretching ten, twenty metres high. Vulnerable to fire and singed before, they clung to the banks to sprout new growth. Some of them had fallen over, leaving roots and earth upended. We left them where they lay, part of the unfolding landscape now, their jagged death intertwined with the living; we'd clamber over them on our dawdles down the creek. Sometimes the creek flowed and sometimes it didn't, exposing its underbelly of roots, earth and dross.

On my walks along the dry creek bed I'd think about the nurses – country girls many of them. Could hear their laughter, their laconic cadence. Bud, jaunty, hat set at an angle, pushing the uniform regulations. Perched on a fallen trunk, her legs swinging, ciggie in mouth and shotgun slung over her shoulder – the one that Dad had handed in after the Port Arthur Massacre during the national gun buyback. I didn't know it then, just told Dad, 'Get rid of them, we don't want guns lying around the house.' What I would give to study it now, look it over, hold it in my hands. Bud was there and then not. The faces of the others, twenty of them, passed like shadows over ghost-like gums. They were present here. I did not feel them in the city, or in the empty Shrine of Remembrance.

Melbourne

April 2019 – Mid 2022

A few days later, I asked my cousin Tim, who was now an air commodore in the air force, if he would try to find out about this unit to which we could, supposedly, report 'new historic allegations'. He did some internal inquiries and came back with the following:

> I spoke to my Inspector General ADF contact and, while fascinated by the claim, he said that this is well outside their scope. He suggested a couple of options, but none really fit perfectly:
>
> 1. The Defence Abuse Reporting Taskforce (DART). This was set up to investigate cases of historical abuse, but may have wound up. As the incident was not an internal issue, this is probably a dead end.
>
> 2. Dept of Veterans' Affairs. Again, probably not their lane.

3. Minister for Defence. A Ministerial requires an answer, but I suspect that whomever is tasked to investigate would have access to the same archives as the general public, given the timeline.

The articles are interesting. The comment from the 'ADF spokesperson' suggests that there is a path available ... I'm just not exactly sure what it is. Could you contact the Minister's office and start there?

I felt like I was living in an episode of *Utopia*.

Lynette forwarded me an email she'd received after the publication of *Angels of Mercy*. It was from Barbara Barlow, who had been a clerk at the Repatriation Department in South Melbourne in the late 1960s (it became the Department of Veterans Affairs in 1976). Barlow recalled a conversation she'd had with her boss, Bill South, who told her he had to hurry and get Matron Bullwinkel's file back into the safe in Conde's office – Conde being the deputy commissioner. She had asked why and was told, 'Bullwinkel – she was raped by the Japs on Bangka, you know.' She had not known anything about this at the time, or understood why the file was so sensitive. Later, Barlow told ABC journalist Ellen Fanning, 'That a file should be held under security was unheard of. All department files were stored in the central file office.'

Another confirmation from another source. I wondered if this file still existed, or if it had been conveniently disposed of. Lynette told me she had not applied for the file herself because she didn't think she would be granted access to these personal records. However, as a relative of the nurses, I thought I might be.

'Will you support me to launch an FOI to try and get Vivian's files?' I emailed the group I knew who were related to those killed on the beach. The vast majority said yes, they were prepared to put their names on the letter. They wanted whatever had been hidden to come out and for this matter to be settled.

In April 2021 I applied under a Freedom of Information request to the Department of Veterans' Affairs, laying out our case to access Vivian's medical and service records, which Barlow had helped Lynette and me to identify.

The response I got was that these files were now in the 'Open Access' period under the Archives Act. So I reapplied under the act in June, hoping that the process was about to get a lot easier but still aware that authorities might decide to redact some parts.

We to-ed and fro-ed via email, the reference officer and I. The officer apologised that this was a lengthy process: that the files were held in both Sydney and Canberra – with a couple on internal computer systems, which couldn't easily be trans-ferred. Also, due to COVID, the research centres were closed (like everything else) and staff were working from home, which meant they couldn't physically get in to 'access examine' these files (access examination is to ensure information that needs continuing protection under the Archives Act isn't released). I had been looking into this for so long – what was a few extra months.

Eventually, just before Christmas, he rang me and said that I was going to be given full access via links to download the files without any information being withheld. I couldn't believe it.

Barbara Barlow, Lynette and I started to work our way through the hundreds of pages of files. Lynette was laser-like and could pinpoint relevant details among masses of pages of medical notes. And Barlow had experience and departmental knowledge.

There were things in Vivian's medical files that, though not conclusive, pointed to her having been raped. In her army medical record, called her 'Hospital Or Sick List – Record Card', which was filled out post-war with Vivian providing the medical information and chronology to the medical officer herself, her periods, 'menses' as they are referred to, were described as 'regular till Feb 1942' – the same month the massacre occurred. She lost them that month and then had 'amenorrhoea till October 1942', when her periods started again.[116] That was eight months with no period. Though Vivian was in the camp by the end of February, she was not underweight at that point, so would have been unlikely to have lost her period for that reason.

After regaining her periods in October 1942, she then had them for twenty months, right up until June 1944, when her weight loss started and her periods stopped again – one assumes this time because of malnutrition. Her weight is recorded on 12 April 1944 as '9st 10 pds' (61.7 kilos), and then two months later, on 21 June, as '8 st 8 lbs' (54.4 kilos).

Likely she lost her periods in February 1942 through stress and trauma – known causes of amenorrhoea (functional hypothalamic amenorrhoea) – but it is possible that she could have been pregnant. Distressingly, too, Barlow said to us that she thought the cluster of symptoms Vivian reported having could indicate syphilis: 'furuncles of thigh and tinea of feet', 'tonsilitis', 'tinea of hands', 'gland in left groin … enlarged and painful', 'tropical fever', 'hair came out in handfuls and bald in one spot'.

I felt a familiar sense of dread. My god, I thought, Vivian, was it so much worse for you than we ever imagined? Was this one of the things you referred to that you and the other women never spoke of?

Trawling through these files I was conflicted again: would it be more merciful to let relatives who wanted to remember the nurses with their 'heads held high walking into the water' live with the comfort of partial, more palatable truths? The mythologised version. I was angry, too, that Vivian's medical records were our only portal to understanding what had happened to our relatives and allowing us to bear witness generations later. It was a war crime, I told myself, as I tried to distance myself from the heartbreaking nature of these personal records. We must have an accurate depiction of what actually happened: historical accountability. I held in mind all women who had been raped or kept as sexual military slaves as a weapon of war, not only by Japanese Imperial forces in the Second World War but also in multiple conflicts throughout history; including of course the devastating Frontier Wars in Australia. Right about this time reports of Ukrainian women abused by Russian soldiers were starting to filter in.

Lynette sent the files with Vivian's name redacted to Professor David Lewis, a professor of sexual health at the University of Sydney. He wrote a long email in response to the inquiry as to whether the woman in these files could have had secondary and tertiary syphilis. He said it was impossible to 'diagnose syphilis with certainty on clinical symptoms alone' (that would require a blood test). He thought it was 'quite possible that a fungal foot infection would be the more likely diagnosis than secondary syphilis'. But he agreed with Barlow that 'the presence of "furuncles of the thigh and tinea of the foot" ... could be compatible symptoms for secondary syphilis'. In considering the absence of Vivian's periods for eight months, he thought that was most likely stress-related.

For another opinion Lynette had contacted retired Professor John Hilton (who had previously conducted the forensic work on the bullet holes in Vivian's uniform with Barbara Angell). Professor Hilton told Lynette that symptoms of syphilis were certainly there in Vivian's notes, but as the disease is the great pretender and she was in a tropical place, and there were also vitamin deficiency diseases, he would not be prepared to state that she definitely had secondary syphilis, although it seemed entirely possible.

So if Vivian had been pregnant, could she have had a miscarriage brought on by secondary syphilis? Lewis agreed that if she had been suffering syphilis, there would have been a higher chance of miscarriage, but he also pointed out that any miscarriage could have been 'spontaneous and unrelated to any hypothetical syphilis infection'.

If Vivian did miscarry it would have most likely been when she was hospitalised in the camp hospital in Palembang. She had two hospital stays; the first for almost three weeks: 28 May–22 June ('tinea of feet'). The second for nine days: 17–26 July ('feet').[117] The nuns who ran the Caritas convent hospital would surely have helped her keep it a secret. Vivian would have been in grave danger if it had ever come out that she had survived the massacre.

When I accessed these files, I'd envisaged a clinical note that might confirm the rape, but not all this devastating detail. Barlow told Lynette and me that some files were missing. She identified them as the Pension, Entitlement, Central Office and Hospital files. She said that the one file definitely under lock and key when she worked at the Repatriation Department was the Entitlement file. It was kept in Deputy Commissioner Conde's safe. Presumably this file had something more obvious written on it than anything that existed in the medical files to warrant it being locked away.

I wrote again to the Department of Veterans' Affairs, specifically requesting these files under FOI. In a formal decision letter, dated 4 May 2022, I received the following response:

> After consultation with the Information and Records
> Management Section, I am confident that the Department does
> not hold any further material relating to the late Mrs Vivian
> Statham (nee Bullwinkel). That has not already been provided
> to the NAA.

I can only assume these files no longer exist. That they have been disposed of.

*

I wrote to the Japanese embassy on behalf of the Friends of Bangka Island – as we were now calling ourselves – and conveyed that we would like to work towards Japanese representation for the upcoming eightieth-anniversary memorial service. We invited a representative from the embassy to come on a reconnaissance trip for the seventy-eighth anniversary in 2020 and Mr Takonai Susumu from the embassy of Japan in Indonesia was nominated to attend. But at the last minute I was unable to go: one of my daughters was unwell and starting her last year of school. I stayed with her. As well as being a senior diplomat, Mr Takonai was a historian and a gracious man. Judy and Arlene looked after him as he did not know anyone, and was (I think) brave to go. He and Gary Quinlan, the Australian ambassador to Indonesia, planted a tree of peace. Judy sent me a photo of them standing side by side. Clearly, he was moved by what he had now witnessed.

It was a step.

Ultimately it is an acknowledgement that we seek.

Very shortly after the seventy-eighth anniversary, COVID hit. By February 2022 the pandemic was still affecting international travel enough that we organised for the eightieth-anniversary memorial service to be transmitted via Zoom rather than with us all there on the beach. Like so many things during the COVID years, our plans were diminished.

Yuki Tanaka, whom through a piece of happenstance I had now befriended – he is the next-door neighbour of one of my clients – played a piece at the Zoom service on his *shakuhachi* (bamboo flute). The haunting strains traversed the screen. Yuki said he plays this piece to appease the souls of the victims of Japanese atrocities during the Second World War.

Cheshunt, Victoria

March 2021

I'd wanted to visit Cheshunt since first being drawn into Bud's story. I'd intended to go in January 2020, but there were bush-fires burning fiercely. I postponed to September 2020 but, due to COVID, we weren't allowed to leave our 5-kilometre zone. I moved the trip to February 2021, it was all booked with Sally, but then she telephoned to say she couldn't come – she and Clive were moving into a retirement home.

'It's okay, I understand,' I said, deleting the dates from my calendar with a click of resignation. The window of her and Clive's mobility had been closing and I hadn't squeezed through.

Instead, I visited Cheshunt with Kingsley to see where Bud was from. It was also our anniversary – 'We'll make a weekend of it,' we said, 'stay a night at the art deco hotel in Corowa.'

*

Stringybarks lined the winding road as we drove past farms where cows and sheep ambled. Occasionally we passed a Hilux ute. I let the window down, felt the cold wind ping my face – the fresh air of possibility. The hamlet of Cheshunt – population 213, according to the 2021 census – sits on the flood plain in the upper King Valley. State forest to the west, Black Ranges to the east, and Wobonga Plateau and the Alpine National Park to the south. Floods were common, Dad and Sally said, the water used to come right up to the step of Willow Cottage. What were once mixed farms – Dadee was a tobacco farmer who kept cattle as well – were now wineries with Italian names: Pizzini, Dal Zotto, Francesco and Ciccone; I mouthed their pleasing sounds. Tobacco kilns like tall corrugated sheds studded the landscape. No longer in use, they had been worked into accommodation for gastro-tourists who came on the weekends. Shadows on the alpine foothills danced in front of me through the windscreen and patches of light wove a tapestry of tonal green.

'Slow down,' I snapped at Kingsley – clearly I was on edge – as we approached, with the map that Sally had drawn in hand, checking and rechecking it with the landscape. We crossed two tributaries of the King River, my anticipation rising. After the third crossing, of the King River itself, there was a house on the right which, if x marked the spot correctly on Sally's map, should be Willow Cottage. This was the house that Jean and Dolly had built, that Mummum and Dadee had moved into when Bud had gone to the war. Where she sent all her letters. The Willows, their first house and farm in Cheshunt, had burnt down in the 1939 bushfires.

I sat up, pressed my face forward to the window, fogged it up a little.

'That's it, I reckon.' I could just make out a weatherboard two-storey through the trees that shrouded the house. As we pulled over on the side of the wet dirt road full of puddles, a white ute passed too close and sprayed the car.

'Dickhead,' said Kingsley.

I got out, smelt the damp, decomposing soil. It was fertile up here beside the King River. Soil of sandy loam and river silt, where camellia trees shot up high. An acorn dropped on the roof of the car with a clonk. Was that from *the* oak tree, I wondered – there were a few around me. There was an old oak Dad and Sally told me about, that Jean and Dolly planted, and two willows by the river. No willows here now, and as we approached I was thrown when the sign on the house read 'Old Bridge House'. Still, I was fairly certain it was Willow Cottage. Mesmerised by the house, we walked closer. A plaque beside a big oak tree to the right of the gate was inscribed 'Quercus Robur (English Oak) circa 1920 significant tree 2020'. Must be it. I pulled big metal gates open and an English pointer came to welcome us, placing a paw on my leg. The off-white weatherboard in front of me didn't look particularly old, and as my eyes darted around it was hard to tell where the front door was. Finding the closest door, I knocked.

'Hello.' I called out hopefully. 'Helloooo.'

Silence. I frowned. This wasn't what I'd imagined. Opening a small note book, I ripped out a page and scrawled my phone number, explaining that my great-grandparents used to live here.

'We are staying at the Whitfield Pub until tomorrow, when we go to Corowa. Would love to see the house, if it's not inconvenient.'

'Let's just check around the back,' I said to Kingsley.

We crunched over gravel, through a well-tended garden, to the stables. The dog trailed us without a bark. A Range Rover and Discovery were parked, and we could see a man with grey curls wearing a striped blue shirt and jeans tinkering in the garage.

'Hello,' I said, trying to sound like someone you would invite in.

A woman strode out from the depths of the garage. Lean, with short, grey hair and thoroughbred energy, she introduced herself as Ginny.

'My great-grandparents used to live here,' I explained, 'the Elmes.'

Ginny looked us over. By this stage the man had emerged from the garage. He introduced himself as Chris. He had an earthier energy, quieter, drier.

'You've met my Aunt Sally before, showed her around ... My great-aunt Bud was the one who was killed in the war.'

'Ah yes ... I remember,' Ginny warmed up. 'Would you like to come in?'

I spun on the gravel and heard my boots squeak.

I stepped inside through the back door and paused. My eyes adjusted to the filtered light. Willow Cottage wrapped around me with its warmth and wooden cabinetry, its colours that calmed. I inhaled. Ginny, previously an architect, had pulled the threads together like a master weaver to create this late Edwardian, French country, post-Depression cottage. Above me a skylight had been cut into the low kitchen ceiling, and as I went upstairs behind her, my eyes soared up through big panes of glass to the oaks, gums and dogwood towering above. I stood and stared.

Though the house was still modest-ish – conditions were basic, Dad and Sally said – it had been rebirthed with a second storey. The old incorporated into the new. Floorboards and a chimney were the obvious remnants of the original. If I was here alone I would place my head against the chimney, lie down on the wooden floorboards beside the hearth, and let the house cradle me. Or just sit and settle, attune my breath. Turn my ear to the stories of the house. Creep upstairs and be awed by the swaying canopy, the symphony of green. Watch the river flow, its cold, clean water twist, turn and tumble.

Downstairs, Chris made us a coffee and we chatted at the kitchen table where an open-spined Margaret Atwood book lay. Grim, he said. Mummum and Dadee would have sat here at their kitchen table too. Opened breezy letters and packaged trinkets from Bud, stamped Malaya and Singapore. Lined up the trinkets on a shelf – like the shelf I could see above the hearth: the brass woven basket with four glass bottles, the tiny bronze Buddha. Until one day the telegrams started, delivered from the exchange nearby, perhaps slid under the door in the corner of this room, or handed over solemnly. Then the grieving began too. Sobs and wails were now embedded in these walls, underneath the carefully chosen paint.

But there were other memories.

Back outside in the garden, I looked across the river to the flat plain on the other side, hugged by foothills. 'What happened to the willows?' I asked. Dad said there were two weeping willows down by the riverbank, and another, a large osier, in the backyard.

'They've been taking them out,' Chris said. 'They disrupt the flow of the river.'

Willow Cottage without the willows. It dinted the ideal. 'Shame.' But if they were changing the course of the river …

'Their first property must've been over there somewhere.' I pointed to where Dad had described his memory of its location. Pictured Bud roaming that land, Bid, their English setter, trailing her in this Eden; her physical prowess, her long striding walk – though she was decidedly awkward in anything but flats, Smithy had told Sally later in life.

Was it here Bud tasted her first lick of adventure, the freedom the landscape afforded hinting at more, at beyond? I could feel the pull too. Wanted to propel myself into the wide expanse, whirl through the trees, screech like a cockatoo. Lie myself down in the cold, clear river where Bud learnt to swim, and let it carry me downstream. Wash and wring me out, like a drip-dry cycle.

Bud travelled north to Corowa aged twenty-one to be trained as a nurse. Then the call of duty came – she was very keen to sign up for active service, Smithy had said. Appointed to the Australian Army Nursing Service in November 1940, Lieutenant Elmes departed Sydney Harbour on the *Queen Mary*, on 4 February 1941, as the band played 'Auld Lang Syne' and 'The Maori Farewell'. She did not know her destination.

*

We wandered up to Cheshunt Hall, a building of white weatherboard with a slaty-green trim, its tin roof stained with age. Plonked right out the front, marring the vista, was a large generator mounted on a concrete platform.

Two claret ashes were planted to the side of the hall, memorial trees with plaques to dedicate them:

Ash trees
planted in the
hall centenary year of 1995
in memory of
Dorothy Elmes and Caroline Ennis
who gave their lives during World War 2

Two of the sixty-five *Vyner Brooke* nurses were from Cheshunt? I hadn't known that. But afterwards I found out more about Caroline Ennis: she was born in Swan Hill, Victoria, and when she was about nine her widowed mother remarried Joseph Graham of Cheshunt. Caroline was last seen floating out to sea on a raft, cradling two small children with Matron Paschke.

An urge to scatter soil or sand from Radji Beach came over me, though I didn't have any, and Parks Victoria would not have thanked me. If I'd been able to, I would have knelt down, grabbed a handful of topsoil from the base of the claret ash, and blended the sand and soil one with the other. Tilting my head back, I looked up at Bud's tree. Its leaves had shot way above the hall and had turned to autumn colours.

*

That night at the Whitfield Pub, dehydrated from the Pizzini nebbiolo we had drunk with dinner, I dreamt of bushrangers. Harry Powers and Ned Kelly had staged hold-ups nearby. Earlier in the day we had visited Powers Lookout and passed flocks of king parrots and a dead black snake with its guts splayed open on the road. The Elmes family had picnicked at this spot where Harry, Ned's mentor, surveyed the district. Holed up in his bush camp, police captured him asleep on an inclement morning when the usual dog-bark-warnings could not be heard. The year was 1870.

About two a.m. I woke up, sat up, drank some water, lay back down, sat up again.

'I have to go back to Willow Cottage.'

'What?' Kingsley startled and turned over.

'Sorry … didn't mean to wake you … tell you in the morning.'

'I'm awake now,' he replied, grumpy.

'I have to go back to Willow Cottage.'

'Why?'

'Don't know … something …'

'Okay,' he said, touched my shoulder gently and went back to sleep.

Kingsley sat in the car outside – he wanted to keep things moving. We were due soon at Corowa Hospital, where Bud had nursed with her 'old hounds', and had labelled her patients' special delicacies that she stored in the fridge for them, 'Dogs' meat. Do not touch.'

In the morning dew, I approached Willow Cottage and looked up at the giant oak – the 'significant tree' that Jean and Dolly had planted. I knelt down out the front where its boughs draped over the fence, and placed my hands on layers of composting leaves. Light refracted through the branches, bent and changed directions till it came to rest. A kookaburra flew laughing in the wan sun of autumn.

This should have been Bud's final resting place. I stood up and scratched around with my foot, searching for an acorn. 'Has to be from this tree.' I discarded one that had fallen from another oak nearby.

'We've already got an oak tree,' Kingsley said, still sitting in the car idling beside the nature strip, 'at Kyneton. Plenty of acorns.'

'It's not the same,' I protested. My unfocused eyes saw only piles of fallen leaves. I brushed them with my boot. 'Can't find one. Can you help me?'

Kingsley got out of the car and searched the ground methodically. 'Here,' he said and handed me two.

I held out my palms. Smooth and round with tough, chestnut-coloured outers, my fingers closed around them. 'We can try to propagate them.' What were the chances? I could hardly bear the thought of it not working.

As I turned my back to Willow Cottage and walked towards the car, I knew I would never stop trying – to get information out, to get an acknowledgement and work with the families of those impacted by these terrible events to make a mark in history. But I also knew that I was leaving lighter. That different conversations in our family had opened up and that some of the grief handed to me, as Sally put it, was staying here. Piled up with the rocks on the river bank, draining back into the gurgling King River, thrown out into the flood plain, and laid down beside the old oak tree, the seedlings of which my daughters will one day, hopefully, tell their grandchildren about.

And I could picture Bud roaming the landscape, her physical prowess, her long striding walk.

The Walk for Humanity

These words have been written by the Friends of Bangka Island and are read before every Walk for Humanity on Bangka Island.

On 16 February 2017, when many people from many countries, including Indonesia, gathered on this beach to mark the seventy-fifth anniversary of the Radji Beach massacre, twenty-two modern day Australian Army nurses joined hands and spontaneously walked into the water in a moving re-enactment of the Australian nurses walking to their death all those years ago.

This act, as well as the generosity of local Indonesian doctors and nurses who came to conduct their own memorial service, inspired us, the relatives of those who died here, to enshrine the Walk for Humanity as part of every commemorative event on this beach.

The Walk for Humanity stands 'for life', just as the motto

of the modern-day Australian Army nurses, 'Pro humanitate', declares. It stands for unity, our common humanity binding us beyond race, religion, country or culture. The walk breaks down barriers and builds goodwill and understanding between people.

The Walk for Humanity also honours the many wonderful people from around Muntok and Bangka Island who experienced great suffering during World War II; and the thousands of military personnel and civilians from many countries who died on and around Muntok and Bangka Island while escaping from Singapore in 1942.

It is said that the beaches around Muntok and the Bangka Straits were just one mass grave.

Above all, the walk today is an act of positive defiance. It says that we, the relatives and our friends who will join us, stand here today and say, 'Brutality will not have the last word on Radji Beach.'

Let us now all come to the beach, join hands and walk to the water; remembering all those who suffered so terribly around these waters and on Bangka Island in 1942.

Postscript

In February 2023, in the process of fact checking for an article journalist Ellen Fanning was writing for the ABC, Lynette Silver called a retired army officer, Major Patricia Hincks, with whom she had previously been in contact after the publication of *Angels of Mercy*. Hincks had briefly met Vivian at the officers mess in Fremantle's Leeuwin Barracks in 1991 ahead of the publication of Vivian's biography, *Bullwinkel*, by former army officer Norman Manners. Hincks had asked Vivian how her book was going and, Hincks said, Vivian responded by saying that she was having a dispute with some of its wording because she wanted to make sure her story was told truthfully with all the facts. Hincks said Vivian told her that Manners did not want to publish the whole truth about the massacre, on the basis that it would upset the relatives of the murdered nurses. Hincks subsequently said that Vivian told her that Manners wanted to 'flower it up', and that the truth was too political. Hincks could sense that Vivian was upset.

It was another confirmation that Vivian had wanted to speak up about exactly how the nurses had suffered. But Hincks had more to say. Lynette asked if I was sitting down.

Apparently, Vivian had gone on to tell the major, 'We weren't made to walk into the sea. We were tortured and raped. We were then marched out to sea and shot.'

I was immobilised on the other end of the phone. Had I heard correctly?

Later, Ellen Fanning also got hold of the series of taped interviews that Manners had conducted with Vivian as research for *Bullwinkel*, but the tapes do not have a record of any of these conversations.

What Vivian told Hincks fitted with Tanemura's statement in his reinterrogation about 'hearing screams coming from nearby houses', and what Weston had said to Lynette: 'There are some things [*plural*] about that case which I had to keep secret and cannot talk about.' Also, it quite possibly explains why the report by Jean Williams, the wife of war crimes investigator Major Harold Williams from 2 AWCS, had five centimetres cut off the top.

Was this now the whole brutal account? Taken out of the box of discarded and unpalatable historical truths. Twenty-two nurses have spoken through one, who felt that 'she had been allowed to live so that she could be a messenger'.

I wanted to look away, it was so desperately sad, but I also felt that finally their full experience had been told. I hoped this was the end of it.

Appendix

There were, of course, many others who made it ashore to Bangka Island from the *Vyner Brooke* but managed to avoid the massacre. So what was their fate?

The party we met in Part One, who walked off the beach, including women and children, were taken to prisoner-of-war camps, first in Muntok and then in Sumatra. Izzy Warman (who was three at the time) is still alive at the time of publication. Mrs Warman died in Muntok from an abscess of the lung or pneumonia a couple of weeks after the group handed themselves in.

Captain 'Tubby' Borton (Lieutenant Richard Edward Borton, RNR) made it to land and was interned in Muntok, then Palembang and finally transferred to Changi. He survived the war.

Mrs Annabelle Bull had three children with her on the *Vyner Brooke* – Hazel, Molly and Robin. When the ship sank, she was separated from Molly and Robin. She thought they were dead. She and Hazel were interned in the POW camps in Muntok and Sumatra. After the war they were reunited with Molly and Robin, who had been picked up by a raft and taken to Java.

The sixty-five nurses who were on the *Vyner Brooke* when it was bombed suffered different fates. Schuey, Marjorie Schuman, perished after the ship sank and there are no known reports of how she died. Matron Olive Dorothy Paschke died after the sinking, too – she was last seen floating out to sea on a raft. Mary Clarke, Betty Jeffrey, Iole Harper and Gladys McDonald were also seen on the raft with Caroline Ennis and Matron Paschke. Hilda 'Millie' Dorsch and Annie Merle Trenerry were alongside in the water hanging on to trailing ropes. The bodies of Sister McDonald and two other unidentified nurses were found on a raft in the Indian Ocean a few weeks later. Iole Harper got separated from the raft, made it ashore to Bangka Island with Betty Jeffrey and they became prisoners-of-war. It is uncertain what happened to the others. It is possible some may have come ashore and been executed. Sister Dorsch's identity disc was found on the beach by Ralph Armstrong's mother. Most likely it would have been ripped or cut off to have become separated from her uniform.

Those who were killed during the bombing or after the sinking were:

Louvima Mary Bates
Ellenor Calnan
Mary Dorothea Clarke

Millicent Hilda Marie Dorsch
Caroline Mary Ennis
Kathleen Kinsella
Gladys Myrtle McDonald
Matron Olive Dorothy Paschke
Lavinia Jean Russell
Marjorie Schuman
Annie Merle Trenerry
Mona Margaret Wilton

Other nurses who survived captivity in various prisoner-of-war camps in the Dutch East Indies were:

Carrie Jean Ashton
Kathleen Constance Blake
Jessie Jane Blanch
Vivian Bullwinkel
Veronica Ann Clancy
Cecilia May Delforce
Jess Gregory Doyle
Jean Keers Greer
Janet Patteson Gunther
Ellen Mavis Hannah
Iole Harper
Nesta Gwyneth James
Agnes Bettina Jeffrey
Violet Irene McElna

Sylvia Jessie Mimmi Muir
Wilma Elizabeth Forster Oram
Christian Sarah Mary Oxley
Eileen Mary Short
Jessie Elizabeth Simons
Valerie Elizabeth Smith
Ada Corbitt Syer
Florence Elizabeth Trotter
Joyce Tweddell
Beryl Woodbridge

In the first four months of 1945, four nurses died in the prisoner-of-war camp in Muntok, Bangka Island:

Dora Shirley Gardam
Pauline Blanche Hempsted
Wilhelmina Rosalie Raymont
Irene Ada Singleton

Between May and August 1945, four nurses died in the prisoner-of-war camps in Belalau, Loeboek Linggau, Sumatra:

Winnie May Davis
Rubina Dorothy Freeman
Gladys Laura Hughes
Pearl Beatrice Mittelheuser

Notes

PART ONE

1   Gurvich, Victoria, 'Old letters unearth a nursing wartime hero', *The Age*, 1 January 1996, p. 2.

2   Angell, Barbara, *A Woman's War*, New Holland, Sydney, 2005, pp. 131, 147.

3   The names and numbers of nurses in each category are from Manners, Norman, *Bullwinkel*, Hesperian Press, Western Australia, 1999, pp. 225–6.

4   Adam-Smith, Patsy, *Prisoners of War*, Penguin, Victoria, 1992, p. 461.

5   Darling (nee Gunther), Patteson, Janet, *Portrait of a Nurse*, Don Wall, New South Wales, 2001, p. 81.

6   Tebbutt was the Australian liaison officer for the Far East Combined Bureau (FECB). Silver, Lynette, *Angels of Mercy*, Sally Milner Publishing Pty Ltd, New South Wales, 2019, p. 225.

7   Simons, Jessie Elizabeth, *While History Passed*, William Heinemann, Melbourne, 1954, p. 111.

8   Shaw, Ian, *On Radji Beach*, Pan Macmillan, Sydney, 2010, pp. 289–90.

PART TWO

1   Bullwinkel, Vivian, Board of Inquiry Sworn Statement, NAA: MP742/1, 336/1/1976, Part 5, 29 October 1945, p. 4.

2   Smyth, Sir John, *The Will to Live*, Cassell, London, 1970, p. 59.

3   Noyce, Michael, 'The First Ever Commemorative Service at Radji Beach', Muntok Nurses and Internees Facebook page; facebook.com/983774011682886/videos/1298673700192914, accessed 10 November 2022.

4   Convention for the Amelioration of the Condition of the Wounded and Sick in Armies in the Field, Geneva, 27 July 1929, Chapter III: personnel – Article 9.

5   Manners, Norman, *Bullwinkel*, Hesperian Press, Western Australia, 1999, p. 80.

6   Lawrence, Tess, 'Vivian Bullwinkel, the Bangka Island Massacre and the Guilt of the Survivor', *Independent Australia*, 19 February 2017.

7   Shaw, Ian, *On Radji Beach*, Pan Macmillan, Sydney, 2010, p. 321.

8   Letter from Frank Statham to Sally Alsop, 5 March 1996, Banks personal archives.

9   Abjorensen, Norman, 'Murdered nurses were probably raped by Japanese officers, says academic', *Canberra Times*, 22 September 1993.

10 Tanaka, Yuki, *Hidden Horrors*, Rowman & Littlefield, Maryland, 2018, p. 96.

11 MacKay, James, *Betrayal in High Places*, Tasman Archives, Auckland, 1996, p. x.

12 Ibid., p. 242.

13 'Bullwinkel, Vivian, Direct Examination, International Military Tribunal for the Far East', NAA: MP742/1, 336/1/1976, Part 4, 20 December 1946, pp. 13, 457.

14 Captain Godwin, J. G., and Sergeant Weston, A. H., 'War crimes – Weekly reports of investigations by 2 Australian War Crimes Section: Reports of investigation', NAA: MP742/1, 336/1/1965, Parts 4 & 11.

15 Hadley, Gregory and Oglethorpe, James, 'McKay's' Betrayal', *Journal of Military History*, 71, April 2007.

16 Angell, Barbara, 'Appendix B, A Hypothesis, Concerning the Bangka Island Massacres', Vivian Bullwinkel, Angell Productions, 24 September 2016; angellpro.com.au/bullwinkel.htm, accessed 22 February 2017.

This website is no longer in use by Angell. The National Library of Australia has archived it. A copy of the content of an earlier version, 9 April 2008, which contains Appendix B, is in the Banks personal archives.

17   Ibid.

18   Simons, Jessie Elizabeth, *While History Passed*, William Heinemann, Melbourne, 1954, preface, p. ix.

19   Adam-Smith, Patsy, *Prisoners of War*, Viking, Melbourne, 1992, p. 456.

20   Bullwinkel, Direct Examination, pp. 13, 458.

21   Manners, *Bullwinkel*, p. 84.

22   Lloyd, Ernest Alexander, Statement, NAA:MP742/1, 336/1/1976, Part 2.

23   Wilding, William Dick, Statement, NAA:MP742/1, 336/1/1976, Part 2.

24   Smyth, *The Will to Live*, p. 59.

25   Ibid.

26   Lloyd, Statement, NAA:MP742/1, 336/1/1976, Part 2.

27   Germann, Eric, Affidavit, NAA: MP742/1, 336/1/1976, Part 5.

28   Wilding, Statement, NAA:MP742/1, 336/1/1976, Part 2.

29   War crimes – Banka [*sic*] Island – Massacre of 21 Australian nurses and murder of Australian trade commissioner Mr Bowden, NAA: MP742/1, 336/1/1976, Part 2.

30   Balcombe, Judy, *The Evacuation of Singapore to the Prison Camps of Sumatra*, Pen and Sword Books, Barnsley, 2023.

31   Hamilton, Thomas, *Soldier Surgeon in Malaya*, Angus & Robertson, Sydney, 1957, p. 216.

32   40 Australian War Graves Unit, 'Report on Recce of Bangka and surrounding Islands: Bangka Island 5.', NAA:MP742/1, 336/1/1976, Part 5.

33   Smyth, *The Will to Live*, pp. 57–60.

34   Mukwege, Denis, Nobel Lecture, Nobel Peace Prize 2018; nobelprize. org/prizes/peace/2018/mukwege/lecture/, accessed 20 November 2022.

35   Ibid.

36   Murad, Nadia, Press Release, Nobel Peace Prize 2018; nobelprize.org/ prizes/peace/2018/press-release, accessed 20 November 2022.

37   Murad, Nadia, Nobel Lecture, Nobel Peace Prize 2018; nobelprize.org/ prizes/peace/2018/murad/lecture/, accessed 20 November 2022.

38 Tanaka, Yuki, Introduction in Henson, Maria Rosa, *Comfort Woman*, Rowman & Littlefield, Maryland, 2017, pp. xi–xiv.

39 Yoshimi, Yoshiaki, *Comfort Women*, Columbia University Press, New York City, 2002, p. 29.

40 Kim, Jimin; Milner Bisland, Beverly; Shin, Sunghee, 'Teaching about the Comfort Women during World War II and the Use of Personal Stories of the Victims', Education about ASIA, vol. 24, no. 3, 2019, p. 58.

41 Angell, Barbara, *A Woman's War*, New Holland, Sydney, 2005, p. 49.

42 Armstrong, Ralph E. H., *Short Cruise on the* Vyner Brooke, George Mann, Kent, 2003, pp. 53–4.

43 Hannah, Mavis, interviewed by Amy McGrath, transcript of oral history recording: TAPE NO.TRC 1087/1, National Library of Australia, 13 July 1981, p. 19; catalogue.nla.gov.au/Record/2205092.

44 Fakhrizal, Abubakar, interview with Mr Idris about Old Kampong Menjelang and Second World War Tragedy, 10 March 2018, copy in Banks personal archives.

45 *Weekly Times* (Melbourne), 19 September 1945, p. 5.

46 *Adelaide Advertiser*, 18 September 1945, p. 5.

47 Manners, *Bullwinkel*, p. 82.

48 'Bombing of Darwin: 70 years on', ABC (online), 17 February 2012.

49 Smith, Emily, 'Shinzo Abe arrives in Darwin for first visit by Japanese leader', ABC (online), 16 November 2018.

50 Pether, Michael, 'The Broad Perspective: An overview of the events that lead to the sinking or beaching of the ships listed below and the aftermath', February 2023, Muntok Peace Museum; muntokpeacemuseum.org.

51 Neiman, Susan, *Learning from the Germans*, Allen Lane, London, 2019, pp. 7–8.

52 Yamazaki, Dr James N., 'Hiroshima and Nagasaki Death Toll', *Children of the Atomic Bomb*; aasc.ucla.edu/cab/200708230009.html, accessed 15 October 2021.

53 Headquarters, Allied Land Forces South East Asia, Letter of Silence, Liberation Ataka Pamphlet, Section 1; fepow.family/Research/Liberation/Pamphlets/Ataka/html/letter_of_silence.htm

54 Kenny, Catherine, *Captives*, University of Queensland Press, St Lucia, Queensland, 1986, pp. xii–xiii.

55 Abjorensen, Norman, 'Biting the Lip on War Crime', *Canberra Times*, 23 September 1995, p. 44.

56 Tanaka, *Hidden Horrors*, p. 120.

57 Twomey, Christina, 'Australian Nurse POW's Gender, War and Captivity,' *Australian Historical Studies*, 36:124, 255–274, DOI 10.1080/10314610408596288, 2004.

58 Letter from Eva C. Macknight to Vivian Bullwinkel, 5 November 1945, AWM PR01216 item 2/4, Bullwinkel, Vivian, Correspondence, November–December 1945.

59 Tebbutt, Major W. A, 'Report by Major Tebbutt', AIF, Evacuation from Singapore and massacre of members of Aust. Nursing Service and others, NAA:MP742/1, 336/1/1976, Part 2, pp. 1, 4.

60 Letter from John Henry Neuss to Vivian Bullwinkel, November 1945, AWM PR01216 item 2/4, Bullwinkel, Vivian, Correspondence, November–December 1945.

61 Letter from Eva C. Macknight to Vivian Bullwinkel, 22 December 1945, AWM PR01216 item 2/4, Bullwinkel, Vivian, Correspondence, November–December 1945.

62 Bullwinkel, *Sworn Statement*, NAA:MP742/1, 336/1/1976, Part 5, p. 4. Vivian also said that Matron Drummond, Sister F. R. Casson and Sister R. J. Wight were killed before they reached the water's edge (Angel, *A Woman's War*, p. 65).

63 'Sister Was Left For Dead On the Beach,' *Sydney Morning Herald*, 18 September 1945, p. 3.

64 Seddon, Robert, Statement, NAA:MP742/1, 336/1/1976, Part 2.

65 Wilding, Statement, ibid.

66 Lloyd, Statement, ibid.

67 Smyth, *The Will to Live*, p. 59.

68 Jacobs organised the prisoners at Palembang into panels to collect information about war crimes and this account by Stoker Lloyd was one of them; Jacobs, G. F., *Prelude to the Monsoon*, University of Pennsylvania Press, Philadelphia, 1982, pp. 130–31.

69 McDougall Jr, William H., *By Eastern Windows*, Charles Scribner & Sons, New York, 1949, p. 152.

70 *Argus*, 28 July 1956, p. 9.

71 Richardson, Hal, 'The Japanese leopard with unchanging spots.', *Sun*, 8 September 1946.

72 Butler, Janet, 'Report on Searches', unpublished, December 2020, Banks personal archives.

73 Richardson, Hal, *Into the Fire*, Benchmark Design, Canberra, 2000, p. 70.

74 40 Australian War Graves Unit, 'Report on Recce of Bangka and surrounding Islands', NAA:MP742/1, 336/1/1976, Part 5.

75 'Nurses Return to Bangka Island: Memorial to comrades dedicated in Indonesia', Vetaffairs, Department of Veterans' Affairs, March 1993, p. 3; Silver, Lynette Ramsay, *Angels of Mercy*, Sally Milner, NSW, 2019, p. 364.

76 Shaw, *On Radji Beach*, p. 202.

77 Bullwinkel, Sworn Statement, NAA:MP742/1, 336/1/1976, Part 5, p. 2.

78 McDougall, *By Eastern Windows*, p. 145.

79 Ibid., p. 144.

80 Ibid., p. 147.

81 Bullwinkel, Sworn Statement, NAA: MP742/1, 336/1/1976, Part 5, p. 4.

82 McDougall, *By Eastern Windows*, p. 148.

83 Smyth, *The Will to Live*, p. 58.

84 Shaw, *On Radji Beach*, p. 205.

85 Manners, Bullwinkel, p. 84.

86 Bullwinkel, Sworn Statement, NAA:MP742/1, 336/1/1976, Part 5, p. 5.

87 Shaw, *On Radji Beach*, p. 205.

88 McDougall, *By Eastern Windows*, p. 145.

89 40 Australian War Graves Unit, 'Report on Recce of Bangka and surrounding Islands', NAA:MP742/1, 336/1/1976, Part 5.

90 Ibid.

91 Bullwinkel, Sworn Statement, NAA:MP742/1, 336/1/1976, Part 5, p. 4; Smyth, *The Will to Live*, p. 58.

92 Boss, Pauline, 'Speaking of Psychology: Ambiguous loss and the myth of closure', with Pauline Boss PhD, American Psychological Association; apa.org/news/podcasts/speaking-of-psychology/ambiguous-loss, accessed 21 January 2023.

93 Memorandum No. 510 for the Secretary, Department of External Affairs, Canberra, ACT, 'War Crimes Suspect a Suicide', from Patrick Shaw, Head of the Australian Mission in Japan, Tokyo, 13 September 1948, NAA:MP742/1, 336/1/1976, Part 1.

94 Information Concerning 229 INF RGT, Japanese Army and the murder of Australian nurses on Bangka Island collected and compiled by Capt. R. L. Watts, Appendix C, History of 229 INF RGT, NAA:MP742/1, 336/1/1976, Part 5.

95 Letter to Kent Hughes from the Minister of the Army, 3 February 1950, NAA:MP742/1, 336/1/1976, Part 1.

96 Tanaka, Yuki, Re-examination of the Massacre on Banka [*sic*] Island: A Case of Japanese Military Violence against Women; http://yjtanaka. blogspot.com/2021/09/re-examination-of-massacre-on-banka.html.

97 Summary of Examination of Paymaster Capt, Shibayama Sukezo, NAA:MP742/1, 336/1/1976, Part 5.

98 Bullwinkel, *Sworn Statement*, NAA:MP742/1, 336/1/1976, Part 5, p. 4.

99 Weston, Sergeant A.H., Weekly Investigation Reports, NAA: MP742/1, 336/1/1965, Part 11, week ending 20 January 1950.

100 Ibid.

101 Silver, *Angels of Mercy*, p. 251.

102 *Sun*, 'Net Draws in on Killers of Aust. Nurses', 29 August 1946, p. 3.

103 Weston, Weekly Investigation Reports, week ending 25 November 1949.

104 Morris, Narrelle, 'Japanese War Crimes in the Pacific: Australia's investigations and prosecutions, Appendix B: Index of accused Japanese war criminals by name', NAA: Research Guide, 2019, pp. 276–371.

105 Dower, John, in Tanaka, *Hidden Horrors*, p. xii.

106 Banka [*sic*] Island Atrocities, Orita, Masaru, NAA:MP742/1, 336/1/1976, Part 1.

107 Barlass, Tim, 'Australian nurse was ordered to keep war crimes secret', *The Age*, 8 April 2019.

108 Silver, *Angels of Mercy*, p. 361.

109 Barlass, 'Australian nurse was ordered to keep war crimes secret'.

110 Silver, *Angels of Mercy*, p. 356.

111 Ibid.

112 Ibid, p. 355.

113 Kenny, *Captives*, p. 21.

114 Majeed, Zaini, 'Ukraine's First Lady Demands Global Response to Alleged Sexual Crimes Committed During War', *Republic World*, 8 December 2022; republicworld.com/world-news/russia-ukraine-crisis/ukraine-first-lady-demands-global-response-to-alleged-sexual-crimes-committed-during-war-articleshow.html, accessed 18 January 2023.

115 Nunn, Gary, 'Bangka Island: The WW2 massacre and a truth too awful to speak', *BBC News*, 18 April 2019.

116 'Hospital or Sick List – Record Card', Army Medical Record of Vivian Statham (formerly Bullwinkel), World War II Army Service documents, NAA: A14472, VFX61330, clinical notes, pp. 1–3.

117 Ibid.

Bibliography

Most of the official documents I have used for my research are held in the National Archives of Australia (NAA) and the Australian War Memorial (AWM). Newspaper articles quoted in the text have, for the most part, been accessed via Trove. I have also used family papers, and a number of other sources. Our family papers are held in personal archives.

Family papers

I have included in the text letters and telegrams. Unless otherwise referenced in the endnotes, the letters from Sister Dorothy 'Bud' Gwendoline Howard Elmes to her family, telegrams associated with her death and whereabouts, and other letters between family members are held in our family's personal archives.

Other sources related to Bud

- Elmes, Dorothy Gwendoline Howard, Service Record, NAA: B883, NX70526.

- Elmes, Dorothy G., Service Documents, Department of Veterans Affairs: SD0251563.
- Letters from Sister Dorothy 'Bud' Gwendoline Howard Elmes, 1941–42, to her friend Jean Smithenbecker: AWM PR88/108.

Sources related to the *Vyner Brooke* nurses

The Australian War Memorial Research Centre contains a plethora of material related to the nurses. Many of the *Vyner Brooke* nurses (particularly those who survived captivity) are represented in these archives. Private Records (PR) can be anything of a personal nature – diaries, photos, momentos, letters, logbooks, medals. Manuscripts (MSS) can be a couple of pages or an entire manuscript. The most substantial collections are:

- PR 01216 Vivian Bullwinkel
- PR 01780 Betty Jeffrey

In the National Archives of Australia, the main series to consult for further information on the War Crimes Investigations related to the nurses are:

- NAA: MP 742/1, 336/1/1976, War Crimes – Banka [*sic*] Island – Massacre of 21 Australian Nurses and murder of Australian Trade Commissioner Mr Bowden.
- NAA: MP 742/1, 336/1/1965, War Crimes – Weekly Reports of Investigations by 2 Australian War Crimes Section.
- NAA: MP 742/1, 336/1/1289, Part 1, Affidavit File – Directorate of Prisoners of War and Internees – Investigation File Sumatra 1; Basic Documents relative to War Crimes.

- AWM 54 1010/6/128, War Crimes Investigations – Information concerning 229 Infantry Regiment, Japanese Army and murder of Australian Nurses on Banka [*sic*] Island, compiled by Captain R.L. Watts.

Books

Adam-Smith, Patsy, *Prisoners of War: From Gallipoli to Korea,* Viking, Melbourne, 1992.

—, *Australian Women at War,* Penguin, Melbourne, 1996.

Angell, Barbara, *A Woman's War: The Exceptional Life of Wilma Oram Young, AM,* New Holland, Sydney, 2005.

Armstrong, Ralph E. H., *Short Cruise on the* Vyner Brooke, George Mann Books, Kent, 2003.

Balcombe, Judy, *The Evacuation of Singapore to the Prison Camps of Sumatra,* Pen and Sword Books, Barnsley, 2023.

Bassett, Jan, *Guns and Brooches: Australian Army Nursing from the Boer War to the Gulf War,* Oxford University Press, Melbourne 1997.

Burchill, Elizabeth, *Australian Nurses Since Nightingale 1860–1990,* Spectrum Publications, Victoria, 1992.

Cohen, David and Totani, Yuma, *The Tokyo War Crimes Tribunal: Law, History and Jurisprudence,* Cambridge University Press, Cambridge, 2018.

Darling (née Gunther), Patteson, Janet, *Portrait of a Nurse: Prisoner of War of the Japanese 1942–1945,* Don Wall Publishing, Sydney, 2001.

Hamilton, Thomas, *Soldier Surgeon in Malaya,* Angus & Robertson, Sydney, 1957.

Henson, Maria Rosa, *Comfort Woman: A Filipina's Story of Prostitution and Slavery under the Japanese Military,* Rowman & Littlefield, Maryland, 2017.

Jacobs, Gideon Francois, *Prelude to the Monsoon: Assignment in Sumatra*, University of Pennsylvania Press, Philadelphia, 1982.

Jeffrey, Betty, *White Coolies,* Angus & Robertson, Sydney, 1954.

Kenny, Catherine, *Captives: Australian Army Nurses in Japanese Prison Camps,* University of Queensland Press, St Lucia, Queensland, 1986.

MacKay, James, *Betrayal in High Places,* Tasman Archives, Auckland, 1996.

Mann, Arthur John, *One Jump Ahead: Escape on the* Vyner Brooke, Harry Nicholson, Kindle Edition, 2020.

Manners, Norman, *Bullwinkel,* Hesperian Press, Perth, 1999.

McDougall, Jnr William, H., *By Eastern Windows: The Story of a Battle of Souls and Minds in the Prison Camps of Sumatra*, Charles Scribner's sons, New York, 1949.

Neiman, Susan, *Learning from the Germans: Confronting Race and the Memory of Evil,* Allen Lane, London, 2019.

Nelson, Hank, *Prisoners of War,* ABC Enterprises, Sydney, 1985.

Rees, Lawrence, *Horror in the East: Japan and the Atrocities of World War II,* BBC Books, London, 2001.

Richardson, Hal, *Into the Fire,* Benchmark Design, Canberra, 2000.

Ruff-O'Herne, Jan, *Fifty Years of Silence: The Extraordinary Memoir of a War Rape Survivor,* William Heinemann, Sydney, 2008.

Schwab, Gabrielle, *Haunting Legacies: Violent Histories and Trans-generational Trauma,* Columbia University Press, New York, 2010.

Shaw, Ian, W., *On Radji Beach: The Story of the Australian Nurses After the Fall of Singapore,* Pan Macmillan, Sydney, 2010.

Silver, Lynette Ramsay, *Angels of Mercy: Far West & Far East*, Sally Milner, New South Wales, 2019.

Simons, Jessie Elizabeth, *While History Passed,* William Heinemann, Melbourne, 1954; reprinted as *In Japanese Hands,* 1985.

Smyth, Sir John, *The Will to Live: The Story of Dame Margot Turner D.B.E., R.R.C.*, Cassell, London, 1970.

Tanaka, Yuki, *Hidden Horrors: Japanese War Crimes in World War II*, Rowman & Littlefield, Maryland, 2018.

Twomey, Christina, *Australia's Forgotten Prisoners*, Cambridge University Press, Melbourne, 2007.

Volf, Miroslav, *The End of Memory: Remembering Rightly in a Violent World*, William B. Eerdmans Publishing, Michigan, 2006.

Walker, Allan Seymour, *Medical Services of the Royal Australian Navy and Royal Australian Air Force with a Section on Women in the Army Medical Service*, vol. IV, *Australian Medical War History*, Australian War Memorial, Canberra, 1961.

Warner, Lavinia and Sandilands, John, *Women Beyond the Wire: The True Story of Japan's Women P.O.W.s that Inspired the Motion Picture* Paradise Road, Arrow Books, London, 1997.

Wigmore, Lionel, *The Japanese Thrust: Official History of Australia in the War of 1939–1945*, Australian War Memorial, Canberra, 1957.

Williams, Jennifer, *Victoria's Living Memorial: History of the Nurses Memorial Centre*, 1948–1990, Nurses Memorial Centre, Melbourne, 1991.

Yoshimi, Yoshiaki, *Comfort Women: Sexual Slavery in the Japanese Military During World War II*, Columbia University Press, New York City, 2000.

Articles and Papers

Arthurson, Lex, 'The Story of the 13th Australian General Hospital: 8th Division A.I.F., Malaya, (unofficial)'; pows-of japan.net/articles/AUSTRALIAN_GENERAL_HOSPITAL.pdf

Fulford, Sarah Margaret, 'Training Ethos, Camaraderie and Endurance of WWII Australian POW Nurses', unpublished thesis, Department of Social Sciences and Security Studies, Curtin University, 2016.

Fletcher, Angharad, 'Sisters Behind the Wire: Reappraising Australian Military Nursing and Internment in the Pacific during World War II', *Medical History*, 2011, 55: 419–24.

Hadley, Gregory and Oglethorpe, James, 'MacKay's' Betrayal', *Journal of Military History*, 71, April 2007.

Kim, Jimin; Milner Bisland, Beverly; Shin, Sunghee, 'Teaching about the Comfort Women During World War II and the Use of Personal Stories of the Victims', Education about ASIA, vol. 24, no. 3, 2019.

Morris, Narrelle, 'Japanese War Crimes in the Pacific: Australia's Investigations and Prosecutions, Appendix B: Index of Accused Japanese War Criminals by Name', NAA: Research Guide, 2019.

Twomey, Christina, 'Australian Nurse POW's Gender, War and Captivity', *Australian Historical Studies*, 2004, 36: 124, 255–274, DOI 10.1080/10314610408596288.

Moremon, Dr John, Reid, Dr Richard, 'A Bitter Fate: Australians in Malaya and Singapore, December 1941 to February 1942', Commemorations Branch, Department of Veterans' Affairs, February 2002; anzacportal.dva.gov.au/sites/default/files/docs/a-bitter-fate-2002.pdf

Websites

Australian Nurses Memorial Centre: australiannursesmemorial centre.org.au

Australian War Memorial: awm.gov.au

Human Rights Watch: hrw.org

Malayan Volunteers Group: malayanvolunteersgroup.org.uk

Muntok Nurses and Internees Facebook page: facebook.com/
    Muntok-Nurses-and-Internees-983774011682886/

Michael Pether's work on the evacuation of Singapore has been
    invaluable. You can find his passenger lists, including that
    of the *Vyner Brooke*, on the Muntok Peace Museum website:
    muntokpeacemuseum.org

National Archives of Australia: naa.gov.au

Nobel Prize: nobelprize.org

Trove: trove.nla.gov.au

Women's Active Museum on War and Peace in Tokyo:
    wam-peace.org

Acknowledgements

Thanks to Sally for gifting me Bud's story and the precious cache of letters. For letting me write so much about our conversations and allowing me to put her vulnerability on the page.

To Dad, for whom I know this was not an easy intrusion, I thank him for allowing questions and volunteering information. To both Dad and Mum for encouraging a family culture of reading – other writers have been my greatest teachers.

To the relatives of the nurses and others either killed on Radji Beach or interned on Bangka Island – Michael Noyce and Judy Balcombe, first and foremost, whose passion and tireless work over many years has cemented both our memorialising and our relationships on Bangka Island. Philippa and James Dickson, David Man, Kate Neuss, Lorraine Curtis, Eve Balfour-Ogilvy, Kate Newton, Joan Wilson, Stoker Lloyd's granddaughters Helen Webb and the late Sarah McCarthy, Emily Malone, David and Di Hick, all of you have played an important part.

Also, Arlene Bennett for her tireless work as the (former) president of the Australian Nurses Memorial Centre and the late Bruce Bird for his contribution.

To Michael Pether for his painstaking research and expert read and for inviting me to the seventy-fifth memorial service in the first place.

To Lynette Silver for her detective work and determination over many years to put the clues together.

To Yuki Tanaka for his analysis, bravery and commitment to peace. Ian Shaw, whose book *On Radji Beach* galvanised my interest. Historian Dr Janet Butler for helping with historical searches and analysis.

Thanks to the late Ralph Armstrong who generously shared his memories of his time on the *Vyner Brooke* and in the camps, despite his fall, and to Verna for welcoming us into their home.

The Australian, British and New Zealand embassies and the Australian and New Zealand defence attachés, who have supported and assisted our yearly services. Thanks to Mr Takonai Susumu from the embassy of Japan in Jakarta for attending the service in 2020.

To the staff at the National Australian Archives in Melbourne and the Australian War Memorial in Canberra for your preservation of our historical documents and for helping me navigate my way around them.

To our friends in Muntok, Mr Fakhrizal Abubakar, your work as a historian and director of the Timah Tinwinning Museum and your wonderful team were a great help. Members of the Red Cross and the Muntok History Volunteers Group. Marc and

Yanni for feeding us at D'Orange Café and your work coordinating our activities. Henri and the staff at the Hotel Yasmin, Muntok – our home away from home. PT Timah Indonesia for developing the Vivian Bullwinkel Gallery in the Timah Museum and for hosting us over many years. West Bangka Tourism Department, Bupati of West Bangka Province and the Governor of Bangka Island.

Antoni Jach, my writing teacher and mentor, who welcomed me into Melbourne's writing scene when I was a newbie and gave me a seat at the table.

My writing group, Jane Leonard and Tali Lavi, Ellie Nielsen, Peter Kenneally, Louise Bassett and Jacinta Halloran. We've sampled the pub fare of the northside, and you have patiently guided me to become a decent writer. Thank you for your feedback and friendship, your kindness and bluntness when required. Plus a few of you have done significant editing on this work: Peter, Tali and Jane – I love your track changes.

Writers Victoria and my Glenfern studio buddies; Jane and Tali once again, Bram, Isabel, Stephen, Anna, Ally, Rose, Martine, Melissa, Tanya, Katrina, Jim, Iola and Fiona. For the sense of community, inspiration and our monthly lunches. Varuna and my week spent in the Blue Mountains where Australia's literati whisper from the walls. Nadine Davidoff for your insight and structural edit – even though I did sob through my feedback session – you helped me to find the Georgina voice. Marion Potts who read and gave wonderful feedback.

My sister Imogen who did the same and for all your insightful advice. Amanda, my sister-in-law, who took the first trip to

Muntok with me. Adam Chernok for pro bono legal advice. Kate Hoy, Louise Sweetland, Neil Conning and Matthew Kelly, who helped me get published.

To my publisher Ali Urquhart at Penguin Random House, for your professionalism and calm approach and for backing a new author. Catherine Hill, my brilliant editor, who polished up my manuscript. Jo Baker and team, Veronica Eze and Bella Arnott-Hoare – all powerhouses and a delight to work with. Alex Ross for my beautiful cover. The talented Sally Coggle for my author photos. To Pippa Masson at Curtis Brown for being the dream agent.

Thank you to my early writing advisors, Anna Funder, Fiona Higgins, Cathy Gowdie and Ned Manning, and to Julia Baird for her generous reading, insight and endorsement.

To my business partner Sam Crock for supporting and cheering me on in this substantial side gig.

To my family and friends who have encouraged and tolerated me over the last five years as I inhabited this world of war crimes and obsessive research. Thank you for your unwavering kindness and interest.

To my daughters, I know this has consumed me over a long time and I am so grateful for your love and support.

To Kingsley, who always believed I could do it even when I didn't know myself. Thank you for your encouragement, love and your engineering-type edits.

Born in Sydney, Georgina left at nineteen to study acting in New York at the Neighbourhood Playhouse and then worked as a performer throughout her twenties. She worked mainly in theatre for companies such as Sydney Theatre Company, Playbox and Theatre South, and in television for shows like *A Country Practice* and *Outback*.

Interested in what makes people tick, subsequently she changed direction and went back to university to study Applied Psychology. She then co-founded her consulting business, Changeable, in which she combines her psychology background and facilitation skills to enable meaningful change for individuals, teams and organisations.

Now Melbourne based, Georgina has two daughters in their early twenties. When she has time she likes to escape with her husband to their block of land near Kyneton.

Georginabanks.com.au
georginabankswriter

Discover a
new favourite

Visit **penguin.com.au/readmore**